Educative Lead

Acknowledgments

The Editors wish to record their sincere thanks to a number of people:

to those who contributed to this text, especially for their responsiveness to our editorial feedback;

to Cindy Strahle and the staff of the University of New England's Computer Centre, who helped to assemble some of the chapters of this text;

to our one-time colleagues in the Department of Administrative, Higher and Adult Education Studies, and to the University of New England for their support and contributions to research in educational administration; and

to our loved ones who support us in our pursuit of new and trustworthy ideas.

Educative Leadership:
A Practical Theory for New Administrators and Managers

Edited by

P.A. Duignan and R.J.S. Macpherson

 The Falmer Press

(A member of the Taylor & Francis Group)
London • Washington D.C.

UK   The Falmer Press, 4 John Street, London WC1N 2ET
USA   The Falmer Press, Taylor & Francis Inc., 1900 Frost Road, Suite 101, Bristol, PA 19007

© Selection and editorial material P.A. Duignan and R.J.S Macpherson 1992

All rights reserved. No part of this publication may be reproduced, stored in a retrieval system, or transmitted in any form or by any means, electronic, mechanical, photocopying, recording or otherwise, without permission in writing from the Publisher.

First published in 1992

A catalogue record for this book is available from the British Library

Library of Congress Cataloging-in-Publication Data are available on request

ISBN 0 75070 058 0
ISBN 0 75070 059 9

Jacket design by Benedict Evans

Typeset in 9.5/11 Times by
Graphicraft Typesetters Ltd., Hong Kong

Printed in Great Britain by Burgess Science Press, Basingstoke on paper which has a specified pH value on final paper manufacture of not less than 7.5 and is therefore 'acid free'.

Contents

Contents

Chapter 1

Creating New Knowledge about Educative Leadership

P.A. Duignan and R.J.S. Macpherson

Introduction

It was not by accident that the first of the eight major recommendations of the National Commission for Excellence in Educational Administration (1987) in the United States of America was that educational leadership should be redefined. As the Commission evaluated the quality of educational leadership in the USA, it became particularly troubled by the absence of conceptual clarity throughout the field of what constituted 'good' educational leadership. And while the Commission courageously offered remedial strategies — a National Policy Board, the remodelling and dramatic rationalisation of preparatory programs, the equalisation of selection outcomes, the establishment of grounded and recurrent education for administrators, and new 'licensure programs' for neophytes — it ended its work by again posing the basic question: what is 'good' or 'excellent' educational leadership?

The Educative Leadership Project (ELP) was mounted in 1986 by the editors and three state education systems in Australia to attend to this very question. Hence, while the ELP processes and findings outlined in this chapter must be understood in terms of their Australian context, and therefore used elsewhere with caution, they offer an approach whereby different yet socio-politically specific answers to the Commission's basic question could be generated.

It must also be understood that the ELP strategy and findings reflect a research design based on a set of assumptions held by the co-directors of the project (the co-authors of this chapter). The first assumption was that the wisest approach to leadership in education should be *educative* in intent and outcome. Another was that theory-building about educative leadership should come after new syntheses of experience, research and theory on major dilemmas of leadership had been generated afresh and tested through in-service activities and analysis by postgraduate students.

A third precept was that the most trustworthy base for theory-building about educative leadership was the refined collective wisdom of specialist theorists and exemplary practitioners. A fourth precept was that if the practical and theoretical products of the ELP were to be valued and applied widely the project would require substantial support from education systems and should

1

demonstrate an uncompromising attitude to scholarly standards. The co-directors' fifth precept was that as schools are not natural systems, but cultures, educative leadership should constitute both philosophical and practical action directed at cultural elaboration. To prevent the ELP strategy being adopted uncritically, the background to these precepts is now clarified.

The Theoretical Turmoil

Since Greenfield's (1975a; 1985; 1988a) dramatic refutation of natural systems ideology, and since Bates' (1980; 1982; 1984) introduction of New Sociology into educational administration, the agendas of researchers and theorists in educational administration have diversified sharply. The simplisms of behaviourism have been challenged (Gronn, 1982; 1983; 1984; Macpherson, 1986). But how administrators might resolve the dilemmas of practice, and compromise in a morally defensible manner when facing politically critical, socially critical, economically critical, managerially critical and educationally critical imperatives, remain as major new agendas largely unaddressed by the field.

Although the field of educational administration has been singularly lacking in its use of philosophical machinery (Macpherson 1985), there are strong indications that this deficit is being addressed (e.g. Rizvi, 1985a; Miklos, 1985; Holmes, 1985; Hodgkinson, 1985; Greenfield 1985b; GREAT Conferences 1984, 1985, 1986; Greenfield, 1988b). Nevertheless, as these academic initiatives unfold, there is also the need for projects that bridge the theory-practice gap. This chapter explains the specifications of one such project (Duignan, Gaut and Macpherson, 1986).

The purpose of the ELP was to generate a new synthesis of experience, research and theory on leadership, and to develop complementary in-service and postgraduate learning materials. This chapter presents an overview of the purpose, design and procedures of the ELP. The chapter has five sections. First, there is a discussion of the purpose of the ELP and a working definition of educative leadership is presented. Second, the design for the project is described and explained. Third, there is a discussion on the principles of adult learning which underpinned the product-oriented approach adopted. Fourth, a number of issues related to educative leadership are identified and discussed. Finally, an outline of the project phases and workshop procedures is presented.

Purposes and Emergent Definitions

The ELP sought to break new ground in educational administration. It did this by following the advice given over decades by many respected practitioners and leading academics in the field — that the wisest approach to leadership in education is that it be educative.

Unfortunately, as our own research has shown, the detail of this wisdom remains elusive to many educational leaders today (Duignan, 1985; Duignan, in Simpkins *et al.*, 1987; Macpherson, 1986; 1987a; 1987b). The management recipes in the literature usually apply to selected aspects of specific situations whereas the problems faced daily by practitioners always seem far more complex. Indeed, management techniques are often of little help when a leader has to choose between competing values. When it comes to solving new types of problems in education, it usually means creating new types of understandings. To add to the confusion, the political, economic and social contexts of education continue to change rapidly. Two of the most difficult questions outstanding in educational administration are therefore:

1 How should leaders in education decide what is important?
2 How will they know that they are morally right, when they act?

Unfortunately, administrative practice is often seen to be driven by non-educational criteria, such as bureaucratic efficiency, political expediency and economic constraint. While it would be naive to expect that these criteria will be displaced in the realities of practice, it is time to inject a concern for values into the administration of education, in a practical manner.

The purpose of the ELP was to provide a means by which a 'practical' theory of educative leadership might be developed. We believe that the ideas discussed in this project will be of immediate interest to all who wish to influence the nature and direction of educational administration in the coming decades, simply because educators in administrative positions will continue to prefer being educative leaders, and academic educators will want to assist them in that endeavour.

Our point of departure is that an emergent definition of educative leadership should not just focus on the traditional elements of leadership emphasised in the literature of educational administration, namely, attitudes, styles and behaviours. Instead, we prefer to be concerned with ways of knowing organisations and ways of leading that find expression in the cultural norms of the group, the educational organisation or the system. We do not see organisations as natural phenomena (Greenfield, 1985); instead, we see them as cultures, that is, the concerted imaginations of organised people who share assumptions, values, interpretations of their situation and meanings that they give to their actions (Smircich, 1983; Sergiovanni and Corbally, 1984; Duignan, 1986; Macpherson, 1986).

We believe that cultural elaboration is a dialectical process (Watkins, 1985) of clarifying values and partly resolving inevitable conflict in a way that modifies peoples' patterns of assumptions and relationships. Educative leadership is, therefore, central to the negotiation of what will count as important in education and what will count as morally right. The direct consequence of this type of concerned action is the development of professional values, intentions and practices. Given this view of organisation, what then is our view of leadership?

Educative leadership appears to be a deliberate attempt at cultural elaboration. What people actually attempt in the way of change is, of course, mediated by the culture of their setting and by the wider context. Nevertheless, actions taken by determined people to change the assumptions of others about the situation in which they 'find themselves', inevitably lead to a redefinition of the culture of the setting. As Smyth (1985) has proposed, the difference with educative leadership is that it helps professional educators work with others to shape their purposes and the meanings that they use to make sense of, and to justify, their involvement in and contribution to education.

It follows that educative leadership must closely respond to the cultural context, be critically aware of the long-term practices of participants in educational processes, and when action is proposed, justify ends and processes using an educative philosophy. Educative leadership is therefore far more than a set of social or management techniques evident in the skills or style of an individual, such as a school principal, or in the behaviours of a group comprising the executive team of an institution or system. It is more concerned with ways of knowing, valuing and altering the organisation.

Educative leadership inevitably questions the arbitrary exercise of social power. We find it very difficult to assume that wisdom about education is hierarchically distributed in an organisation or that a bureaucratic rationality about structures and functions is self-justified. We hold that the responsible use of social power in education is an essential feature of educative leadership.

As noted above, we see educative leadership as part of the processes of modifying or maintaining an organisational culture (Purkey and Smith, 1983; Saphier and King, 1985). The linking of culture and organisation helps focus attention on the subjective and interpretative aspects of organisational life (Jelinek *et al.*, 1983). Educative leaders, within a cultural framework, are seen as symbolic leaders who pay attention to important cultural details (Deal and Kennedy, 1983). In this sense, educative leadership is part of a group phenomenon whereby a shared reality of meaning and of what is right is regularly renegotiated and reaffirmed. The use of the adjective 'educative' thereby implies the active involvement of all members of an educational organisation as philosophers, planners and policy makers. Educative leadership is, therefore, concerned about right and wrong, justice and injustice, truth, aesthetics and the negotiation of practical ideals in education. It is concerned with an active analysis of the way things are, the way they are seen to be, and with the creation of preferred ways of doing things. In this visionary work (Starratt, 1984), the educative leader focuses on what is right, nurtures acceptance of these ideas and protects them. Hence, educative leadership implies a responsible involvement in the politics of organisation.

As the culture of an organisation evolves, so should the nature and ends of educative leadership change. While being sensitive to the valued history and traditions of the setting, the educative leader is critically aware of the implications of cultural change. People can too easily be trapped by history. In the everyday world, educators and their leaders can also become desensitised to the tyrannies of routine. Too often, educators become slaves to dull routines and, as a result, lose their sense of excitement at being professional educators. This can have a prejudicial effect on their service to clients. Educative leaders help to inject a sense of excitement into the performance of routines.

To summarise so far, we envisage an educative leader as one who communicates a sense of excitement, originality and freshness in an organisation. We believe that an educative leader is a person who challenges others to participate in the visionary activity of defining 'rightness' and preferred ways of doing and acting in education (Starratt, 1984). Finally, we see an educative leader as a person who challenges educators to commit themselves to approaches to administration and professional practices that are, by their nature, educative. We are not denying that leaders in education need to be efficient but we are convinced that there is much more to educative leadership than managing for efficiency (Miklos, 1983).

We noted above that our vision of a 'practical' theory of educative leadership was emergent; indeed, we anticipated that the ELP would elaborate these ideas. The project design criteria and the principles of adult learning consistent with our emergent position are presented in the next two sections.

Project Design Principles

Eight design principles were identified to ensure that the organisation and ethical assumptions of the ELP were consistent with our primary purpose — to create a new 'practical' theory of educative leadership. Given the priorities and nature of the host institutional and system settings of the project, and the need for the continuing and active support of Departments of Education, practitioners and academics, the first principle of project design was that the enterprise had to be efficiently planned, directed and marketed. Other sections of this chapter set out interrelated sets of assumptions, activities and systems of accountability consistent with the primary purpose of the enterprise.

The second principle was that the articulation of educative leadership should be concerns-based; a practical theory driven by educational issues and problems. To this end we asked policymakers and key administrators in three states to identify the most challenging areas for leaders in their systems. The issues discussed in Chapters 2, 3, 4, 5 and 6 are those selected by these key practitioners.

The third principle was that the products of the project should be creative and stimulating. It was felt that there was a need to offer fresh, challenging ideas, together with exemplars of educative leadership practice, all consistent with the values implicit in the emergent concept of educative leadership. To do this did not, however, mean ignoring the wisdom so painfully acquired in the past. Indeed, the fourth principle was that the project should provide for the systematic review, refinement and incorporation of prior knowledge to do with educative leadership. This implies a critical awareness of the values served by the ideas, the approaches and the solutions devised for past problems.

It was also recognised that searches for solutions to complex educational problems have never ceased. The fifth principle was, therefore, that the project should incorporate the best informed synthesis of recent research, thinking and practice in each of the immediate issues of concern. Given the diversity of concerns associated with educative leadership, this implied the involvement of academic specialists of national and/or international standing with respect to each issue. The sixth principle of the project's design was to ensure that the ideas drawn from prior knowledge and recent research and reflection were consistent with the experiences of exemplary practitioners. It was seen to be so important that the theory products of the project should be grounded in exemplary practice, that exemplary practitioners were involved in the design and development of materials on each issue.

Associated with these ideas was the seventh principle; that the project should produce both practical and academic outcomes of high quality, mindful of the different criteria used in each general setting to define excellence. The seventh principle of project design was that all phases and activities should be consistent with the principles, derived from recent knowledge, of how adults learn best. This task was considered so crucial to the project design that a discussion on adult learning follows.

Principles of Adult Learning

An initial assumption was that professionals would want to take primary responsibility for their own in-service education. This means that the content and processes of in-service education had to be sensitive and responsive to learners' perception of needs. It also implied that these in-service activities had to be seen as opportunities for real growth along intellectual, emotional, social, educational, aesthetic, skills and career dimensions. An associated assumption was that the way that individuals and groups respond to the opportunities for professional growth would be in part a reflection of the quality of the approaches, the materials, the processes and the experiences selected, developed and used. It follows therefore that the materials designed for the ELP should incorporate a review of prior knowledge and examples from the current experiences of exemplary practitioners.

From our own experience, we also took the position that the context of adult learning must also be carefully planned. A supportive social climate had been shown to be crucial to participants' willingness to experiment freely, to learn from each other (Macpherson, 1983; Barnett and Long, 1986), to give and accept constructive criticism in a non-threatening manner, and to reappraise deeply embedded assumptions about their professional self, actions and values. There had also to be substantial latitude for learners to be self-directing and self-regulating. One consequence of these assumptions was that adult learners, provided with such resources, would develop their understandings of what they do, refine their knowledge of the organisational, cultural and moral implications of their actions, and relate their contribution to education to themselves and to the wider contexts of systems, and society.

This meant that in-service should help learners develop their tools of ethical and organisational analysis. In-service was therefore defined as philosophy-in-action (Hodgkinson, 1983). We also assumed that adult learners preferred a stimulating, challenging and experimental context that directly related to their career and work world. For this reason, we did not see in-service education as a series of discrete and occasional activities removed from the continuing processes of professional growth.

To summarise our position, we saw in-service education as a sophisticated and effective means by which adult learners could research, refine and review educational and administrative wisdom, plan and debate the making and implementing of policies so that considered and value-based decisions could be internalised and so that the new synthesis of experience and reflection would inform subsequent leadership practice. The content and processes of the ELP were expected to reflect this position. Indeed, the criteria that we used to identify the issues and the participants in this project are outlined in the next section to illustrate one application of these ideas.

Issues and Personnel

Without implying priority, the following criteria for the selection of issues (areas of concern, problems, current pressure points) were identified. Each issue had to be:

> defined in a way that was consistent with the emergent definition of educative leadership;
> have an identifiable and developed theory base;
> be seen as practical and relevant to multiple audiences;
> be discrete and manageable in terms of scope, given the restrictions of product specifications; and
> lend itself to the development of in-service and postgraduate learning materials assuming the use of modern communication technologies.

When viewed as a whole, the issues given priority had to be comprehensive and coherent enough to provide for a new gestalt of educative leadership.

The criteria for the selection of project personnel related to their crucial roles as either academic specialists or exemplary practitioners.

Academic Specialists

Academic specialists were required to bring to the project an overview of prior knowledge and the latest research findings on specific issues. The criteria for their selection were that:

> each was a nationally recognised authority on the issue under consideration;
> his or her personal views of the purposes of educational administration and of administrative practice had to be compatible with the emergent definition of educative leadership above;
> each had to declare a willingness to work within the specifications of the project and meet the terms of a workshop contract;
> each had to declare a willingness to work as a peer in a team situation; and
> each had to have the demonstrated ability to write in a style that is readily understood by multiple audiences.

Exemplary Practitioners

Exemplary practitioners were required to ensure that exemplary practice was consistently used as the point of reference in the revision of the ideas and the preparation of materials developed on each issue. Criteria identified to select practitioners were as follows:

> their practices were esteemed by professional colleagues, inspectors, regional and system leaders;
> their attitudes and practice were consistent with the emergent definition of educative leadership above;

their involvement in this project was supported by others in their system, sector and setting;

they declared a willingness to comply with the project specifications and workshop contract;

they declared a willingness to work as peers in a team situation; and

they had the demonstrated ability to write in a style that is readily understood by multiple audiences.

Despite widespread consultations, and the diversity of interests discovered, a relatively limited list of issues emerged as the basis for units in the ELP. At the time of writing, five units have been completed: 'educative leadership and the quality of teaching' and 'educative leadership in a multicultural context' (sponsored by the New South Wales Department of Education); 'educative leadership and curriculum development' and 'educative leadership and the rationalisation of education services' (Australian Capital Territory Schools Authority); and 'values and valuable leadership action (Ministry of Education, Victoria). The theoretical framework for, and an elaboration of each issue, are presented in Chapters 2, 3, 4, 5 and 6.

Project Phases and Workshops

The first of the ELP phases was concerned with project design. The co-directors developed draft project specifications at a two-day workshop after some six months preparatory thinking (Duignan, Gaut and Macpherson, 1986). The objectives of the workshop were to:

define educative leadership;

define principles of in-service education consistent with educative leadership;

define selection criteria and processes to identify issues, areas, problems and current pressure points in educative leadership;

plan selection criteria and processes to identify at least three exemplary practitioners and one research-theorist of national standing with respect to each issue;

design project specifications and plan subsequent phases in outline.

The second phase was principally given over to negotiations. The co-directors made draft specifications available to education systems in three states for consultations in April 1986. Subsequent negotiations by the editors modified the specifications and led to substantial resource commitments, and the active involvement of participants from New South Wales, Australian Capital Territory and Victoria.

The third phase was where new syntheses of experience, research and theory were created. Five-day workshops for teams of four or more, comprised of one researcher-theorist and at least three exemplary practitioners, focused on each of the issues identified above. In brief, in the areas defined, each team created new syntheses of educative leadership that were converted into a range of in-service materials.

Each workshop had four major objectives. First was the sharing of experiences and knowledge on the issue. The theorist's state-of-the-art paper, distributed prior to the think tank, was then given sustained and detailed scrutiny. The second objective was the negotiation and writing of a coherent discussion, usually based on the theorist's paper, that related the best of prior knowledge and current research to the experience of exemplary practitioners.

The third objective was the drafting of a lecturette that introduced, in direct language, the key concepts and arguments of the position paper. The lecturette text was then elaborated with overhead transparencies and a workbook, with an audio-taped version for isolated users. The fourth objective was concerned with the production of in-service and postgraduate learning materials. A professionally produced video was designed to introduce, in a dramatic manner, the major concepts, values and educative leadership strategies associated with each issue. The in-service package also contained structured workshop activities, the monograph (with selected articles from the literature), and assignment questions available for those who wish to use the package as a unit of tertiary education. In the final stages of materials production, the state-of-the-art papers and monographs were re-edited into this text for a national and international academic and practitioner audience. The final chapter in this book presents a new practical theory of educative leadership.

The fifth phase is concerned with in-service and postgraduate education. The materials have been made available to institutions, systems, and regional and local in-service educators in a planned way. The materials have also assisted with peer consultancies for educative leadership and school development issues by examining the implications, at all levels, for educative leaders in a multicultural society.

From the outset of this project, it was assumed that these materials would be appropriate for the gaining of credit or advanced standing in postgraduate programmes of educational, administrative and policy studies; an assumption evidently warranted by their extensive usage. This view is consistent with the implications of the Coulter and Ingvarson Report (1984) and those in the joint CTEC/CSC Report on funding tertiary and in-service education. The point here is that the ELP's design has been validated to the extent that the materials have become multi-media vehicles for tertiary coursework as well as the basis for systemic and institutional development programmes.

To further assist other possible projects, the detail of the workshops is now summarised in terms of purposes, objectives, workshop activities and contract.

The aim of each workshop was to generate a new synthesis of experience, research and theory that would provide an adequate base for subsequent materials production and contribute to the development of a 'practical' theory of educative leadership. The objectives of each workshop were to:

review the nature of the Educative Leadership Project;
review the nature of each issue as defined in the Project Specifications;
share the experience of practitioners;
review the state-of-the-art of research findings and theory;
negotiate and design a team position;
draft a monograph for a general practitioner audience, and then;
draft a video treatment to convey the major ideas of the monograph.

A typical workshop schedule was:

Day 1 a.m. Review Educative Leadership and the Issue — Co-Directors.
p.m. Reports from Practitioners and Academic Specialist.
Day 2 a.m. Team Negotiations on content.
p.m. Draft Position Paper
Day 3 a.m. Writing and Editing.
p.m. Complete First Draft. Discuss with Communications Technologists.
Day 4 a.m. Editing Team stays with position paper while Lecturette Team begins work.
p.m. Brainstorm Video Treatment with Communications Technologists.
Day 5 a.m. Draft Monograph and Lecturette Package assembled. Production Planning begins.
p.m. Closing Reports and Discussion.

To clarify the extent to which the writers made their expectations extant, an extract from the think-tank contract entered into by all participants follows:

This is to confirm that I have read the detail of the Educative Leadership Project Specifications and that I declare my willingness to serve within the terms of these specifications.

In particular, I note that this means that Practitioners will bring to the 5 day Workshop, draft accounts, cameos, case studies and papers summarising the best of current practice. I also note that, for Academic Specialists, it means bringing appropriate background material and a draft position paper summarising the state-of-the-art of research findings and theory pertinent to the unit topic.

Finally, I understand that my contributions to this Project will be used in the production of in-service and postgraduate materials as indicated in the specifications, and that such contributions will be duly acknowledged. (Duignan and Macpherson, 1987)

Problems Encountered During the ELP

There were three major sources to the difficulties that arose during the ELP: those that derived from the nature of individuals involved and from how they interacted during their involvement; those that reflected the histories and assumptions of the three systems that sponsored the project; and those that stemmed from the processes used during the production and implementation phases.

People

It was noted above that specific criteria were developed to select individuals; criteria that were, in almost all cases, validated by the performance of individuals. Without exception, as the following chapters illustrate, the specialist theorists produced original and challenging material. They responded well to critical feedback from the writers prior to the workshops although one had not budgeted adequate time for this process. The real difficulties came, however, at the workshops when 'truth' claims were subjected to unremitting scrutiny by initially sceptical practitioners.

It took time for some of the theorists to accept the fact that the exemplary practitioners had highly sophisticated 'theories-in-use', and that their ideas could not be dismissed arbitrarily or easily explained away. There were times when a practitioner's explanatory scheme was demonstrated to be naive, and quickly conceded as such when a more effective explanation was offered.

However, when the converse situation prevailed, and this was not uncommon, there was far less evidence of cheerful pragmatism. Some theorists had to be helped through the processes of making compromises on intellectual grounds. As the hours together unfolded, the practitioners almost invariably became adept at handling flashes of intellectual arrogance, flights into abstraction and examples of *argumentum ad hominem* and *argumentum ad argumentum*. From the outset, the editors took turns at process facilitation, while being fully engaged in the debate.

It is important to note that practitioners quite regularly expressed their concern at being 'out of their depth'. On most occasions this related to the depth and intensity of the theorist's position or unfamiliarity with the language used. Humorous devices were developed to signal an intuited problem. Some practitioners were reluctant to suspend disbelief in a proposal that contradicted received wisdom, although all came to enjoy the exercise of exploring and then critically evaluating an alternative theory. Decoding, paraphrasing and assumption-testing processes proved invaluable.

On the other hand, it quickly became evident in two workshops that a practitioner participant lacked the capacities implied by the selection criteria. In both examples, discreet inquiries confirmed that the recommended criteria and selection processes had not been adhered to, and an additional person was nominated at short notice.

System Cultures

The second major source of difficulty stemmed from the unique organisational histories and cultures of the sponsoring systems. The three systems had administrative mindsets with little in common. The differences made themselves felt in different ways.

Victoria's administrators had experienced three major restructurings since the late 1970s. They seemed comparatively at ease with new ideas and yet, in a context of structural ambiguity, found it difficult to identify the most appropriate reform strategy or process. Those from New South Wales tended to be in the converse situation, that is, initially uneasy with new policies and yet very clear on patterns of formal authority and appropriate implementation processes. Those from the ACT, a tiny system by comparison, with intimate relationships, spoke confidently of possibilities. In general, there was an inverse relationship found between structural rigidities and a willingness to consider new ideas.

Other problems arose as the ideas in ELP units began to challenge long-standing policies. Unit 1, for example, showed that in-service education and training policies that favour extracting professionals from their service context, a widespread practice, are fundamentally flawed. Unit 2 showed that the atomisation of curriculum on disciplinary grounds, a virtually unquestioned premise in all systems' policies, fails to cohere with modern learning theories or theories of knowledge. Unit 3 challenged all professionals to underpin their practice with an appropriate moral culture. Unit 4 demonstrated why liberal multiculturalism should be displaced by a critical interculturalism, while Unit 5 showed that administrators have to, and should know how to, take responsibility for the effects of rationalisation. In most cases where the problems were formalised, negotiations with system leaders saw the ideas explicitly or implicitly accepted as new policy. In one instance, a senior official who was obstructing the ELP was redeployed, and production of the unit proceeded.

While system mindsets were very evident in many responses, we also noticed other influences at work. Involvement in the project was one determinant of attitude. All of those who had been involved in a workshop, those at institutional and regional levels who had used the materials, and those at senior executive levels who had commissioned and directed the project, remained very supportive of the project and its products. Others at intermediary levels sometimes took other positions.

There were those in all three systems who exhibited gate-keeping attitudes and practices. Others took the role of guardians of past approaches and beliefs. Some intuitively resisted the suggestions of those they saw as 'outsiders' while responding more positively to the involvement of highly respected local practitioners. There was as much caution shown to those from 'academe' as to those from another state. We were not able to establish the origins of these responses, but the nature of three myths involved became manifest.

First was the myth that 'we in this system know best'. It was used to ingratiate the arbitrary use of vetoes, selective inattention, concerted ignorance and collective denial about expertise elsewhere. Despite this, the evidence in the problem areas nominated by systems for attention invariably indicated a policy vacuum and a situation where professional skills were becoming obsolete or where they were at an early stage of development.

Second was the myth of the 'professional veto'. This myth legitimated people or groups setting aside ideas, strategies or formal policies, however explicitly mandated or warranted, on the grounds that they had not been consulted or involved during development. In some systems, the power of this myth reached well beyond any appropriate balance of interests.

The third myth was that 'professionals will do the right thing'. It shrouded the problems of symbolic supervision and minimal monitoring. We became aware of variations in fidelity during implementation. There were even occasions where the ELP materials were used in ways that contradicted the educative philosophy they explicitly championed.

While such events distressed the editors, it must be noted that, from the outset of the ELP, their efforts ended with the production of materials. Nevertheless, despite having no formal role in the management of implementation, they found means of making their views known, even to the extent of revisiting system leaders.

On a number of occasions, naive users unwittingly generated hostility in audiences when they disregarded suggestions on how best to introduce and to pace the video-tapes and case studies. Such problems tended to be self-correcting. No problems have been reported by users in higher education.

More seriously, however, the management structures that administered the ELP in each of the systems became accidental casualties during restructurings. In all three systems there were major reforms to administrative policies and practices triggered by political intervention unrelated to the ELP. Remedying these accidents and re-establishing priorities proved very time-consuming and present an ongoing problem.

The most challenging type of problem concerned the abuse of positional power. On one occasion, regional and local practitioners used ELP arguments to question manipulative practices at central levels over the implementation of ideas about educative leadership. They pointed to the mismatch between words and deeds. Intervention at the most senior executive levels had to be mounted to preserve the integrity of the project.

Processes

The third major source of difficulty stemmed from the processes used during the production and implementation phases. It will be recalled that the three systems involved had unique patterns to the distribution of powers, resources, responsibilities and communication links. Assembling the required commitment and resources in each organisational setting was a complex task. Generating managerial structures to coordinate the ELP across state boundaries proved extremely difficult, but not impossible, although there were examples of poor supervision of production processes leading to less than ideal quality output. However, when the coordination problems were compounded by the effects of gate-keeping, the myths noted above, the ownership contest over the ELP ideas, and the seemingly random effects of systemic restructurings, it meant that an inordinate amount of time had to be devoted to project maintenance.

In sharp contrast, workshop participants worked in near-ideal settings. The workshop processes were highly geared and, given the sophisticated feedback from participants, settled onto standard patterns. An issue that arose with the first three groups was their relative lack of expertise in designing video treatments, particularly their general inability to 'Think Pictures.' Since very few had experience of multi-media instructional design, the workshop format was altered so that participants could focus on tasks that took advantage of their skills and understandings; writing and editing case studies, and drafting the text and illustrations of a lecturette that summarised the key arguments of the monograph.

Involving creative experts to develop a dramatic video presentation of each unit's ideas brought a new suite of problems. We soon discovered, through a series of false starts, that talent is not necessarily or even positively correlated with ego in the television world. We also found that the film crews and production staff in large systems can be neutralised by limited talent in critical areas, such as script writing, direction and production management. There were also, at the time, state government monopolies on video production, but of doubtful quality, that could only be evaded with considerable difficulty.

One of the greatest problems encountered to do with video treatment was to do with the use of humour. It was decided that the only way that some hitherto inadmissible topics could be raised for treatment was to make a deliberate use of gentle parody shot in real settings. The potential for offence was considerable, particularly if users did not prepare audiences or allow them to read the introductory notes on the video tape.

A series of experiences suggest that parody in situational humour can be extremely effective as a teaching aid, particularly if the tape is stopped after each incident to allow for progressive analysis. It is, however, counterproductive for stereotypes to come close to becoming stand-up comics. Such scenes are seen to belittle the complex dilemmas involved or to degrade the roles being played. We were surprised how sensitive some position-holders were to a portrayal that presented a less-than-ideal stereotype. In essence, when the humour denigrated an aspect of ideal self it generated anger, and moved attention from the substantive argument implied by the screen play to a proactive defence of self-worth.

Concluding Note

A review of the problems encountered drew attention to two fundamental issues. First, it was notable how closely the processes used cohered with the design principles outlined above. Or to put it another way, whenever processes deviated from the messages of the literature, the project suffered.

Second, it was a constant task for the editors to help participants to discover touchstone. The theorists were generally reluctant to consider the implications of their ideas in the leadership of schools and education systems, and practitioners were often reluctant to make radical analyses of current leadership dilemmas. Exemplary practitioners had to learn effective ways of challenging theorists' basic assumptions. Leading theorists had to learn how to come to terms with the ability of practitioners as theorists.

The primary outcomes of each workshop, theoretical position papers on educative leadership, follow as the next five chapters. The editors were closely involved in the development of these position papers, in the design and management of the project, and in the generation of a variety of materials for the implementation of the ideas. They also had a major interest in generating a coherent over-arching theory. To promote that coherence, it was decided to preface each chapter with a synthesis and a commentary. A concluding chapter provides a summary of a *practical theory of educative leadership*.

This project has been the outcome of a concern that the rapid development of theory in recent years has yet to be made available to practitioners or to reflect exemplary practice. As the specifications made available here were being negotiated, we were pleased to find our concerns widely shared by those in education systems and those consulted in academe. The outcomes can now be introduced.

The structure of the following chapters signals an argument. Chapter 2 is concerned with an appropriate moral framework for educative leaders. Chapter 3 develops a system of knowledge, an epistemology of educative leadership, which both justifies a particular path to trustworthy knowledge and applies the approach to curriculum development. Chapter 4 uses this same approach and provides a constructivist theory that links educative leadership to the quality of teaching. Chapter 5 moves from the classroom and school to system level to articulate a responsible role for educative leaders in the rationalization of educational services. Chapter 6 illustrates the interconnectedness of societal and education policy, and further, reflects this holism in a practical theory of educative leadership presented in Chapter 7.

Notes

1 An earlier version of this chapter was presented to the 1986 combined Conferences of the Philosophy of Education Society of Australasia and the Group for Research in Education and Administration Theory, Armidale 1–7 September, and later published in *Educational Management and Administration*, 1987, **15**, 49–62.
2 Colin Gaut, Head, Continuing Education, Department of Education, NSW, was initially a co-director of the project. Further, the support of the New South Wales In-Service Education Committee, the advice of the then Director of Services of the NSW Department of Education, Trevor Harrison, and the active involvement of David Francis from the ACT Schools Authority and Ron Ikin from the Ministry of Education of Victoria, are gratefully acknowledged.

References

BARNETT, B. and LONG, C. (1986) 'Peer assisted leadership: Principals learning from each other', *Phi Delta Kappan*, May, **67**, 9.

BATES, R.J. (1980) 'New directions — The new Sociology of Education', *British Journal of Sociology of Education*, **1**, 1, 67–79.

BATES, R.J. (1982) 'Towards a critical practice of educational administration', *Studies in Educational Administration*, **27**, September, Armidale: CCEA.

BATES, R.J. (1984) *Educational Administration and the Management of Knowledge*, Geelong: Deakin University.

COULTER, F. and INGVARSON, L. (1984) 'Professional Development and the Improvement of Schooling: Roles and Responsibilities', A Report to the Commonwealth Schools Commission, Canberra, November.

DEAL, T.E. and KENNEDY, A.A. (1983) 'Culture and school performance', *Educational Leadership*, **40**, 4, 14–15.

DUIGNAN, P. (1985) 'Near enough is not good enough: Developing a culture of high expectations in schools', *Studies in Educational Administration*, **37**, May, Armidale: CCEA.

DUIGNAN, P. (1986) 'The culture of school effectiveness', in SIMPKINS, W.S.,

MAS, E.B. and THOMAS, A.R. (Eds), *Principal and Change: The Australian Experience*, Armidale: UNE Press.

DUIGNAN, P.A., GAUT, C. and MACPHERSON, R.J.S. (1986) *Educative Leadership Project: Project Specifications*, Armidale: UNE Press.

DUIGNAN, P.A. and MACPHERSON, R.J.S. (1987) 'The Educative Leadership Project,' *Educational Management and Administration*, 15, 1, 49–62.

EVERS, C.W. (1986) 'Hodgkinson on ethics and the philosophy of administration', *Educational Administration Quarterly*, 22, 1.

FIRESTONE, W.A. and WILSON, B.L. (1983) 'Using bureaucratic and cultural linkages to improve instruction: The high school principal's contribution', *Center for Educational Policy and Management*, Eugene: University of Oregon.

GALBRAITH, J.K. (1984) *The Anatomy of Power*, London: Hamilton.

GREAT — The Group for Research in Education and Administration Theory have held three conferences: in 1984, 'Ethics and Educational Administration' at the Institute of Educational Administration at Geelong; in 1985, 'Applied Philosophy and Educational Administration' at the University of Tasmania in Hobart; and in 1986, in conjunction with the Philosophy of Education Society of Australasia Conference in Armidale. Between conferences the GREAT regularly heard the papers of members of Deakin, Melbourne and Monash universities.

GREENFIELD, T.B. (1975) 'Theory about organizations: A new perspective and its implications for schools', in HUGHES M.G. (Ed.) *Administering Education*, London: Althone Press, 71–99.

GREENFIELD, T.B. (1985a) 'Putting Meaning Back into Theory: The Search for Lost Values and the Disappeared Individual', paper presented at the Canadian Society for the Study of Education Conference, Montreal, May.

GREENFIELD, T.B. (1985b) 'Theories of educational organisation: A critical perspective', *International Encyclopedia of Education: Research and Studies*, Oxford: Pergamon.

GREENFIELD, T.B. (1988a) 'The decline and fall of science in education administration', in GRIFFITHS, D.E., STOUT, R.T. and FORSYTH, P.B. (Eds) *Leaders for America's Schools: The Report and Papers of the National Commission on Excellence in Educational Administration*, CA: McCutcheon.

GREENFIELD, W.D. (1988b) 'Moral imagination, interpersonal competence, and the work of school administrators', in GRIFFITHS, D.E., STOUT, R.T. and FORSYTH, P.B. (Eds) *Leaders for America's Schools: The Report and Papers of the National Commission on Excellence in Educational Administration*, CA: McCutcheon.

GRONN, P.C. (1982) 'Neo-Taylorism in educational administration', *Educational Administration Quarterly*, 20, 1, 115–129.

HODGKINSON, C. (1983) *The Philosophy of Leadership*, Oxford: Basil Blackwell.

HODGKINSON, C. (1985) 'New Directions for Research and Leadership: The Triplex Bases of Organisation Theory and Administration', paper presented at the Canadian Society for the Study of Education Conference, Montreal, May.

HOLMES, M. (1985) 'The Revival of Traditional Thought and its Effects on Educational Administration: The Case of Decision Making', paper presented at the Canadian Society for the Study of Education Conference, Montreal, May.

JELINEK, M., SMIRCICH, L. and HIRSCH, P. (1983) 'Introduction: A code of many colors', *Administrative Science Quarterly*, 28, 331–338.

LAKOMSKI, G. (1985) 'Critical Theory and Educational Administration', paper presented to the AERA, Chicago, IL, 31 March–4 April.

LIPHAM, J. (1981) *Effective Principal: Effective School*, NASSP, Reston, VA.

LUKE, S. (1974) *Power: A Radical View*, Hong Kong: Macmillan.

MACPHERSON, R.J.S. (1983) 'The W.A. Peer Process Consultancy Project: Action

Research as INSET for Principals', *British Journal of In-Service Education*, **9**, 3, 141–149.

MACPHERSON, R.J.S. (1985) 'Values, ethics and the Journal of Educational Administration', in RIZVI, F.A. (Ed.) *Working Papers on Ethics in Educational Administration*, Geelong: Deakin University, School of Education, 15–34.

MACPHERSON, R.J.S. (1986) 'Talking up and justifying organisation: The creation and control of knowledge about being organised', *Studies in Educational Administration*, **41**, May, Armidale: CCEA.

MAZZARELLA, J.A. (1985) 'The effective high school principal: Sketches for a portrait', *Perspectives*, Winter, Center for Educational Policy and Management, Eugene: University of Oregon.

MIKLOS, E. (1983) 'Alternative images of the administrator', *The Canadian Administrator*, **22**, 7, 1–4.

MIKLOS, E. (1985) 'Comments on The Re-emergence of Values and the Transformation of Administrative Theory', paper presented at the Canadian Society for the Study of Education Conference, Montreal, May.

PURKEY, S.C. and SMITH, M.S. (1983) 'Effective schools: A review', *The Elementary School Journal*, **83**, 427–452.

RIZVI, F.A. (Ed.) (1985a) *Working Papers in Ethics and Educational Administration*, Geelong: Deakin University School of Education.

RIZVI, F.A. (1985b) *Multiculturalism as an Educational Policy*, Deakin University School of Education, Geelong.

SAPHIER, J. and KING, M. (1985) 'Good seeds grow in strong cultures', *Educational Leadership*, **42**, 6.

SERGIOVANNI, T. (1984) 'Leadership and excellence in schooling', *Educational Leadership*, February, **41**, 4–13.

SERGIOVANNI, T. and CORBALLY, J.E. (1984) *Leadership and Organisational Culture: New Perspectives on Administrative Theory and Practice*, Urbana: University of Illinois Press.

SHARPE, F. (1986) *Quality Leadership — Quality Education*, Occasional Paper No. 5, Department of Education, NSW.

SHEARS, L.W. (1984) *Administrative Structures in Education. A Report to the Hon. R. Fordham, Minister of Education*, Office of the Coordinator-General of Education, Victoria.

SMIRCICH, L. (1983) 'Concepts of culture and organisational analysis', *Administrative Science Quarterly*, **28**, 339–358.

SMYTH, W.J. (1985) 'An educative and empowering notion of leadership', *Educational Management and Administration*, **13**, 3, 179–186.

STARRATT, R. (1984) 'Educational Leadership', a presentation to a Seminar at Catholic College, Sydney, August.

WATKINS, P. (1985) *Agency and Structure: Dialectics in the Administration of Education*, Deakin University Press, Geelong.

Values and Valuable Leadership Action: A Synthesis and a Commentary

P.A. Duignan and R.J.S. Macpherson

As noted in Chapter 1, administrative practice is often seen to be driven by non-educational criteria, such as those manifest in bureaucratic rationality, in political expediency, and in calls for economic restraint. While noting that it would be naive to expect that these criteria will be easily replaced in the realities of practice, we argue that there is a need to explore ways and means of rekindling a concern for values in the administration of education. Like Evers *et al.*, we recognise this as an intrinsically philosophical and practical task. Essentially, it is philosophy-in-action (Hodgkinson, 1981).

In recent years, economic-driven criteria have become the benchmarks by which the management of schools is being judged. School leaders are being encouraged to believe that an efficient use of resources, or a set of well ordered administrative routines, are distinguishable signs of an effective school. Many believe otherwise. They believe that school leadership should focus on what is worthwhile and on what is worth doing. These are value-driven criteria which force a school community to engage in systematic evaluation of purpose and practice. This does not, of course, exclude the necessity for sound management practices — efficiency and effectiveness can have a moral face. It merely means that other educational values, such as quality, equity and choice, should have a higher profile.

The practicalities of educative leadership mean focusing on what is worthwhile and what is worth doing in a group or large organisation. To question what is being done and how it is being done with a view to doing it better implies the need for a comparative understanding of educational, social and ethical values, ideologies and practicalities (Lakomski, 1985). Examples follow.

How can peoples' valuing of education be changed in ways that are educative?

What examples illustrate how educational communities come to recognise that there are 'right' things to do and 'right' ways of doing them?

If educative leadership is to be philosophy-in-action, what are the values that set it apart from other approaches to leadership?

What non-educational demands are made of leaders of education and how can the legitimacy and the power of these claims be evaluated, accommodated or deflected?

How can leaders reconcile legitimate alternative demands on their actions with educative priorities?

These are complex questions that admit of no easy or ready answers or solutions in theory or practice. Each question must be considered in the light of its detailed circumstances. However, as Evers *et al.* argue in Chapter 2, regardless of the precise nature of these details, questions and issues concerning values in education do permit a 'unified approach or perspective' as well as 'the use of a general coordinating strategy for finding answers, or at least knowing where to look'.

Evers *et al.* contend that most decisions made by leaders have a moral dimension and should, therefore, be subject to moral appraisal. And as educative leadership is a process of creating, promoting and applying knowledge, such an appraisal should be conducted in accordance with a moral theory that values problem solving and the growth of knowledge. A key point follows.

The moral knowledge on which educative leaders base their actions and judgments about whether something is right or wrong, is not a separate and distinct form of knowledge. Rather, it is part and parcel of their total pattern of knowledge, understandings and beliefs — their web of belief (Quine and Ullian, 1978). The growth and development of this web of belief are continuous and part of the same broad principles that govern the growth of knowledge in general.

While Evers *et al.* argue that educative leaders must be held accountable for their actions, and the judgments upon which they are based, they acknowledge that many would argue that administrators are expected to carry out the policies of their organisation, and are, therefore, only partly responsible for their actions. The diffusion of responsibility, especially in large organisations where many people contribute to outcomes, creates problems for moral appraisal.

Who do you praise? Who do you blame?

The answers developed are that leaders should be open to moral appraisal to the extent that they have decision-making control. Their contribution should be appraised for the extent to which they enhance the growth of understanding and knowledge about the organisation and its learning systems. Evers *et al.* also show that this appraisal would help educators discover the essential information linkages in an organisation and how they operate. Knowledge about who does what, and why, in an organisation would then become educative information and help with structural reform.

Educative leaders help create the conditions to make this form of learning possible by being personally educative, that is, by creating and promoting learning throughout all levels of their organisation. Such learning has to be enhanced by informed feedback from all those affected by decisions. Indeed, as decisions with a moral component have consequences for others, there is an obligation on those who make decisions to be sensitive to how others are affected and to the effectiveness of feedback processes. As Evers *et al.* point out, for leaders to claim they are educative means they must be able to develop and maintain a climate that promotes inquiry, values problem solving, welcomes criticism and encourages participation and learning about organisation. Openness to criticism and an ability to learn from mistakes becomes the basis for more valuable leadership action and cycles of reflection and decision making.

Evers *et al.* conclude their argument by suggesting that educative leaders should be judged by five criteria. These are:

> their ability to develop and maintain an effective inquiry and problem-solving culture in their domain;

> their respect and tolerance of different points of view and an acceptance of criticism as the key ingredient in the growth of knowledge within the organisation;

> their ability to adapt to challenges and provide for change in policy or practices through participative feedback and reflection;

> their concern to ensure that people have the freedom to fully participate in this process of learning and growth; and

> their commitment to the holistic belief that their decisions can be defended on the basis of their contribution to the benefits of long-term learning within the organisation.

References

HODGKINSON, C. (1981) *Towards a Philosophy of Administration*, Oxford: Basil Blackwell.

LAKOMSKI, G. (1985) 'Critical Theory and Educational Administration' paper presented to the AERA, Chicago, IL, 31 March–4 April.

QUINE, W.V.O. and ULLIAN, J.S. (1978) *The Web of Belief*, second, revised edition, New York: Random House.

Ethics and Ethical Theory in Educative Leadership: A Pragmatic and Holistic Approach

C.W. Evers

in association with David Dillon, Pat Duignan, Margaret Long, Mac Macpherson, Michael Norman and Judy Williams.

Introduction

Importance of Leadership Appraisal

The exercise of leadership in most contexts involves scope for decision making and influential action, either directly or indirectly through the initiation of acts and events by others. What those in leadership positions decide and do, when mediated and extended by a large organisational context, can also have extensive consequences for others. That consequences may be extensive, however, is not just a matter of the size of an organisation or the way and extent to which the behaviour of its members has been influenced. It is also a question of the extent to which networks of coordinated activity typical of organisational behaviour shape the framework, or set of options, in which others in the wider community can act: what realistic choices they actually have, and know about, and desire to choose.

A further and quite fundamental source of consequences for leadership actions concerns those which have some bearing on how people learn. For what is subject to influence here is not just access to and choice among some static or fixed range of options, but a capacity to develop or change the very framework that currently conditions thought and deed. Decisions that affect how and what people learn have very long-term consequences, for they shape not only the choice of solutions a community may adopt to solve its problems, but the very formulation of those problems and the way in which a community conceptualises its needs, including what it needs to learn to solve its problems.

For these reasons, what leaders do, particularly those in educational organisations or contexts, comes under, and ought to come under, close scrutiny. Communities that have no mechanism for evaluating decisions that can influence decisively their long-term well-being, or have no way of learning from mistakes with that effect, place that well-being at further risk. Fortunately, when it comes to educational decisions, both the community and particular educational organisations have in the past adopted a range of evaluation criteria and associated practices. For example, as an item of public (and private) expenditure, it has been customary to evaluate the effectiveness of educational leadership in terms of the efficient utilisation of resources. Sound educational management practices therefore urge the securing of educational goals through an optimal use of resources. Within the terms of this kind of evaluation there is even some scope for trading off goals against alternative configurations of resource use (Simon, 1976:257–78).

A further type of evaluation, often focused at the goals or aims of education itself, is moral evaluation. At this level, decisions made may be reckoned as just or unjust, right or wrong, good or bad, these being the traditional terms of moral appraisal. We may also use these terms to evaluate the desirability of efficiency as a coordinating strategy for resource management (Goodwin and Wilenski, 1984). Indeed, such is the possible scope of moral appraisal that we may even raise questions about the conditions under which it is desirable to promote human well-being as a goal. Whether the whole practice of moral judgment and evaluation of leaders in their organisational life is ultimately defensible is, of course, controversial, but there can be little doubt that most people expect those in leadership positions to do right rather than wrong, to promote good rather than evil, and to act justly rather than unjustly. And whether and how it is possible to meet this expectation is the principal concern of this discussion.

Outline of Argument

In this chapter it is argued that the moral appraisal of leaders is: (i) possible; (ii) desirable; and (iii) something that should be conducted according to moral theory that values problem solving and the growth of knowledge as goods.

The argument, which is reflected in the main structure of this chapter, proceeds as follows:

(a) Moral knowledge, the basis of our judgments and appraisals, is not a separate and distinct form of knowledge. Rather it is knowledge that is part of, and continuous with, our whole web of belief. Its growth and development is governed by the same broad principles that govern the growth of knowledge in general. This position is defended by claiming that all moral judgments are embedded in or depend on further underlying theories which in turn need to be assessed as knowledge. Whole classes of possible underlying theories have been ruled out by those who believe in the Naturalistic Fallacy and the is/ought dichotomy. These doctrines are therefore challenged.

(b) Leaders can be appraised morally to the extent that they have control over the circumstances of organisational life, including the circumstance of leaving organisational life. Diffusion of responsibility, created by many hands contributing to organisational behaviour, creates problems for moral appraisal. But there is at least one good moral reason for closely identifying and appraising the contribution that individuals make: such identifications enhance the growth of knowledge.

(c) Organisations, like individuals, families, teams, cultures and even species, face and solve problems. The growth of knowledge, of problem-solving means and resources, proceeds in general by a process of conjecture and refutation. Organisations need, therefore, to be able to *learn* from the consequences of organisational activity (Argyris and Schon, 1978; Evers, 1990). For this to be possible organisational leadership should be *educative*, creating and enhancing the possibility of learning, through informed feedback, at all levels of organisation. This is also a requirement for the improvement of moral knowledge which is a part of our total web of belief.

(d) How, then, should we morally appraise educative leadership? Classical utilitarian theories advocate the promotion of human happiness as the fundamental moral good. More recent utilitarian theories speak of maximising expected utility through rational choice. The Kantian tradition also offers standards of moral valuation, though based on theories about the nature of rationality, rather than consequences. A recent influential example of moral principles being justified by a particular theory of rationality, is Rawls' theory of justice.

Both recent utilitarian theories and Kantian theories however, depend, to some extent, on a separation of principles of rationality from the particular *content* of rational choice. When content is taken into account, rational choice becomes a matter of following the advice of our best global theory.

(e) There is much controversy over what theories to count as our best guides for action. But, whatever our starting point in theory and practice, it is claimed that the growth of knowledge, the improvement of problem-solving practices, can be recognised as touchstone or commonly shared theory. As such, it can be regarded as a primary good, the promotion of which is fundamental to other achievements.

In morally appraising educative leaders, what is of interest, therefore, is the extent to which they are able to promote the conditions for effective learning; to what extent problem-solving in organisational life mirrors the social relations of effective inquiry. Since the good of effective inquiry involves learning from criticism through informed feedback, educative leaders need to promote a range of values. These will include: fair distribution of knowledge and access to conditions of learning, respect and tolerance for different viewpoints and experiences, and freedom of thought, inquiry and expression.

Some Issues in Moral Philosophy

The belief that administrative leaders be morally accountable for their leadership actions, or subject to moral appraisal, is predicated on a number of assumptions. The first of these concerns whether moral judgment and evaluation forms a distinct and coherent category — whether it is a distinct and separate form of knowledge.

Quite plainly, there is some theoretical integrity to the patterns of ordinary moral discourse we regularly employ to make judgments. For a time there was wide belief in a particular philosophical theory of meaning. It held that the meaning of moral terms could be known by a careful analysis of how they were used in ordinary discourse. In systematising and classifying these patterns of usage, philosophers and logicians have made detailed studies of what they call 'the logic of moral discourse' or, more ambitiously, 'deontic logic' (Hare, 1952; Hintikka, 1969).

Nowadays, it is better to see discourse as expressing or being underpinned by some theory (or theories). What consistency, structure or pattern there is to be found in discourse reflects the systematic properties of the underlying theory. This view offers an important advantage, namely, that while moral discourse is embedded within a theory, it is not immune from review, criticism, feedback or refutation. It is still an open question whether the underlying theory is mistaken, consistently wrong, or whether it is partly or wholly reducible to some other theory.

Some theories make for radical revisions of our ordinary moral judgments and some do not. Writers as diverse as Skinner and Rawls attempted to explain moral terms by reducing them to some other terms. An example of a reducing theory, proposed by B.F. Skinner in *Beyond Freedom and Dignity*, seems drastic enough to require the wholesale elimination of familiar moral usage.

Good things are positive reinforcers. (p. 103)

When we say that a value judgment is a matter not of fact but of how someone feels about a fact, we are simply distinguishing between a thing and its reinforcing effect. Things themselves are studied by physics and biology, usually without reference to their value, but the reinforcing effects of things are the province of behavioral science, which, to the extent that it is concerned with operant reinforcement, is a science of values. (pp. 103–104)

To make a value judgment by calling something good or bad is to classify it in terms of its reinforcing effects (p. 104).

Skinner has analogous reductions/eliminations for 'justice', 'right', and 'ought', as well as behaviouristic causal analyses for a variety of moral judgments. If this theory is true, there would be so little left in our familiar categories of moral appraisal and their relations to one another, that a moral assessment of what leaders do would be as inappropriate as a moral assessment of the doings of some complex piece of machinery.

Not all reducing theories have such drastic consequences. Varieties of utilitarianism that define good in terms of maximising human happiness, for example, are often tested for adequacy against our ordinary moral language and experience, against the qualified judgments of our folk moral theory (e.g. Brandt, 1959:241–270). Of course, some utilitarians (e.g. Smart, 1956), like Skinner, recommend revising folk theory where conflicts occur. A more generous accommodation with folk moral theory can be found in the theory of justice developed by Rawls (1971). It asserts that our best moral judgments are likely to be those that result from a kind of 'reflective equilibrium' between folk theory and the dictates of a proposed theory's formal principles of justice. Accordingly:

> From the standpoint of moral philosophy, the best account of a person's sense of justice is not the one which fits his judgments prior to his examining any conception of justice, but rather the one which matches his judgments in reflective equilibrium. (Rawls, 1971, p. 48)

The Naturalistic Fallacy

Although we have spoken freely of reducing theories, there exists an argument in moral philosophy to the conclusion that reduction is impossible for a very wide range of alternatives, notably naturalistic theories of ethics. Thus consider definitions of 'good' like: (i) good is a positive reinforcer, or (ii) good is the greatest happiness for the greatest number. Now positive reinforcement and human happiness are part of nature, part of the natural order of things. However, G.E. Moore (1903:5–15) pointed out that for any such naturalistic definition of good, it always makes sense to ask whether it really is true, whether good really is the natural quality the purported definition claims it to be. The significance of this lay in the fact that for Moore, and many others, it was not possible to challenge a correct definition. For definitions, in Moore's sense, were always analytic, or true in virtue of the meanings of their terms, and could be denied only on pain of contradiction, in the same way that it is apparently contradictory to deny (iii) a triangle is a three-sided figure whose interior angles sum to 180°. Because of this, naturalistic definitions of 'good' were said to commit the naturalistic fallacy. In fact, Moore went on to argue that 'good' cannot be defined.

In criticising this argument we can note that it is sustained by a theory of meaning that distinguishes analytic statements or truths from other (synthetic) statements or truths. Nowadays, thanks to the work of Quine (1951; 1960) this distinction, at least in the form required to run the naturalistic fallacy, is widely regarded as untenable (Evers, 1985).

A better view is to see definitions as equivalences constructed within theories. The definition of 'triangle' in (iii), for example, is located within Euclidean geometric theory, but not in non-Euclidean geometries where interior angles generally sum to more than 180° or less than 180°. And since our world is non-Euclidean then the definition in (iii) will serve, in description, as an approximation. Similarly, for ethical terms we construct our definitions within the different (reducing) theories, guided by the systematic dictates of each theory. In this way, definitions will be judged inadequate or not by virtue of the relative advantages of their corresponding embedding theories. And in this regard, moral definitions are no different from definitions of other terms. Moreover, successful reduction in ethics no more requires conservation of meaning than does successful reduction in science — as evidenced by the reduction of, for example, temperature to mean kinetic energy. (On reduction, see Churchland, 1985, and Hooker 1981a, 1981b, 1981c.)

The Is-Ought Dichotomy

A further important view often used to defend the claim that moral discourse and its expressed judgments form a distinct category, is the so-called 'is-ought dichotomy'. First expounded by the eighteenth century philosopher, David Hume, it asserts that there is a radical separation of what *ought* to be from what *is* the case. In moral philosophy this is sometimes expressed as the doctrine that one cannot logically derive an 'ought' from an 'is', or in other words, that no factual premise, or set of premises, is ever sufficient to entail a moral conclusion.

If moral statements are identified as moral solely because they contain (non-logical) moral vocabulary then the doctrine is false. Elementary logic does, in fact, permit the deduction of sentences containing moral words from sentences containing non-moral words. These deductions are sometimes regarded as trivial, and hence not a threat to the is-ought dichotomy. But instead there is now a problem about distinguishing trivial from non-trivial valid deductions. Here the story becomes complicated and the is-ought dichotomy loses its initial appeal. In fact, it begins to beg the question in favour of the autonomy of ethics (Evers, 1985).

The naturalistic fallacy, the is-ought dichotomy, and belief in a theory of meaning that discerns analytic truths in ordinary discourse, conspired to give philosophers an unwarranted confidence in the truth and integrity of the folk moral theories of everyday moral discourse. With the failure of all three positions, this confidence needs either to be earned anew, or relocated in some other moral framework.

In the light of these arguments we may summarise the situation for valuing administrative leadership as follows. Networks of moral claims, judgments, or statements in their various interconnections, we may call a moral theory. In being a theory about aspects of human thought and action, it is embedded in some further, underlying substantive theory that deals with such matters as human nature (its origin and development), autonomy, rationality, and the nature and development of reason, feeling, experience, and our capacity for knowledge. Our ordinary folk morality, which tends to sanction the moral evaluation of leaders in the exercise of administrative leadership, is no exception. Whether this sanctioning is reasonable, however, will depend on:

the truth of folk morality's underlying substantive theory, or
the degree to which some better substantive, but reducing, theory sustains, reinforces, or provides new or different grounds for such sanctionings.

We will examine later the merits of three reducing theories and their associated moralities on this issue.

Educative Leadership and Moral Appaisal

We need to examine the issue of whether there is anything about administrative leadership itself that prevents or limits the application of moral terms of appraisal. To do this we note that leadership can be examined from at least two main perspectives. First, it can be analysed in terms of the *psychological* attributes of persons. Thus a person may be said to be a *leader* although that person is in no formal leadership role or office. Leaders in this sense may exercise influence and control informally, in a variety of ways, including influence aimed at securing leadership roles. A second important sense is to see leadership as a function of organisational role, of organisationally sanctioned authority and control in the exercise of power being vested in a person regardless of psychological attributes. Clearly, these approaches are not exclusive. However, when it comes to the question of moral appraisal, of the accountability and responsibility of leaders acting in organisations, it is the second sense of 'leadership' that raises problems. When it comes to the first sense, we assume that except where there obtain certain pathologies not peculiar to leaders, ordinary moral appraisal is appropriate and no more problematic than it is outside organisational life. Hence our emphasis on organisational role in leadership activity and its appraisal.

The argument in this section will be for two conclusions:

The extent to which moral principles are applicable to officials in organisational roles of leadership is an empirical matter to do largely with the amount of control they exercise in their organisational role, including the option of leaving that role or office.

Organisational contexts which permit the exercise of leadership to the extent that some moral evaluation of leaders is possible, are superior in that they imply the relevance of important internal and external *feedback* concerning the performance of both leader and organisation.

We shall argue that provision for this kind of feedback is best realised by the organisational practice of *educative leadership*. Moreover, we shall suggest that for educational organisations, where decisions can have extensive consequences which affect the long term well-being of a community, realising the possibility of moral assessment is itself morally advantageous. In other words, one important way for a community to secure and promote moral virtues in its social life is by having its organisations so structured that officials, and especially leaders, are subject to moral appraisal.

Morality in Organisational Life

In denying the possibility of applying private morality to public or organisational life, some writers employ what may be called the argument from neutrality. (See Thompson, 1985, for a discussion.) This argument makes two claims: first that officials should follow, or at least act within the past and present decision and policy structure of an organisation, not their own moral principles; and second, that it is not officials that should be held responsible, but the organisation (perhaps at most through its formal officers).

In defence of the first claim, it is maintained that opportunities to act within a specific administrative context occur as a result of acceptance of a position or office. Organisational leaders cannot do just anything they please. They are constrained in the exercise of their leadership, their deliberations, thoughts, and judgments, by an organisation's goals and established commitments, by the demands of office. Therefore, moral assessment is reasonable only at the points of entry or exit, whether to accept a job or whether to resign from it. It is at these points that we register our own valuations of consent or dissent, and what moral unease leaders may feel about aspects of their organisational role is best construed as the moral judgment error of misplaced consent. Where this unease is great 'the choice for the administrator remains to obey or resign' (Thompson, 1985:556).

In responding to this argument it should be noted that in saying officials should act within organisational constraints, there is an ambiguity between social/physical constraints and moral constraints. If 'should' here means 'ought' then the claim amounts to the assertion of a moral imperative for officials to obey or resign. To defend this claim we would have to show that the *carte blanche* approach of initial consent is morally superior to the application of continuous moral review of performance in office. While there may be no problems for closely specified jobs, those that involve initiative, leadership and wide scope for action and decision can result in outcomes not easily predictable at the time of initial consent. To leave officials, in the face of unforeseen circumstances, with only two morally appropriate responses — obey or resign — seems unnecessarily restrictive and inflexible. On the other hand, if 'should' means 'must' in the sense that officials have no choice but to act within organisational constraints, there is still the possibility of morally evaluating not only initial consent, but all that a leader chooses to do within those constraints. The greater the scope for action the more appropriate the practice of wide-ranging moral appraisal. (For examples, see Graham, 1974.)

The second claim of the neutrality argument, that it is organisations which are responsible and not officials, has been defended most frequently by an appeal to the complex structure of organisational decision making. A condition for attributing moral responsibility, as Thompson (1985:559) pointed out, is that a:

> person's actions or omissions ... [are] ... a cause of the outcome. However ... because many people contribute in many different ways to the decisions and policies of an organisation, we may not be able to determine, even in principle, who is morally responsible for those decisions and policies.

And so, it is concluded, the moral evaluation of officials in their organisational lives is inappropriate.

Although organisational activity can be so structured that the delineation of causal chains becomes not only difficult, but perhaps impossible, at least for the purpose of attributing responsibility at a level more fine-grained than the whole organisation, this argument nevertheless gains some unwarranted plausibility through a conflation of two sets of conditions. For example, it is an *ontological* question, a question of how the world is, whether a person's actions matter in the production of an outcome or not. And presumably there is a fact of the matter about this. But whether one can know this fact of the matter is an *epistemological* question that complexity obscures or renders difficult.

Armed with this distinction one may be tempted to conclude that the problem of complexity is not unlike the problem of finding the responsible party to an act when that party's action has been obscured or disguised by their being hidden in a crowd. We know there is some one person responsible, say; we just have a problem of identification. One may be so tempted, but one would be mistaken. The real difficulty the problem of many hands poses, is not the epistemic one of identification, but the ontological one of individuation. For the locus of moral attribution in our folk morality (and also in many other moral theories) is the individual, and when an individual's identifiable action is only part of the causal fabric of larger organisational outcomes that locus blurs and becomes attenuated.

Where familiar exemplars fail to guide, are there any defensible criteria for individuating clusters of causal chains in an apparently continuous causal network, so as to sustain the practice of moral evaluation of officials? There are several things to be said here. For a start, the problem is relatively benign for officials who are *leaders*, since the actions of leaders are more individually prominent in the production of organisational outcomes. This prominence is a natural consequence of the causal role of leaders in organisational life, and undercuts any appeal to moral neutrality. A second point to note is that if criteria are to be found at all, they will be embedded in some *moral theory*. Where our present intuitions on attribution are uncertain, or even indeterminate, we have the option of drawing more heavily on a more elaborated moral theory to guide our folk-informed intuitions. What the criteria are, of course, will depend on the preferred moral theory. (There is a more fundamental theoretical, and somewhat technical, reason for preferring theories that entail the possibility of individuation to those that do not. Such theories do not breach a condition for bivalence, a logical virtue of theories that requires each closed sentence to be either true or false, and each general term to be true or false of each object it denotes (Quine, 1981)).

As well as theoretical advantages of individuation, however, there are moral advantages. That is to say, there are moral gains to be made in so structuring organisational activity that the distribution of responsibility, the application of moral principles, and the practice of moral evaluation, are rendered as clear and as unambiguous as can be achieved.

Educative Leadership and Administration

The place of ethics in administrative theory has been relatively minor until recently. That this should be so reflects the dominance of a so-called 'scientific' view of administration. Perhaps the best known and most influential theory in this tradition is that developed by H.A. Simon, initially in *Administrative Behaviour* (1945) and continuously since then forming part of the work for which he was awarded the Nobel Prize in economics. In Simon's theory, the most important feature of administrator behaviour is *decision making*. If an organisation is to be improved, one obvious place to begin therefore, is to ensure further resources and opportunities for sound decision making, to structure an organisation so that it may, through the exercise of rationality, effectively and efficiently achieve organisational goals (Simon, 1945:1–19).

In evaluating an administrator's decisions however, Simon's theory contains two important strictures. First, because of complexity, and the need to decide many matters quickly, administrators should not try to *optimize*; rather they should try to *satisfice*. Most organisational decisions are made under conditions of bounded rationality: limited time, limited information, limited conceptual resources. Since decisions must be made, the more realistic requirement is that they be *satisfactory* rather than *optimal*. Simon's theory of administrative behaviour is a theory of decision making under conditions of bounded rationality (Simon, 1945:80–96; 1956).

The second stricture concerns moral evaluation. In evaluating an administrative decision, strictly speaking what is evaluated for Simon is the factual relationship that is purported to hold between a decision and its aims (Simon, 1945:49). Inasmuch as aims involve a values dimension, they are either 'given' or else are a *means* to achieve further 'givens'. Where the regress halts ultimately is in subjective human feelings of preference (as manifest in judgments) concerning which there is no fact of the matter as to their correctness. At the level of rational decision making in organisations, the regress halts earlier, and decisions 'must take as their ethical premises the objectives that have been set for the organisation' (Simon, 1945:52; Evers, 1987).

Now notice that when it comes to the evaluation of a leader's decisions, what this model of administrative science evaluates is the rational quality of the relationship between means and ends, not the moral worth of ends or alternative means. This is because Simon holds a view of ethical claims that requires they be eschewed from administrative theory. In a nutshell, his early logical empiricist theory of meaning, still influential in administrative theory, denies that ethical claims are items of knowledge because they do not correspond one-to-one with some observable state of affairs. In proposing an alternative to this theory of administration, the task will be, not to deny the importance of the theory of bounded rationality, but to champion certain modern holistic theories of meaning that do permit ethical judgments to count as knowledge. Indeed, in a view we defend in a later section, ethical claims not only count as knowledge, but they are known and justified in much the same way as all the other claims that comprise our web of belief (Evers and Walker, 1983; Evers, 1988, 1991; Evers and Lakomski, 1991).

If we assume this unity of knowledge, it has major consequences for how we conceive the role of moral appraisal in organisational leadership. For example, decision making can now be construed more generally as *problem-solving*. Correspondingly, an important feature of organisational leadership will be the leader's role in facilitating the problem-solving process. In performing this kind of leadership, however, it's not just a matter of applying existing knowledge and skills to the resolution of organisationally specified problems. There are at least two further issues. First, we now know from epistemology, especially as informed by philosophy of science, that a major element in the growth of knowledge is the process of learning from mistakes, or more grandly in Popper's (1963) terminology, the process of conjecture and refutation. A well structured organisation will, therefore, contain the resources, the administrative structures, to learn from the consequences of its own actions. Indeed, without the opportunity for feedback, an organisation's capacity to learn, or to improve its problem-solving skills, is seriously impaired. (See Simon, 1956, for a related discussion on human problem-solving.)

Second, not all, or even most, of the problems that organisations deal with are pure organisational creations. All problems have social contexts, due partly to the causal embedding of organisations in a wider community and partly to the network of non-organisationally conditioned conventions, expectations, beliefs and feelings that people bring to their jobs. Indeed, on a holistic view of knowledge, the justification of organisationally relevant knowledge owes much to the way it coheres systematically with this broader, prior network of theory that people hold (or, at least, what is best in it). Since an account of the growth of knowledge (or problem-solving potential) broadly, in terms of conjectures and refutations, places a premium on feedback and making correct responses to it, this account may also serve as a model for evaluation (Phillips, 1983; 1985). An important corollary of this epistemic holism is that just as nature may be said to evaluate a scientist's proposals by sometimes being recalcitrant to the point of falsification, so a community and its physical circumstances can expect to be a significant source of feedback to organisationally structured problem-solving. And this will be particularly so if organisations are limited directly by charter to the solution of community-wide problems, such as the effective provision of educational opportunities. The securing of feedback from those most reliably placed to experience the effects of proposed solutions is, therefore, an integral part of promoting the growth of knowledge and enhancing the quality of organisational leadership, decision making and problem-solving (Evers, 1990).

However, as should be clear, this evaluation is not restricted to the so-called empirical consequences of policy and administration. Granted the by now widely accepted blurring of the theory/observation distinction, it is not epistemically feasible to isolate criticisms to the allegedly empirical parts of a theory. There is no such distinct part. Rather it is whole theories, including those sentences couched in familiar moral language, that have (theoretically describable) observable consequences (Quine, 1951; Evers, 1985, 1986; Walker and Evers, 1982). This means that evaluation is a species of theory competition, and one should expect, indeed encourage in the hope of improvement, criticisms at all levels of theory, including obviously enough, the moral. And if our moral judgments lend themselves to improvement through corresponding improvements in our whole theoretical perspective then, as Dewey saw, there are good moral grounds for promoting the growth of knowledge. Indeed, this cannot occur without also promoting the practice of moral appraisal or evaluation, especially of those acting in leadership roles.

The view of organisational functioning presented here lends itself to a corresponding view of organisational leadership. Just as, for Simon, leadership is a matter of facilitating, by example or otherwise, sound organisational decision making, so on the pragmatic and holistic view of knowledge growth through feedback enhanced problem-solving, the leader's central task is the provision of *educative leadership*. That is, as someone concerned with creating, promoting and applying knowledge, a leader must also be an *educator*. As most organised problem-solving is very complex, to enhance learning, administrative leaders should aim to achieve at least two conditions though subject to a general constraint:

> that in the problem formulation and solution planning stages there are identifiable administrative divisions of labour corresponding to designated

tasks and with designated areas of responsibility and standards of achievement. In the absence of these it is difficult to apply evidence of success or failure in any constructive and systematic way; and

that provision be made for the application of evaluative procedures at *all* levels of theory and practice. These procedures will include the creation of opportunities for criticism and the means for *learning* from criticism.

The constraint concerns the fact that if evaluation is part of the learning cycle, where it is placed can affect how efficiently knowledge grows. Theories, practices, the business of problem posing and trying out solutions, all take time. Premature testing could therefore tell against knowledge under development. Some principle of learner autonomy seems to be required to balance error feedback. Nature solves this problem at the level of brain processes in human learning by striking a balance between neural plasticity and neural stability. The need for some such balance, even a constantly shifting one, in organisational learning, must be borne in mind.

In applying feedback at all levels there is clearly no way of insulating an organisation's aims or goals, as distinct from its means, from scrutiny and evaluation. Nor can moral appraisal be ignored, especially when it is of aims or goals and, especially, when it comes from groups directly concerned with or affected by the consequences of those aims. Educative leadership is, therefore, not only epistemically progressive, but by being epistemically progressive it creates through the provision of moral evaluation, *the opportunity for more valuable leadership actions*.

Some Theories of Moral Appraisal

Organisations and their officials are currently subject to moral judgment in a great variety of ways and circumstances. For example, a community may take steps to protect its well-being by legislation, requiring formal independent evaluations of decisions according to criteria that reflect a moral perspective. Instances of this include evaluating the environmental impact of corporate development proposals, compulsory auditing of certain financial records, or product evaluation according to fixed standards to protect consumers. In these kinds of cases the law may be said to enforce a *minimal morality*. Other ways in which moral suasion may be exerted on administrative leaders can range from the slightly less formal, as in the use of codes of professional ethics to regulate and set bounds to behaviour, through to the thoroughly informal influence of community standards and moral climate. However, in all cases, what is important for the practice of problem-solving, is whether the moral principles being applied in the evaluation of conduct are themselves warranted.

In considering this broad issue, we examine three theories of moral justification. The *first* is utilitarianism, which, because of its influence, we consider in some detail. The *second*, Rawls' theory, is an example from the Kantian tradition. And the *third*, which is advocated here, is drawn from the traditions of both Dewey and Popper.

The aim of this section is to:

demonstrate how moral reasoning and decision making is conceived within some major intellectual traditions, and

indicate some broader grounds for preferring a pragmatic and holistic approach to moral theory that is based on theory of knowledge.

Utilitarian Theories

Ethical theories characteristically divide into a theory of value, usually concerned with the nature of good, or right, or justice, and a theory of obligation, which sets out what we must do, or what we are obligated to do (Frankena, 1963:1–46). Teleological or consequentialist theories usually define 'good' as some quality, natural or non-natural, and then evaluate actions in terms of the amount of good produced, or the resulting balance of good over evil. These theories also tend to be monistic, with 'right' or 'just' being defined, derivatively, in terms of 'good'.

The most influential teleological theory has been utilitarianism, or better, varieties of utilitarianism, since it exists in a number of forms. A number of classifications of these forms are possible, but for our purposes we distinguish hedonistic from preferential theories, and within each of these, rule from act theories. With regard to the first division, the Bentham-Mill tradition adopts a theory of value that equates good with maximising human happiness or, more precisely, the greatest balance of pleasure over pain. Mill (1861) makes the identification at one remove, equating good with what is desirable and pleasure with what all people desire and, consequently, incurs the wrath of those sensitive to the naturalistic fallacy by equating what is desirable with what is desired. In any case, on this theory of value, pleasure, or happiness, and these are to be understood very broadly, function as intrinsic good.

On the question of obligation, what ought to be done, what constitutes the right thing to do, is that course of action which brings about the largest amount or quantity of human happiness. Although there may be problems *determining* when this condition is met, nevertheless, theoretically there is a fact of the matter about whether an action is right or wrong. The next problem is the epistemological one of knowing what the relevant quantities are prior to their summation. This problem is made severe by noting that happiness may not be a sensation (with intensity and duration) that lends itself to quantitative summation. For example, pleasures appear to be qualitatively different. Mill expresses his concern over this point by claiming that Socrates dissatisfied is better than a fool satisfied. Unfortunately, pleasures that are qualitatively different do not lend themselves to addition. Is the pleasure derived from an elegant proof of a theorem comparable to the pleasures of good food? If the latter is a sensation, then it is doubtful that the former is, or at least not the same *kind* of sensation; that is, it differs on more than just intensity and duration. However, even if all happiness, even broadly construed, is sensation of the same kind, then being essentially a matter of private experience, it would seem impossible to know the amount of sensation involved beyond one's own experience. The assumption of intersubjective equivalence seems at odds with behavioural manifestations of great variety in tastes and preferences.

Assuming that these problems can be solved, there is then a further difficulty to do with the nature of the utilitarian reduction of folk morality. If it is construed as a largely conservative reduction (as most theorists do), then it will be presumed to leave intact the bulk of our ordinary moral judgments. We must try then to make the two sources of judgment — utilitarian and folk — cohere where there appear to be conflicts. For example, if utilitarianism is concerned exclusively with maximising happiness, then that is a consideration that appears to be independent of *distribution* of happiness. Indeed, some ways of maximising happiness can be profoundly unjust. The classic case is scapegoating, perhaps the sacrificing of an innocent person in order to placate an angry mob. Other examples include breaking promises or telling lies, which are sanctioned every time an increase in utility results.

To avoid this sort of difficulty, it is standard to distinguish act utilitarianism from rule utilitarianism. The above conflicts with folk morality appear to be generated by applying the principle of utility to each individual act. However, the rule utilitarian requires only that moral *rules or principles* be justified by the principle of utility (Rawls, 1955; Mabbott, 1956). On this theory, in deciding what we ought to do in a given situation, we look for moral guidance from a set of rules that are in turn justified. And here justification consists in showing that following some favoured set of rules will produce more happiness than following any other set. Thus a society with a rule of justice requiring fair distribution of happiness is happier than one without such a rule. And similarly for justification of truth telling and promise keeping.

This sounds well but complications emerge when we consider problems created by exceptions. For example, why cannot we permit exceptions to a rule where the exceptions are justified by the principle of utility? Truth telling may be a justifiable practice in general but there are clearly cases where breaches will engender much greater happiness. The same point holds, perhaps to a lesser extent, with the practice of justice, or promise keeping (Smart, 1956). The challenge for the rule utilitarian here is to devise some way of either admitting exceptions without rule utilitarianism collapsing back into act utilitarianism, or prohibiting exceptions without undermining the point of utilitarian justification, namely the appeal to human happiness.

One important move is to claim that just as, say, truth telling is a practice, so truth-telling-with-exceptions is an alternative practice. The rule utilitarian then attempts to adjudicate the merits of these distinct practices on the basis of the principle of maximising utility, usually deciding in favour of exceptionless practices. Some writers (e.g. McCloskey, 1957) have observed, however, that this move rests on a confusion between constitutive rules and regulative rules. Constitutive rules *define* a practice, and make it what it is; for example in the rules of chess, or golf. Regulative rules, on the other hand, do no such thing; they are like rules of thumb, functioning to regulate behaviour. Critics of pure rule utilitarianism deny that truth telling, promise keeping, and the like are practices defined by constitutive rules which admit exceptions only in the form of alternative constitutively defined practices. These practices may reflect agreed social practices or conventions, but they are regulative nonetheless. It is worth noting that in either case, if the rule utilitarian is after a conservative reduction there is considerable scope for conflict with our ordinary moral judgments.

For someone like Smart (1973) who favours a more radical reduction, conflicts with folk morality are not so important. Where the appraisals of his act utilitarianism run counter to the demands of commonsense morality, Smart concludes instead, 'so much the worse for our ordinary moral judgments'. His point is that we should be using utilitarianism to inform and correct our folk morality rather than vice versa. The main worry with this bold approach is that any number of moral theories can entail major differences with folk theory. Why should we choose act utilitarianism? Clearly some pretty major theoretical advantages need to accrue in order to make a radical reduction attractive.

Although this issue is not developed in detail in the hedonistic tradition, what we earlier called the 'preferential' tradition does provide some interesting possibilities. On this more recent approach to utilitarian ethics, the epistemological problem of knowing magnitudes of sensations is by-passed by dealing directly with *expressed preferences*. As Beauchamp and Childress (1984:46–47) remark:

> The major alternative approach is to appeal to the language of individual preferences. For this approach, the concept of utility refers not to experiences or states of affairs, but rather to one's actual preferences, as determined by one's behaviour. To maximise a single person's utility is to provide what one has chosen or would choose from among the available alternatives that might be produced. To maximise the utility of all persons affected by an action or policy is to maximise the utility of the aggregate group.

These remarks are very general. To give a more detailed account of how modern preference utilitarianism works, as well as some of its theoretical advantages, we shall sketch some of the main features of the influential theory developed by Harsanyi (1977; 1980a).

In the case of maximising a single person's utility, Harsanyi (1977:43) considers three broad conditions under which the rationality of expressed preferences can be defined:

(i) under conditions of *uncertainty* where some or all probabilities are unknown;

(ii) under conditions of *risk* where all probabilities of outcomes are known, an individual's preferences are assumed to *maximise expected utility*, and

(iii) under conditions of certainty where all outcomes are known, an individual's preferences are assumed to *maximise utility*.

Decision theory deals with the problem of maximising expected utility under conditions of risk and uncertainty, although for Harsanyi, more is required for *moral* decision making. Where a single person is engaged in rational interaction with one or more other persons, each rationally pursuing his/her own objectives, the problem of determining strategies, or preferences, which are assumed to maximise expected utility is a matter for that part of decision theory known as the mathematical theory of games. Again, Harsanyi does not consider game theoretic constraints sufficient to constitute *moral* decision making.

What he requires for ethics is 'a theory of rational behaviour in the service of the common interests of society as a whole' (Harsanyi, 1977:43). Thus, consider a person x, rationally deciding which of two social systems or arrangements to prefer. If x knows what position he/she would occupy in each system then x would presumably decide on the basis of the expected utility maximisation decision rule. But while this is certainly a judgment of personal preference, it is hardly a *moral* value judgment. However:

> in contrast, most of us will admit that he would be making a moral value judgment if he chose between the two social systems without knowing what his personal position would be under either system. (Harsanyi, 1975:45)

Under this condition of ignorance, however, where each society has, say, n individuals in positions from the worst-off to the best-off, x must assume that the probability of being in any position in either society is $1/n$, a condition Harsanyi calls the *equi-probability assumption*. He then goes on to argue (p. 45) that an individual who chooses between the two systems on the principle of maximising expected utility, but under the assumption of equi-probability,

> would always choose that social system which, in his opinion, would yield the higher *average utility level* to the individual members of the society.

Applied to individuals in society, what this means is that making rational moral value judgments will involve maximising the average utility level of *all* individuals in society. According to Harsanyi, on this criterion rule utilitarianism is rationally (and morally) preferable to act utilitarianism, so in practice it is best to interpret the principle of maximising social utility as a constraint on proposed moral rules.

For those using the theory to evaluate the actions of organisational leaders, it sanctions some controversial moral decisions. As a theory of value that equates good with maximising average utility of *all* individuals in society, leaders are under no obvious obligations to help those who are worse off, or even at the bottom of the social heap. Indeed, the practice of positive discrimination, not just in education, but in employment and welfare generally, would appear not to maximise all individual welfare functions. Of course, differences in felt need are relevant to satisfaction, and hence utility, but then a very greedy person would arguably require more goods than a poor or a sick person for a corresponding increase in utility. There are other consequences too, but some of these should emerge when this theory is seen against a major deontological rival. Note however, that what plausibility it may lose in appearing to be a more radical reduction of folk morality, it gains in grounding moral decision making in a general theory of rationality. Its moral judgments are supported then partly in virtue of the broad theoretical soundness of the theory of rationality.

Deontological Theories

Generally speaking, deontological theories of moral appraisal hold that some actions are right or wrong independent of their consequences. The usual pattern of deontological moral justification is to show how right actions are those that are entailed or sanctioned by a theory of reason. Thus Kant, a rule deontologist, held that moral rules were justified if they conformed to a single categorical imperative, which required that rules should be universalisable. And to be universalisable, a rule must be able to be conceived and willed to be acted upon by all without contradiction. To see how this works, consider Kant's (1947:85–86) objections to a rule for making promises that will later be broken.

> How would things stand if my maxim became a universal law? I then see straight away that this maxim can never rank as a universal law of nature and be self-consistent, but must necessarily contradict itself. For the universality of a law that everyone believing himself to be in need can make any promise he pleases with the intention not to keep it would make promising, and the very purpose of promising, itself impossible, since no one would believe he was being promised anything, but would laugh at utterances of this kind as empty shams.

Rather than dwelling on the various problems of the categorical imperative as a standard of moral justification, we shall instead consider what is probably the most influential deontological theory of recent times, namely that developed by Rawls (1971). Because of their structural similarities, Rawls' theory will provide some interesting comparisons with Harsanyi's theory.

What Rawls is primarily concerned with is demonstrating what principles of social justice would be chosen by rational persons reasoning in an impartial way. To simulate impartiality he conducts a thought experiment where people are to choose the basic principles of justice regulating social life from behind a 'veil of ignorance' (Rawls, 1971:136–42). This amounts to Harsanyi's condition of not knowing what one's social position will be in the span of options from the worst-off to the best-off. However, the principle of rationality for Rawls is not Bayesian rationality; rather it is the *maximin* rule. According to Rawls (1971:152–153):

> The maximin rule tells us to rank alternatives by their worst possible outcomes: we are to adopt the alternative the worst outcome of which is superior to the worst outcome of the others.

To see how this rule works consider how it guides action in a simple case. We have a choice of carrying an umbrella to work or not. If it rains and we are without the umbrella we could catch cold and may even become seriously ill. On the other hand, if we carry the umbrella and it fails to rain we merely have the inconvenience of extra baggage. Since the worst outcome of carrying an umbrella is always superior to the worst outcome of not, rationally, we should always carry an umbrella to work.

Now Rawls (1971:302) uses this principle of rationality to argue that two (ordered) principles of justice would be chosen. They are:

> each person is to have an equal right to the most extensive total system of equal basic liberties compatible with a similar system of liberty for all; and

social and economic inequalities are to be arranged so that they are both

to the greatest benefit of the least advantaged consistent with the just savings principle, and

attached to offices and positions open to all under conditions of fair equality of opportunity.

The central idea of Rawls' (1971:303) theory is that:

all social primary goods — liberty and opportunity, income and wealth, and the bases of self-respect — are to be distributed equally unless an unequal distribution of any or all of these goods is to the advantage of the least favoured.

It is easy to see how these principles could be applied to administrative contexts in education. Indeed, Rawls (1971:107) himself draws a number of conclusions:

Thus, for example, resources for education are not to be allotted solely or necessarily mainly according to their return as estimated in productive trained abilities, but also according to their worth in enriching the personal and social life of citizens, including here the less favoured.

He also observes (p. 101) that his 'derivative principle' (choosing an equal distribution unless another distribution makes all parties better off):

would allocate resources in education, say, so as to improve the long-term expectation of the least favoured.

Historically, deontological arguments have tended to support minimum standards of basic educational provision for all, and equality of opportunity for all where educational provision is scarce. In these broad moral aims they cohere with much that is found in our ordinary folk morality. Perhaps because of this agreement, dissent from Rawls's theory is often directed at his theory of rationality.

As the example of the umbrella makes clear, maximin does not appear sensitive to the question of the *probability* of worst outcomes. For while it seems to be a rational decision rule in, say, Melbourne, it would be decidedly eccentric in, say, Alice Springs or any other place that does not enjoy Melbourne's capacity for unpredictable weather. Other difficulties with maximin are canvassed in the literature, but since modern moral theory is so sensitive to theory of rationality, it may be useful to dwell a while on two important points about rationality.

First, methodologically, theories of rationality involve a study and refinement of folk theoretic rational practice, the fundamental example of which is goal directed behaviour. But generating a theory of rational behaviour that is relatively free from the specific contexts and problem situations in which people act, calls for a fair measure of abstraction. Not surprisingly, an empirical gap emerges between content-specific problem-solving practices and decision making, and the dictates of abstract rationality (Davidson, 1974). One solution to this gap problem is to see the abstract theory as a *normative* theory that may be called upon to correct or improve our content-laden reasoning. A better solution, in our view, is to deny the distinction between rationality and content, or substantive theory. Where a particular type of reasoning appears ubiquitous we have, instead, evidence of common or *touchstone theory*. Where ubiquity lapses, content exerts its pull. Promoting good standards of rationality is therefore a matter of promoting the kind of reasoning employed in and exhibited by our best theories. Indeed, it will involve a further willingness to engage in epistemological practices aimed at improving those theories.

Second, since the growth of reasoning occurs along with the growth of knowledge, indeed is part of that process, empirical theories of human reasoning and knowledge growth, how people actually learn and think, assume a fundamental importance. (For examples contrary to rationalistic abstract models see Tversky and Kahneman, 1981; Stich and Nisbett, 1980.) Since ethical theory (as well as rationality theory) is part of the more elaborate global theory of the world that we all build up from infancy onwards (and hope now to continue improving), we propose to conclude by examining the kind of moral issues and precepts that appear basic to any improvement of reasoning or, in fact, of knowledge in general. We shall argue that leadership should be educative, and that it should aim to meet these precepts whatever else it does.

Pragmatic Holism and Moral Procedures for Leaders

Earlier, we argued that organisational activity directed at problem-solving should mirror certain epistemological strategies for promoting the growth of knowledge. The model of educative leader was based on these strategies and, therefore, educative leaders were claimed to have an organisational role in promoting institutional learning. Since the overriding epistemological structure of such learning is the general schema of conjecture and refutation, its organisational instantiation requires the provision and maintenance of informed feedback to organisations from all relevant sources. In this section we want to suggest some broadly moral requirements for the existence and maintenance of organised learning or problem solving and propose that these requirements be used to morally evaluate educative leadership. The approach we adopt is in a pragmatic realist tradition that draws heavily on Dewey and Popper. It also owes much to the work of J.C. Walker (1983, 1987).

Organised (or even individual) learning is a social activity that (i) takes place in a network of social relations of inquiry, and (ii) assumes some prior distribution of knowledge. We also know that some distributions of knowledge diminish opportunities for learning. For example, knowledge vital to the solution of problems may be concentrated in certain specialised groups, such as professions, or kept exclusively in the hands of experts, where its further distribution is subject to regulation, perhaps the payment of tariff. The problem-solving resources of a well educated community constitutes a powerful consideration in making knowledge as widely available as possible. Even where it is arguable that expertise only develops under conditions of restricted distribution, it does not follow that *opportunities* to gain expertise should be restricted. On the matter of distribution of knowledge therefore, an individual, an organisation, and a community's capacity to develop successfully will depend on the provision of:

> access for all to the conditions of learning and when, and only when, these are restricted; and
> equal opportunity for access to the conditions of learning.

Participation in the social relations of effective inquiry also carries some moral requirements. For example, respect and tolerance for different points of view is the cornerstone of a theory that sees criticism as the key ingredient in the growth of knowledge. Like-mindedness may be a virtue in consolidating, or even developing to a certain point, a particular perspective, but without criticism its testable consequences are diminished by default. Errors can thus remain to live on unchecked in like-minded solutions.

Like Popper's open society, the open organisation or community will be concerned primarily with *democratic reform*, with maximising provision for the correction of policy and practice through informed participative feedback from those most concerned with the consequences of policy and practice. There is, therefore, also a premium on *freedom* as a virtue, being a requirement for full participation in a fundamentally *epistemic* community governed by the social relations of effective inquiry. Everyday school practice should reflect an appropriate epistemology. The educative leader should prefer and promote approaches to learning that are based on dialogue, on conjecture and on refutation.

It is against the maintenance of these relations that educative leaders should be evaluated.

Although the theory we have sketched in outline will lend itself to more detailed working out in relation to specific problems and issues of practice, we propose to conclude by locating the theory in our earlier taxonomy of moral theories. Pragmatic holist moral theory is first of all a consequentialist or teleological theory, though of a non-utilitarian kind. It is pragmatic in holding that all our beliefs are in principle open to revision. It is holistic in that principles of revision include the consistency, coherence, comprehensiveness, and simplicity of our total belief system, including our moral beliefs. On theory of value it follows Dewey in identifying good with problem-solving — a value that is arguably *touchstone* for any comprehensive account of the human condition. This view of value should not make for too radical a departure from certain widely held moral values, such as altruism, fairness, and concern for human well-being. For evolution, itself an example of conjecture and refutation, though at the biological level, could be expected to favour some moral dispositions over others (Ruse and Wilson, 1986). And, it is, perhaps, these initial dispositions (or epigenetic rules) overlaid merely with further learning and experience, that explain our present folk morality and the direction of attempts to revise and reduce it.

Because the theory deals with very general constraints on problem-solving, it is best defended as a form of *rule-consequentialism*. That is, the touchstone virtue of problem-solving, of promoting the growth of knowledge, is used to adjudicate rules or principles of social practice, to determine whether they are fundamentally *educative*. Such a defence presumes that alternative short cuts and quick fixes, while they may maximise, for example, short-term happiness, do not make for sound long-term progress. And it is against the provision of long-term learning that educative leaders in *educational* organisations should be evaluated.

References

ARGYRIS, C. and SCHON, D. (1978) *Organisational Learning: A Theory of Action Perspective*, Menlo Park, CA: Addison-Wesley.

BEAUCHAMP, T. and CHILDRESS, J.F. (1984) 'Morality, ethics and ethical theories' in SOLA, P.A. (Ed.) *Ethics, Education and Administrative Decisions*, New York: Peter Lang.

BRANDT, R.B. (1959) *Ethical Theory*, Englewood Cliffs: Prentice-Hall.

CHURCHLAND, P.M. (1985) 'Reduction qualia, and the direct introspection of brain states', *Journal of Philosophy*, **82**, 1, 8–28.

DANIELS, N. (1975) *Reading Rawls*, Oxford: Basil Blackwell.

DAVIDSON, D. (1974) 'Psychology as philosophy' in BROWN, S.C. (Ed.) *Philosophy of Psychology*, London: Macmillan.

EVERS, C.W. (1985) 'Hodgkinson on ethics and the philosophy of administration', *Educational Administration Quarterly*, **21**, 2, 27–50.

EVERS, C.W. (1987) 'Philosophical research in educational administration' in MACPHERSON, R.J.S. (Ed.) *Ways and Meanings of Research in Educational Administration*, Armidale: University of New England.

EVERS, C.W. (1988) 'Educational administration and the new philosophy of science', *The Journal of Educational Administration*, **26**, 1, 3–22.

EVERS, C.W. (1990) 'Schooling, organisational learning and efficiency in the growth of knowledge', in CHAPMAN, J.D. (Ed.) *School-Based Decision-Making and Management*, London: Falmer Press.

EVERS, C.W. and LAKOMSKI, G. (1991) *Knowing Educational Administration*, Oxford: Pergamon.

EVERS, C.W. and WALKER, J.C. (1983) 'Knowledge partitioned sets and extensionality: A refutation of the forms of knowledge thesis', *Journal of Philosophy of Education*, **17**, 2, 155–170.

FRANKENA, W.K. (1963) *Ethics*, Englewood Cliffs: Prentice-Hall.

GOODWIN, R.E. and WILENSKI, P. (1984) 'Beyond efficiency: The logical underpinnings of administrative principles', *Public Administration Review*, **45**, 512–517.

GRAHAM, G. (1974) 'Ethical guidelines for public administrators', *Public Administration Review*, **34**, 90–92.

HARE, R.M. (1952) *The Language of Morals*, Oxford: Oxford University Press.

HARSANYI, J. (1975) 'Can the maximin principle serve as a basis for morality? A critique of John Rawls' theory', *American Political Science Review*, **69**, 594–606, cited as reprinted in HARSANYI, J. (1980) *Essays on Ethics, Social Behaviour, and Scientific Explanation*, Dordrecht: Reidel.

HARSANYI, J. (1977) 'Morality and the theory of rational behaviour' in SEN, A. and WILLIAMS, B. (Eds) *Utilitarianism and Beyond*, London: Cambridge University Press.

HARSANYI, J. (1980a) 'Advances in understanding rational behaviour' in HARSANYI, J. (1980) *Essays on Ethics, Social Behaviour, and Scientific Explanation*, Dordrecht: Reidel.

HARSANYI, J. (1980b) *Essays on Ethics, Social Behaviour, and Scientific Explanation*, Dordrecht: Reidel.

HINTIKKA, J. (1969) 'Deontic logic and its philosophical morals', in HINTIKKA, J. *Models for Modalities*, Dordrecht: Reidel.

HOOKER, C.A. (1981a) 'Towards a general theory of reduction I', *Dialogue*, **20**, 1, 38–59.

HOOKER, C.A. (1981b) 'Towards a general theory of reduction II', *Dialogue*, **20**, 2, 201–236.

HOOKER, C.A. (1981c) 'Towards a general theory of reduction III', *Dialogue*, **20**, 3, 496–529.

KANT, I. (1947) *Groundwork of the Metaphysics of Morals*, translated by PATON, H.J., London: Hutchinson and Co.

KURTZMAN, R.D. (1970) '"Is, ought" and the autonomy of ethics', *Philosophical Review*, **79**, 493–509.

MABBOTT, J.D. (1956) 'Interpretations of Mill's "Utilitarianism"', *Philosophical Quarterly*, **6**, 115–20.

McCLOSKEY, H.J. (1957) 'An examination of restricted utilitarianism', *Philosophical Review*, **66**, 466–85.

MILL, J.S. (1861) *Utilitarianism*, 1962 edition, London: Collins.

MOORE, G.E. (1903) *Principia Ethica*, London: Cambridge University Press.

PHILLIPS, D.C. (1983) 'After the wake: Postpositivistic educational thought', *Educational Researcher*, **12**, 5, 4–12.

PHILLIPS, D.C. (1985) 'Is doing evaluation like doing science, or vice-versa?' *Evaluation Research Society Newsletter*, **9**, 2, 1–2.

POPPER, K.R. (1963) *Conjectures and Refutations*, London: Routledge and Kegan Paul.

POPPER, K.R. (1972) *Objective Knowledge*, Oxford: Oxford University Press.

QUINE, W.V.O. (1951) 'Two dogmas of empiricism', *Philosophical Review*, **60**, 20–43.

QUINE, W.V.O. (1960) *Word and Object*, Cambridge, MA: MIT Press.

QUINE, W.V.O. (1981) 'What price bivalence?', *Journal of Philosophy*, **78**, 90–95.

RAWLS, J. (1955) 'Two concepts of rules', *Philosophical Review*, **64**, 3–32.

RAWLS, J. (1971) *A Theory of Justice*, Cambridge, MA: Harvard University Press.

RUSE, M. and WILSON, E.O. (1986) 'Moral philosophy as applied science', *Philosophy*, **61**, 173–192.

SIMON, H.A. (1945) *Administrative Behaviour*, London: Macmillan.

SIMON, H.A. (1956) *Models of Man*, New York: Wiley.

SIMON, H.A. (1976) *Administrative Behaviour*, third edition expanded with new introduction, London: Macmillan.

SKINNER, B.F. (1971) *Beyond Freedom and Dignity*, Harmondsworth: Penguin.

SMART, J.J.C. (1956) 'Extreme and restricted utilitarianism', *Philosophical Quarterly*, **6**, 344–54.

SMART, J.J.C. (1973) 'An outline of a system of utilitarian ethics' in SMART, J.J.C. and WILLIAMS, B. (Eds) *Utilitarianism: For and Against*, London: Cambridge University Press.

STICH, S.P. and NISBETT, R.E. (1980) 'Justification and the psychology of human reasoning', *Philosophy of Science*, **47**, 188–202.

THOMPSON, D.F. (1985) 'The possibility of administrative ethics', *Public Administration Review*, **45**, 555–561.

TVERSKY, A. and KAHNEMAN, D. (1981) 'The framing of decisions and the psychology of choice', *Science*, **211**, 453–458.

WALKER, J.C. (1983) 'Materialism and the growth of knowledge in education', *Occasional Paper*, Sydney University Department of Education, 14–18.

WALKER, J.C. (1987) *Educative Leadership for Curriculum Development: A Pragmatic and Holistic Approach*, Canberra: ACT Schools Authority.
WALKER, J.C. and EVERS, C.W. (1982) 'Epistemology and justifying the curriculum of educational studies', *British Journal of Educational Studies*, **30**, 2, 312–329.
WILLIAMS, B. (1985) *Ethics and the Limits of Philosophy*, Glasgow: Fontana.

Educational Leadership for Curriculum Development: A Synthesis and a Commentary

P.A. Duignan and R.J.S. Macpherson

A major concern for school leaders is the overall content, process, scope, orientation, and value of the curriculum that clients experience. This concern has many facets. For example, educational leaders often face dilemmas to do with what constitutes a valuable curriculum given the demands of clients and their diverse needs, the likely future needs of clients, how clients learn best, as well as the changing priorities of educators, the school system and the host society.

A useful first question is: What criteria should be used to define a curriculum as educational? Second, how should a balance be struck between vocational, neo-classical, liberal, progressive, socially-critical, religious and other values in the curriculum? Third, what is the nature of knowledge that constitutes curriculum? Is this knowledge objective, subjective or dialectical in nature?

The practicalities of curriculum development present a related set of dilemmas. What are the advantages and disadvantages of decentralising curriculum development? Curriculum development can only proceed at the pace at which educators change their philosophies, beliefs and practices. This point then raises a number of questions. What change strategies are available to the educative leader? What examples illustrate effective leadership practices for curriculum development in an educational community? What 'rules-for-success' for educative leadership can be derived from these examples and recent research into curriculum development?

Walker *et al.* in Chapter 3, advocate a strong role for educative leaders in helping to determine what counts as an educative curriculum. They argue that adopting an educative approach demands an examination of the plurality of curriculum values, as well as the selection and organisation of content, materials and teaching and learning practices. In arguing for a coherent and holistic curriculum, Walker *et al.* suggest a problem-solving approach with a pragmatic emphasis on the unity of knowledge — as opposed to using partitionist theories of knowledge. Further, people bring different theoretical perspectives to bear on the dilemmas of curriculum. As Walker *et al.* point out:

> Anyone with an interest in a curriculum situation has a theoretical view, and if that interest clashes with other interests, it is likely that the

theoretical views will clash too, and consequently the view of what
ought to be done.

In order to deal with such pluralistic and often competing value and
theoretical positions, Walker *et al.* argue that educative leaders should try to
identify the common ground, or touchstone, to obtain clues as to where communication, cooperation and progress can begin. This process of developing
touchstone involves a frank and open but rigorous examination of theories in
competition on matters of substance and method. It also means that it is
essential to recognise current structures and how they change, and therefore, to
regularly reconcile views with vertical as well as horizontal negotiations. Hence,
touchstone is a process for making judgments between incompatible theoretical
and practical options, and as such is a valuable tool for the educative leader.

According to Walker *et al.* there are five steps an educative leader can take
in the development and implementation of a pragmatic, holistic and coherent
curriculum:

1 Find out, through situational analysis, what the relevant people in the
situation regard as their problems. The leader's own problems are, of
course, part of this. Identification of perceived problems can be done
explicitly, by obtaining written or verbal accounts from people of what is
preventing them from obtaining their goals, or implicitly, by observing
and interpreting their responses to situations and their more settled
practices;

2 Given their explicit or implicit understanding of what their problems
are, how do they see their options for dealing with them? Can the
educative leader find out what participants in the situation think are
available and practicable solutions to their problems?

3 Analyse each account of perceived problems and solutions (or each
theory of the situation) and assess the degree of internal coherence in
each account. Are there inconsistencies or very loose connections in the
views and practices of the people whose account it is? The assumption,
of course, is that the greater the coherence, the greater the efficacy of
the account;

4 Analyse the relations between these accounts, the different problems-
solutions frameworks of participants in the situation, to determine the
degree of mutual coherence among them. How do the perceived problems and solutions of one individual or group match up with the perceived problems and solutions of other individuals and groups? Where is
the overlap (touchstone) and where is the conflict (theory in competition)?
How much of each is there and how significant, practically speaking, are
they? Since, of course, these are rooted in the practical situation, the
analysis for coherence means addressing the issues of culture, harmony,
diversity or divergence between ways of life present in the situation;

5 Work out what options may be available, either derived from or negotiated through touchstone, for tackling the shared and unshared problems
of the participants in a situation. To maximise touchstone, it is possible
that through further learning and negotiation some participants may

come to see hitherto unperceived solutions to their problems or revise their ideas of what their problems are. If so, competition and touchstone will have been reconstructed.

The challenge for the educative leader is to help create a culture of openness within which individuals are encouraged to state their own accounts of events, explore the positions of other individuals and groups, determine the conflict in the basic assumptions and theories in use of these individuals and groups, and attempt to determine the overlap, the touchstone, which will provide the common ground on which to build pragmatic solutions to complex problems. In Chapter 3, Walker *et al.* provide the rationale, justification and theoretical framework for such leadership.

A Philosophy of Leadership in Curriculum Development: A Pragmatic and Holistic Approach

J.C. Walker

in association with Pat Duignan, Pat Flynn, David Francis, Ron Ikin, Mac Macpherson, Bill Maxwell and Beryl Wade

Introduction

The pressures on leaders in education are often intense, whether in the school or in other parts of the educational system. Responding to a variety of frequently conflicting demands is not easy when decisions must be made. Attempts to persuade others on matters of policy and practice are made all the more difficult when lack of time and resources curtail opportunities for discussion and negotiation.

Yet leadership *in education*, we might expect, should contribute understanding of and respect for genuine differences in needs, problems and opinions. It should facilitate the learning that leads to such understanding within decision making about education as much as in classroom teaching and learning. Leadership in education should be *educative*, in intent and outcome. How is this possible, given the pressures on educational leaders?

We offer some practical solutions to the problems of educational leaders. We argue that by taking a decisive role in curriculum development, school principals, team leaders and system administrators will be better equipped to tackle their problems and promote their roles as educational leaders. In particular, it is in the interest of educational leaders to *take the lead* in public as well as in professional debate about the direction education is going, otherwise they may find that in a context of increasing public concern about and political pressure on education, their roles as educational leaders could slip away from them.

The practical suggestions offered in this chapter flow from a problem-solving approach to educational leadership. This approach is frankly pragmatic. It claims that there is a practical payoff for leaders if they take the trouble to analyse their situation carefully, clarify their own values and views of knowledge and learning, and try to understand the problems of others in education.

We advocate a clear role for educational leaders, consistent with this problem-solving approach. The role is *educative*: the educative leader is a negotiator, an analyst of educational situations, an evaluator of the relative merits of a variety of often conflicting viewpoints, a confident decision maker, a teacher, and, most importantly, a learner. The leader brings all these together in curriculum development.

This role and the problem-solving approach it reflects derive, in turn, from a definite philosophy of educative leadership. Leaders themselves develop their philosophy by critically but practically scrutinising their own educational values, their views of learning and the nature of knowledge. This philosophy, then, makes no bones about insisting on the importance of theory for effective educational leadership. Theory, however, is not merely the product of academic theorists; it is always present in practical decisions and actions. Our actions as leaders reflect our values, our views of learning and knowledge in the curriculum, and our approaches to the politics and administration of education. 'Theory' is used throughout this chapter in a broad sense, the sense in which leaders, whether they like it or not, are theorists.

This being so, the point for an educative leader is to be a practically effective theorist. This means working on your theory by thinking hard about your role in curriculum development. Thus we make no apology for assuming that some hard intellectual work has to be done. Whether the chapter is judged helpful or not should be decided by its contribution to the practical tasks, problems and aspirations of educational leaders.

The chapter commences with a discussion of the scope of curriculum theory, acknowledging the wide variety of views on the topic, and arguing that this variety needs to be taken into account by educative leaders. After examining some strengths and weaknesses of curriculum theory, it broaches the issue of what constitutes an 'educative curriculum', claiming that any answer to the question will involve taking up some theoretical position. Given the variety of possible theoretical views, it is argued, we need some procedure for judging between competing views. A major claim of the chapter is that in considering different views we cannot separate issues concerning decision making from issues concerning curriculum development, especially of content and structure.

Sections dealing with values in the curriculum; learning, teaching and the curriculum; and curriculum knowledge each set out the variety of options in each of these areas, and argue for a holistic, pragmatist approach emphasising the cultural dimension of curriculum and the primacy of problem-solving. Here we explain the role of touchstone analysis, uncovering shared problems and extracting shared standards of inquiry, decision making and development — a central aspect of our pragmatist approach.

The role of educative leaders in the discovery, construction and negotiation of touchstone is then linked to the procedure of situational analysis, in which various features of the school situation, and external factors, are examined to produce effective school-based curriculum development. Situational analysis can also be used at regional, state and national levels. Touchstone and situational analysis are combined in a pragmatic, holistic model of curriculum development interrelating all levels. If we adopt this model, it is pointed out, there are no reasons for thinking that decision making at state or national levels is essentially less democratic than local, nor more efficient. What counts is that the appropriate decisions are made at the appropriate levels.

Since the national level is potentially one appropriate level, given the bearing of national (especially economic) problems on curricula, the holistic model lays the basis for the development of a national curriculum framework, to which the entire educational community, at all levels, can make a contribution. Educative leaders, it is argued, have a vital role to play in the development of such a framework, ensuring that it serves genuinely educational values.

Finally, we argue that, given the pragmatic, problem-solving approach, it is clear that there will be a continual need for flexibility, experiments and productive change. This need can be met only if people are capable of learning new ways of doing things, and are inspired to exercise their own creativity in educational innovation. Such learning and innovation occurs most effectively when educative leaders seek to ensure the continuity of the existing strengths of the educational culture.

The Scope of Curriculum Theory

That there is not one universally accepted definition of 'curriculum' is both obvious and widely acknowledged (e.g. Marsh, 1986, Ch. 1). It follows that there is a variety of views of the scope of curriculum theory and research, especially in open, democratic societies. There is also a diversity of opinion about matters of substance in curriculum in all respects: planning, design, implementation, evaluation, and so on. On this point, we make a basic claim:

Any approach to curriculum development which fails genuinely to acknowledge the plurality of views is doomed to founder.

The acknowledgment must be thorough and inform the whole approach: mere lip service is insufficient. The requirement is not that all relevant views should be reflected in, or written into, all curricula. To the extent that views are incompatible this is likely to produce incoherent curricula. Rather, it is that all relevant views should be considered in the overall curriculum process. Consequently, the above claim has a bearing on the work of educative leaders:

For reasons of both efficiency and democracy, educative leaders might well be expected to be familiar with the current scope and content of curriculum theory, or at least confident that they can take relevant views into account.

Nevertheless, while emphasising the reality of diversity of opinion and approach, it is essential that we take some position on the scope of 'curriculum'. Now if we look at current work in curriculum theory, we find that for some writers 'curriculum' has a restricted reference (for instance, to the content of instruction); for others the scope of curriculum theory would seem to be as wide as the field of educational study as a whole. We will not argue for or against any particular view. Rather, we will suggest a set of theoretically justified *procedures* for dealing with the variety of views on scope.

It is not the case, however, that all views are completely discrepant with each other. For instance, most would agree that curriculum development and theorising is an *enormously complex* business, embracing considerations which range from the nuts and bolts problems of particular classrooms, teachers and pupils to the abstract ideas and procedures of academic disciplines such as philosophy. In between are cultural and social considerations such as subject specialisation among teachers and the variety of subcultures among students. This brings us to another basic claim:

> *As with the plurality of views, any approach to curriculum development and theorising which fails to acknowledge the complexity of the issues is unlikely to succeed.*

The complexity has usually to be managed in a context of policy formation, if not immediate, practical decision making. Consequently, there are understandable tendencies to eclecticism and compartmentalisation in curriculum theorising and development, especially at the level of school and classroom practice.

Eclecticism may be seen in school situations where many different approaches to student learning (exposition, inquiry, graded or descriptive assessment, negotiation, problem-solving, etc.) are applied in different classrooms without any consideration of whether they fit together coherently in the students' learning experiences.

Compartmentalisation is often manifested in, say, secondary schools, in the faculty structure where the approach to curriculum development may be coherent within a faculty but fragmented between faculties. Eclecticism and compartmentalisation may lead to lack of coherence with resultant conflict and the creation of even more problems. This leads us to suggest that:

> *Neither eclecticism nor compartmentalisation is satisfactory, on either efficiency or democratic grounds.*

Strengths and Weaknesses of Curriculum Theory

Amidst the complexity and pluralism, however, there is no doubt about one thing: curriculum theory and development are concerned with the *practice* of education in actual teaching-learning contexts. Decisions *have* to be made and actions *have* to be taken about curriculum in schools. At certain points the insistent obduracy of educational and social reality becomes unavoidable.

So far as curriculum *theory* is concerned, the pressures of practice have had both positive and negative effects. On the credit side, they have functioned as criteria for the selection and evaluation of theoretical ideas and research findings; they have acted as an empirical anchor and reality-check on theoretical work. The field of curriculum theory would seem, in recent years, to have benefited considerably from its relatively tight nexus with educational policy and practice, thus developing a more experimental style. As Skilbeck (1984b:1–2) has put it:

It is indeed one of the characteristic features of curriculum theory that it serves as a bridge between the concreteness and variability of practical activities in teaching and learning, and the systematically analysed research data and constructs of the several branches of educational knowledge.

On the debit side, it would unfortunately be true to say that due respect to the nagging exigencies of practice often results in inadequate attention being given to the current state of the academic resources upon which curriculum theorists and developers must draw. Nowhere is this more apparent than in regard to the fundamental *philosophical* work in ethics, social philosophy, epistemology and the philosophy of science. Here, unfortunately, the study of curriculum, like the study of education generally, remains philosophically backward. We emphasise and develop this point throughout the chapter. But it should be observed here that the current strengths of curriculum theory lie more in its links with practice than in the intellectual merits — logical, semantic and scientific — of the theoretical structures it has so far produced. This chapter, by emphasising certain theoretical constructs, tries to show that:

> *The interests of educative leadership in curriculum development can be advanced by increasing theoretical sophistication, which enhances rather than conflicts with practicality.*

What is an 'Educative Curriculum'?

If we are going to insist that leadership be educative, and that this be linked to the role of leaders in the development of the curriculum, then we need some way of judging the educational worth of curricula.

Anyone familiar with the course of educational theory, especially the philosophy of education over the last quarter-century, will be aware of the raging and largely unproductive debates over what constitutes 'education' as opposed, for example, to 'training', 'indoctrination', 'socialization' or 'miseducation'. Perhaps the major attempt to demarcate 'the educational' from the non- or the anti-educational has been the program of conceptual analysis conducted by certain philosophers of education (e.g. Peters, 1967).

Specifically, the concern was to establish the criteria for the concept of 'education', by logical and linguistic analysis of educational discourse (Hirst and Peters, 1978, Ch. 2). Despite the considerable early influence of the conceptual analytic program, it has been subjected to damaging criticism (e.g. Edel, 1972; Evers, 1979; Walker, 1984), and philosophers are far from unanimous that it has achieved anything. Its major unsolved problem is how to derive, given only the resources of analytic procedures and the existing educational discourse on which they are deployed, criteria for the 'correct' or 'justified' use of a term such as 'education'. In other words, conceptual analysts never succeeded in showing how we would *know* when we had got the 'analysis' of a concept 'right'.

A further problem is the failure to substantiate Hirst's (1974) claim that there are *logically distinct* forms of knowledge, presumably of great significance for curriculum development (Evers and Walker, 1983; Walker and Evers, 1984).

This issue is discussed below in the section on Curriculum Knowledge. The point here is that these failures are almost unrecognised in the literature of curriculum.

Few still believe, then, that we can establish clear and definitive criteria for what counts as educative, which must apply across all theoretical and practical approaches to curriculum. The alternative is to recognise that:

What counts as educative is itself dependent on the theoretical view taken.

Under 'theoretical view' we include ideological, moral and political perspectives on education, the explicit theorising of the conventional disciplines (educational psychology, sociology, philosophy, etc.) and the theoretical assumptions implicit, even if unconsciously, in the educational practices of individuals, groups and institutions. Such theoretical views may be complementary (e.g. when they address different sets of educational problems) or in competition (as when they offer incompatible accounts of the same set of educational problems).

Thus to say that what counts as educative is itself dependent on the theoretical view taken is to acknowledge that to determine what might be an educationally worthwhile curriculum requires us to assess the relative merits of alternative, complementary or competing theories in education. It does not mean that we can arbitrarily please ourselves, or that one view is as good as another.

Rather than a set of criteria for 'education' we need a set of procedures for judging between competing views.

These procedures will have to be practicable: it will be necessary that we are able to implement them in contexts of dispute and uncertainty in curriculum development. It is often the situation, for example, that the school principal is placed in such contexts when working through varying and conflicting inputs from the school environment — community, teachers, students, administrators — while developing the school educational program.

A point of very great importance follows from this.

Because of the practical nature of curriculum theory we cannot separate two apparently distinct questions:
> *What criteria should be used in planning curriculum, selecting content, and in evaluation?*
> *Who should make decisions about curriculum, using what procedures and in what social structures?*

That is to say, in practice our theory of the educative curriculum is tied to our theory of the politics and administration of education, including our theory of educative leadership. What counts as education is something we work out experimentally in classroom, administrative and community practice. Here we are not assuming that all interested parties need to participate in the actual process of curriculum development, although, as stated, the educative leader should take all relevant views into account.

This said, it is uncontroversial that on any view, curriculum development involves making value judgments and selecting and organising knowledge for the purposes of teaching and learning. It may involve more, but these are central. For example, any educative curriculum will be directed to the development in learners of whatever is regarded as valuable knowledge. Competing theories of education are likely to differ on at least this issue, and one way of addressing the question of what counts as an educative curriculum will be to examine some of their differences over values, learning, and the nature and applicability of knowledge.

Values in the Curriculum

It is important to note the range of value positions contending for some influence in the curriculum, and their connection with educational aims. Some of these have even been urged to underpin an approach to the whole curriculum, others to significant aspects of it (i.e. specific curricula). It is not suggested that they are entirely distinct in all respects, nor that they are always in conflict. Nevertheless, they do often conflict, and even when they do not there are questions of priorities and balance. For simplicity's sake we shall extract a major emphasis from each value orientation. Some major value positions follow.

Neo-Classical
In the 'forms of knowledge' approach (Hirst, 1974), for example, or in other revivals of classical liberal education, values tend to be objectivist-absolutist in character, stemming from beliefs about the nature of knowledge and other intrinsically worthwhile activities. The major emphasis is on *conservation of an authoritative cultural tradition.*

Vocational
Whether general and specific vocational education are thought to be compatible or incompatible, the values associated with vocationalism are mainly instrumental, tending to conformity with current social and foreseeable labour markets and enterprise opportunities. The major emphasis is on *individual survival through employment.*

Liberal-Meritocratic
Based on the theory of competitive equality of opportunity, the liberal-meritocratic position advocates values associated with individual rights and equity, anti-discrimination, and reward for effort, in a context of acceptance of inequality of outcomes (at least employment outcomes) and a 'trickle down' theory of social justice and welfare.[1] The major emphasis is on *personal autonomy and egalitarian freedoms.*

Liberal-Progressive
Usually based on theories of individual development, self expression and cultural pluralism, liberal-progressive values, especially in more recent contexts (e.g. MACOS, SEMP, CDC initiatives) are associated with problems of disadvantaged groups and the value of education's potential role in promoting

cooperation, tolerance and understanding rather than competition and elitism. The major emphasis is on *personal autonomy in a context of social and cultural harmony*.

Socially Critical

These values are closely tied with the theory of 'knowledge and human interests', principally as deriving from 'critical theory' (Habermas, 1972). Kemmis, Cole and Suggett (1983) have developed a theory of schooling based on such values, associated with emancipation from social structural roots of inequality and injustice, and the role of the school in promoting critical awareness of society and possibilities of action for social change. The major emphasis is on *social change through educational action*.

Religious

As they are reflected in curriculum proposals, religious values are presented principally as deriving from the organised social practices of religious groups in the society, but with possibility for broader comparative understanding. Values are associated with human capacities and relations which transcend the material context of individual and social living. The major emphasis is on the *development of personal beliefs and attitudes in the context of specific moral and practical commitments*.

Pragmatic

No particular perspective or educational purpose is given overriding or absolute authority or priority. Values are derived from principles for making regular and predictable connections between means and ends so as to increase our chances of solving individual and social problems coherently and democratically.

Let us consider pragmatism in more detail. To take an example, the value of tolerance in the school setting may be justified pragmatically by pointing out that if teachers and students regularly pursue their goals in a way which shows tolerance of each other's goals and views, there will be an element of predictability and reliability in school life. If tolerance is adopted as a value, people will be able to count on each other to act tolerantly, and they will be able to pursue their goals and tackle their problems more effectively and coherently. They will adopt means to their ends which reflect tolerance of each other. Just what the limits of tolerance are should then be considered by relating tolerance to other values, such as efficiency and equity, so as to come up with the most coherent and practicable set of values.

Most pragmatists (e.g. Dewey, 1916, 1948, 1963) have argued that democratic structures and procedures are entailed by pragmatically justified values. Within this perspective there is room for many of the values advocated in the other value positions and an acknowledgment that where value positions clash there should be scope for pluralism (Walker, 1987). The major emphasis is on the *coherent and mutually productive problem-solving and learning capacities of individuals and social groups*.

We should note that each of these value orientations makes certain social and psychological assumptions. Values are neither developed nor put into practice in an empirical or theoretical vacuum. In the educational context, the crucial links, of course, must be with our assumptions about the conditions for learning. For example, the socially critical view assumes that there are social phenomena which need changing and can be changed through practices of critical scrutiny which can be learned in the schools. Religious values make little sense unless our view of human nature has a transcendent, non-material dimension, assuming that this dimension is present and responsive to teaching and learning processes. And so on.

> *Both the justification and the practicality of value judgments requires us to render them coherent with, or at least check them out against, our psychological and sociological knowledge, particularly our knowledge of learning.*

This chapter is written from a pragmatist perspective, in the belief that pragmatism has the best chance of meeting the practical requirements for curriculum theory suggested earlier: that a practicable approach must genuinely acknowledge the plurality of curriculum views and the complexity of curriculum issues. For the pragmatist, pragmatic values are sufficient. They will not, perhaps, be regarded as sufficient by others. But whether or not a pragmatic approach to the question of values in the curriculum is considered sufficient or adequate by, for instance, adherents of socially critical or religious values, a democratic pragmatism would seem the most justifiable position on *procedural* grounds (Walker, 1985a). By this we mean that a democratic and pragmatic approach works best in dealing with plurality and complexity. This need not mean that only pragmatic values are reflected in the curriculum; it will mean that the reasons for the inclusion of values and the procedures for their selection will be pragmatic.

There are four issues requiring consideration here: conflicting values, the weighting of values, the social and political context of values, and the coherence of values with other curricular considerations.

First, a pragmatic approach is a way of taking into account the *fact of difference* in opinion and theoretical view about the curriculum without requiring that all parties agree to all of each other's values.

Second, even in cases where there is no disagreement, pragmatism gives us a method of *weighting* various compatible values not all of which can be reflected to the same extent in the curriculum. Even in cases where instances from some of the above categories do not conflict, it is likely that curriculum priorities and emphases will remain to be sorted out. We therefore need a framework and a set of procedures for assigning priorities as well as for resolving conflicts and establishing workable relationships between different value stances to be reflected in the curriculum.

Third, a pragmatic approach, by emphasising the practical possibilities of actually implementing various combinations and weightings of curricular values, and by recognising their relation to the various individuals and groups whose values they are, is realistic about the *political and social* dimensions of value judgments. For example, practical possibilities are influenced by the power of various groups in the social setting. We need not ask that these go unchallenged; we must face the reality of their existence.

Although such procedures as 'values clarification' may have some place in the curriculum, we need to make decisions about what values *ought* to be in the curriculum. We need to do more than just clarify the values brought to the school context by learners. Here values and ethics overlap with politics, because of the connections of moral and other value positions with different social groups and interests. Pragmatism takes account of the rootedness of values in the material, social circumstances of community groups, curriculum developers, teachers and students.

Fourth, pragmatism addresses the problem of *making our values coherent with other curricular considerations*, such as our knowledge of human learning and development, our social and cultural context and, above all, of our views of the nature of knowledge. It does this by adopting an *holistic* approach to the problems of choosing or justifying values, of weighting them, of judging between competing theories of education, of relating various areas of curriculum content, and of curriculum development and implementation in actual social and institutional contexts. That is to say:

> *Given the variety of value-orientations and the differences of opinion about how to justify particular value judgments as they arise in curriculum development, we need an approach which achieves the most coherent value package possible within a democratic framework.*

For example, a secondary school in an ethnically diverse area of low socio-economic status might develop a curriculum which emphasised values of cultural understanding and tolerance combined with a strong commitment to vocational values relevant to an area of high unemployment, thus achieving some coherence at the local level. The curriculum should also be consistent with regional and national needs, perhaps of an economic and cultural nature. Thus different schools can have different value packages in their curricula, yet fit coherently within broader value packages evolved at regional, state and national levels.

Learning, Teaching and the Curriculum

No curriculum development is possible without assumptions about how learning and teaching can and should proceed. There is a huge variety of views on these questions, and a vast amount of research and theorising has been published (Bower and Hilgard, 1981). Our approach to learning and teaching will also be influenced by our views on motivation, evaluation, classroom management and the institutional and societal contexts (Turney, 1981). Whilst the educative leader cannot be expected to be an expert on all aspects of this, it is important to clarify one's own views of teaching and learning and be able to relate them, in curriculum design and implementation, to the views of others. Thus it will be useful to be familiar with some of the major kinds of view on offer. Examples of views that have been influential follow. Although they differ on some points, there are many common ideas.

Behaviourism
Behaviourism in its strongest form denies the importance of inner, mental forces. Learning is a conditioned *response* to environmental stimuli, in the form

of observable student behaviour. It can be planned and controlled by teaching procedures which stimulate students to respond verbally and in other ways, and which reinforce the desired response. Teaching techniques and programmed material can constitute an educational technology (Skinner, 1968) whereby the students' responses are directed in a sequence of learning which is incremental, proceeding step by step. The teacher's role is mainly that of an instructor, and curriculum content is mostly selected and organised in advance of the teaching-learning situation.

Social Learning Theory
People are neither driven by inner forces nor simply buffeted by environmental stimuli. Rather, learning occurs through a continuous *interaction* between the learner and the environment (Bandura, 1977). Learners select, organise and transform these stimuli through recognisable cognitive processes, and, unless they are subject to the wrong kind of teaching or social influence, can become self-regulating in their learning. The teacher is still a careful designer and organiser of learning experiences, but reinforces those student behaviours which lead to self control. The curriculum must be compatible with careful teacher guidance of learning.

Cognitive Theories
Cognitive theories are much less concerned with stimuli and responses, especially in regard to 'higher mental processes' involving the development of insight and understanding. Gestalt psychologists (e.g. Wertheimer, 1959; Levin, 1935, 1951) emphasise that people perceive situations as *wholes*, interpreting and organising their perceptions into meaningful configurations. This holistic interpretation is closely connected to *problem-solving* in which the development of awareness, or cognition, is central. Problems are solved through insight. For Bruner (1961, 1966) learning is a development of *categories*, or classifications of perception. For Ausubel (1963, 1968) learning has to be *meaningful*, that is, it has to be incorporated into the learner's consciousness. For Piaget (1929, 1971) learning proceeds through a series of cognitive *stages* through which biologically based mental structures grow as the learner adapts to the environment. In general, cognitive theories suggest teachers need to understand learners' cognitive processes, which may not always be directly apparent in behavioural responses. The curriculum must be geared to the development of insight and understanding.

Information-Processing
Learning includes *input, processing and output*, and in these respects people are analogous to machines such as computers. Like the social learning and cognitive theories, information-processing views (e.g. Lindsay and Norman, 1972) emphasise problem-solving and organising experience into categories. They do so by concentrating on the role of *feedback*, through which the effect of output, and therefore the effectiveness of processing, can be evaluated.

Positive feedback maintains present behaviour, but negative feedback indicates the need to revise or replace the program or software through which the processing is being done. Parallels have been drawn between the hardware of computers and the human neurophysiological system (Grossberg, 1982; Evers,

1984). Humans may be regarded as simultaneously hardware, software, and programmers. Teachers, following an information-processing approach, might regard teaching as 'hooking up' learners with each other and themselves, into one complex teaching-learning community, or a set of interdependent information processors. Information-processing always occurs within a framework of social relationships (Weil and Joyce, 1978:3).

Learning as Cultural Action
Learning occurs through shared symbolism (e.g. in language) and other practices of social groups, and is influenced by values and world views. Learning always occurs within a culture, and is therefore always a social activity, having implications for one's relations with others. As learned by the individual, cultural practices may be adapted to personal goals, and the action of people as cultural beings can be seen as a problem-solving activity. Cultural theorists can agree with many of the emphases of other theories on social interaction, understanding, holism, and the importance of feedback through information processing, but they emphasise that the basic *unit* of learning is not necessarily the individual — groups and organisations learn (Argyris and Schon, 1978) and individuals always learn in social contexts using the materials and procedures of their culture.

This chapter is written from a cultural action point of view, incorporating the social learning emphasis on interaction and the importance of self-regulation, the holism and problem-solving emphasis of cognitive theories, and a view of learners as interdependent information processors. This interdependence in learning is a central aspect of cultural analysis. Unless we recognise the cultural context of learning, leadership and curriculum development (Lawton, 1983, 1984) we shall not be able to understand the practical, dynamic *relationships* between individuals and groups with different points of view and material interests, as well as shared and unshared problems. Culture indicates the scope for cooperative educative leadership, as well as the context within which we must pragmatically consider our options for action. By recognising that learning is cultural action and that social relationships and organisations such as schools are outcomes of human learning, we allow ourselves to consider realistically what can and should be changed in the curriculum.

The curriculum itself is a cultural construction, reflecting our attempts to bring our cultural resources to bear upon our present social situation. If we adopt an open, experimental attitude to the culture and subcultures of our society, we will enable learners in all social positions, including educative leaders, to be active inquirers into their social and natural environment. This will promote the kinds of adaptation which are conducive to the development of that human knowledge which is necessary for human progress and even survival (Piaget, 1978).

Active, inquiring learning, then, is required for a creative and flexible culture. A culture, whether it is inclined to conservatism or to change, is the product of the learning of the individuals whose culture it is.

The curriculum cannot but start with the cultural context as it is; what should be conserved and what should be changed has to be sorted out by cultural

action, in which educative leaders, as learners themselves, discover the prob-
lems and possibilities of educational action through curriculum development.

This process of discovery through cultural action, we shall argue, is itself a learning process, through which *knowledge* is produced. The acquisition of this knowledge, obviously, becomes critical for leadership in curriculum development. The knowledge which is selected or developed *in the actual, or 'enacted' curriculum*, that is, what is learned in the classroom, has always been recognised as a fundamental issue in curriculum development. What we are suggesting here is that learning, or the development of knowledge, is also central *in the process of curriculum development*.

It is a major contention of this chapter, then, that our theory of knowledge, or our *epistemology*, is basic to our decisions on matters of value of learning and of the politics and administration of curriculum.

Curriculum Knowledge

Various epistemologies have been influential in contemporary curriculum theory. Both the curriculum and our reasoning and theorising about the curriculum will reflect our epistemological assumptions. The following are some of the major examples which have been recently influential.

Partitionist Theories
Knowledge is held to be divisible into various logically, methodologically or practically distinct 'forms' (Hirst, 1974) or 'realms of meaning' (Phenix, 1964). Such theories regard knowledge, or at least its most significant domains, as 'objective', or 'public' in character. The curriculum must contain this objective knowledge and must reflect the fact that knowledge is partitioned and not a logical, methodological or semantic unity. Hirst's theory has often been associated with neo-classical values.

Recognising the problem of how to bring together the supposedly logically distinct forms or disciplines in curriculum development, Schwab (1969, 1973, 1983) has proposed a focus on 'the practical'. He has suggested a deliberative process of curriculum development in which knowledge from the disciplines is focused on certain kinds of practical concern which come to the fore in curriculum problems. So far as epistemology is concerned, 'deliberative' theorists are best viewed as offering an emphasis on a further kind of cognitive process. More recently other writers, including Hirst (1983), have moved to a similar emphasis.

Phenomenological Theories
Much of the 'new sociology of education' literature (e.g. Young, 1971) and such curriculum theorists as the 'reconceptualists' (Pinar, 1975, 1979) maintain that knowledge grows out of the unique and irreducible experience of the individual, or the irreducible intersubjective or shared experience of social groups. Such theories usually regard knowledge as 'subjective' in character, and are used to

oppose curricula which are based on the supposed objective authority of knowledge enshrined in public traditions or institutions. This theory has often been associated with liberal progressive values as well as more radical positions.

Critical Theory

Much of the 'critical theory' recently influential in education derives from the work of Habermas (e.g. 1972), where knowledge is partitioned according to the kind of human interest each distinct subdivision reflects. Habermas argues that the 'empirical-analytic sciences' embody a 'technical' interest in 'manipulation' and 'control'; the 'historical or hermeneutic sciences' embody the values of a 'practical' interest in open dialogue or 'free communication'; and the 'critical sciences' embody an 'emancipatory' interest according to which knowledge is judged politically by its relation to emancipatory social practices. Often knowledge is regarded as 'dialectical' in nature by adherents of 'critical theory'.

It should be clear that the epistemological distinctions of critical theory underpin the 'socially critical' values mentioned in the previous section. Indeed, the 'socially critical school', as characterised by Kemmis, Cole and Suggett (1983), gives primacy to the assumed emancipatory interest. The distinction drawn between the socially critical and the other two orientations to curriculum identified by Kemmis, Cole and Suggett, namely, the vocational neo-classical and the liberal progressive, is an application of the distinctions between technical, practical and emancipatory interests.

Despite their being critical of some of the more traditional partitionist theories, critical theorists remain partitionist. When it comes to spelling out the relation between knowledge and curriculum development, they resort to a political procedure based on one of the knowledge divisions they recognise as 'critical' knowledge. The domain of knowledge remains fragmented.

Holism

A distinction can be drawn between *foundational* and *non-foundational* epistemologies. The above theories are examples of foundationalism, the view that our claims to knowledge are justified when they can be shown to rest upon secure or at least probable foundations (such as empirical evidence, necessary truths, privileged personal experience or their recognisable contribution to management of practical concerns). Non-foundational theories of knowledge deny that to justify our knowledge claims (or our value judgments, if there is any distinction between the two) we need to derive them from secure foundational items. This chapter is written from a non-foundational point of view.

Foundationalism faces several severe problems (Walker and Evers, 1982), of which the major one is the vicious regress of knowledge claims. For we can always ask of the foundations on which we believe our claims to knowledge rest, why should they be regarded as reliable? What justifies our faith in them? How do we know that the foundations of our knowledge are secure?

For the holist, the very idea of foundations is wrong headed (Quine, 1975; Quine and Ullian, 1978; Walker and Evers, 1984). Instead, we adopt a non-foundational epistemology, emphasising *coherence* among theoretical, empirical and value items. Our beliefs, or knowledge claims, are justified to the extent that they cohere with each other, meaning how logically consistent or tightly integrated they are with each other. Our knowledge claims, including reports of empirical evidence and personal experience, are judged by the degree to which they cohere with the whole of our current knowledge and with the assumptions underpinning the most effective solutions to our practical problems. Thus we judge theoretical views on education by their internal coherence, their coherence with evidence (including practical experience) and their coherence with the rest of 'our theory of the world'. We judge theories as wholes, and as wholes within a whole 'theory of the world'.

However, of course, there can be a variety of incompatible views, or competing theories, in any area of knowledge. As we have insisted throughout this chapter that this is the case in education generally, and in curriculum in particular; perhaps more so than in other areas of knowledge. Just as each individual person needs to judge knowledge claims, whether new or already subscribed to, by their coherence with other considerations (including empirical evidence), so, too, in a collective and social activity like curriculum development, we need to strive to achieve cultural coherence, in what is ultimately developed, between the various inputs of a variety of groups and individuals. Holistic epistemology is well suited to assist in this task.

The holist claims that knowledge grows through the competition between different theories. Coherence is forced upon the overall project of promoting human knowledge (i.e. the cultural project of which research and teaching are two complementary sides in the advancement of learning) through what we call *touchstone* (Walker, 1985b). This derives from the overlap, or sharing, of theoretical assumptions, across competing or complementary views. These assumptions may or may not be explicit. People may not always be aware of the existence of *touchstone*. The overlap occurs because the theories are addressing *common*, or *shared*, *problems*; problem sharing generates touchstone. However, in that they are competing or incompatible theories (i.e. each disagrees with the other on at least one point) they offer *conflicting, logically or practically incompatible solutions* to those shared problems.

How then do we judge between competing theories? How do we apply the coherence test? We extract common standards from the overlapping accounts of shared problems, or we adopt them from other shared areas of the theoretical frameworks of participants. By examining the actual content of touchstone, we discover what values and procedures each of the competing theories is committed to in common with the others, and ask which of the theories comes out best in view of these shared values and procedures. We test the competing theories or divergent solutions to one group of problems by reference to their common solutions to another set of problems.

For example, two scientists with competing theories about the physical and chemical constitution of the planet Saturn may accept, as touchstone, the evidence of a probe sent to Earth by radio signals. They will have achieved some agreement about the problems facing them in understanding Saturn, and they will share the theoretical underpinning of the evidence from the probe, which will include a considerable amount of mathematics, physics (especially optics, if photography is involved) and chemistry. The two scientists are committed to the standards implicit in this touchstone theory. If the theory held by one scientist fits better with touchstone than that held by the other, then the first theory is working better, on that score, in solving the shared problem. If the touchstone actually creates an anomaly for the second scientist's theory, is inconsistent with that theory, the second scientist has a problem — a failure in coherence. The second scientist can try to adjust that theory to square with the evidence, or query the evidence. If the evidence is queried, the second scientist, on pain of further incoherence, has to consider whether this means rejecting other aspects of touchstone, such as the procedures which have produced the evidence, and the theoretical assumptions built into those procedures. The problem facing the second scientist will worsen if some of those procedures were used in identifying the original, shared, problem of understanding Saturn. There will be other moves, perhaps, the second scientist can make, including the rejection of the originally espoused theory and the adoption of the other theory. But short of this admission of error, it is touchstone that brings the two theories into a disciplined competition, and it is the constraint of coherence that forces the two scientists to make their theories square with touchstone, or vice versa, and thus make their relative strengths and weaknesses apparent.

Thus, in the area of scientific research methodology, procedures for gathering empirical evidence may yield findings which constitute anomalies for one theory while they confirm the claims of another. But the evidence counts *as evidence* for or against the competing theories only insofar as they must accept it as touchstone, or if there is some doubt about this, insofar as their adherents have agreed to accept it as touchstone.

Educational practices, policies and curricula can be judged in the same way. For example, a science teacher might approach a school principal complaining that her unruly class is the result of mixed ability grouping. Her solution, that the school adopt a streaming policy, is consistent with her analysis of the problem. Teacher and principal agree that there is a problem but the principal thinks the cause is more likely to be the science teacher's teaching style and relationships with the students than mixed ability grouping. The principal asks the science teacher whether she agrees that the experience of other teachers with the same students would be relevant to assessing the two competing theories — that mixed ability grouping is causing unruly behaviour, and that it is the teacher's approach that is causing the problem. The science teacher agrees that it would be relevant, and consents to the principal's interviewing the other teachers. The science teacher and the principal now have a shared problem, an agreed procedure for investigating it, and a mutual commitment to what is going to count as relevant evidence. They have marked out an area of touchstone. Now suppose that when she interviews the mathematics and English teachers the principal finds that they do not have any problem with that group of students. The principal and the science teacher meet again and it appears that the touchstone procedure has produced evidence which supports the principal's theory and not the science teacher's. The science teacher can try to save her theory by querying the objectivity of the principal's questioning of her colleagues, or perhaps by suggesting that her colleagues haven't revealed the whole story. Perhaps she could modify her theory by claiming that mixed ability grouping creates special difficulties in science lessons which are not shared by mathematics and English teachers. Each of these further claims could be investigated by derived or negotiated touchstone procedures. For instance, the principal could suggest that another science teacher take the same class and see whether their behaviour remained unruly. If it did not, this would be a further anomaly for the science teacher's (now modified) theory. It would also seem, practically, to have solved the problem. But perhaps the debate could go on. It probably would, so long as the original problem, shared by principal and teacher, persisted.

Similarly, imagine a principal trying to take a lead in school-based curriculum development. She is confronted with one set of suggestions from the parents' body, another from her staff, and a third from the regional office. Each group claims its suggestions are theoretically sound and practically implementable. Each agrees that the problem facing the school is to develop a curriculum suitable to its students. To the extent that the three points of view (and maybe the principal herself has a fourth) differ, the resolutions will involve seeking common ground, establishing agreed procedures for discussion and practical experimentation with particular curriculum designs and materials, and so on. As developments emerging from touchstone go for or against the competing views, their advocates have the option of revising them, abandoning them, or renegotiating touchstone. The curriculum situation is more complex than the competition over Saturn or the unruly class, but the role of touchstone in theory competition is the same.

In none of these cases do the competitors have to defer, finally and absolutely, to foundational items of knowledge which stand outside the realm of theory. Rather, they recognise that the evidence itself is permeated with theoretical assumptions, and that choosing the best theory is a matter of coming up with the most coherent overall account of the problem and possible solutions to it. Putting it another way, they recognise that to *justify* one's theory one does not refer to special, authoritative items, but looks at the whole situation. One adopts an *holistic theory of justification* and *a coherence theory of evidence*. In social situations such as the classroom misbehaviour and curriculum development examples, applying this approach is *cultural action* rearranging the ways of life of specific social groups.

It is important to note that to adopt an holistic theory of justification, including a coherence theory of evidence, is a different matter from adopting a coherence theory of *truth*. What makes a claim true is its relation to the world; its truth depends on whether the reference it makes to the world is accurate. (This is known as the correspondence theory of truth.) However, what justifies a claim, what warrants our claim to *know that a statement is true*, is its coherence with the rest of our theory of the world.

Similarly, it is important to note that in adopting a pragmatist position one is not necessarily saying that what is true, or what is valuable, is what works best, and is what best solves our problems. That is not what *makes* statements true, nor what *makes* values sound. Why not? Because there is a real world out there, of which we are of course part, which is the objective origin of the problems which our theories, methodologies and values are addressing.

Thus pragmatic holists can agree with partitionists such as Hirst that knowledge and values can and should be objectively rather than subjectively considered, but not that they can be divided into logically distinct domains. They can agree with deliberative theorists such as Schwab that knowledge is best viewed as a set of solutions to practical problems, but not that practical knowledge is distinct from empirical or theoretical knowledge. They can agree with phenomenologists that the tests of our knowledge are always related to human experience, and that there is no acceptable transcendental or absolute account of objectivity; but they reject the subjectivism of phenomenological views. They can agree with critical theorists that we can know what needs changing in our society, and endorse the importance of a critical perspective, but not that this is a kind of knowledge distinct from or superior to that of the natural sciences or the humanities.

By noting these similarities and differences, we can see the areas of touchstone between our pragmatist holism and the points on which it is a theory in competition with the other theories of knowledge. We make two claims, however, relevant to the areas of difference and the common ground.

The pragmatist holist epistemology is superior to its competitors as an account of the nature of knowledge, methodology and values.

Nevertheless, it is not necessary to accept the epistemology in its entirety to see merit in some of the practical research, development and decision-making principles it generates. These may be found useful by people of various epistemological persuasions.

We should now, therefore, attend more specifically to some of these procedure principles.

Holism, Pragmatism and Curriculum Development

The holistic epistemology supplies both a framework for making decisions about curriculum content and a set of procedures for judging between competing views, whether they concern curriculum, values, knowledge itself, or the desirability of particular decision-making processes and administrative/political structures.

Curriculum Content

The procedure commences with the identification and analysis of practical problems — individual, social, political and administrative — in their cultural context. It applies pragmatic, holistic principles of curriculum design and knowledge selection. Thus *human problems*, present and anticipated, rather than the nature of knowledge, or fundamental values, or the authoritative culture, supply the criteria for curriculum content.

Now assuming that individuals and community groups have varying practical and social situations and needs and varying values and perspectives on knowledge, they will have varying sets of problems in understanding their world and pursuing their goals within it. The school curriculum must reflect these *varying problems*.

However, as members of the same society, all being dependent, for example, for their living on the same economy, they will have certain shared problems. Both shared and unshared problems, then, depend on the perspectives brought to the situations in which the problems arise.

To discover what are the shared and unshared problems in any given situation, we need to conduct a situational analysis.

Skilbeck's influential work on situational analysis is helpful here (Skilbeck, 1976; Reynolds and Skilbeck, 1976), especially for school-based curriculum development (SBCD), (Brady, 1983, Ch. 2; Marsh, 1986:56–59). The situation, or context, in which curriculum is implemented or enacted through teaching and learning, is kept under scrutiny before, during and after each phase of curriculum development; but for each phase it is essential to analyse the factors influencing the situation. This should not be thought of as a mere review of relevant factors upon to keep an eye. For our pragmatic, holistic approach, situational analysis is an explanation of what is going on, an account of how the various elements of the situation affect each other.

For example, we should identify and interrelate *internal* factors, such as the characteristics of teachers and students, the school's ethos and administrative-political structure, its material resources and, especially, the perceived problems of the people in the situation. Internal factors can also, then, be seen in relation to *external* factors such as social and cultural changes and expectations, requirements and policies of the educational system, the changing nature of subject matter, teacher support systems and the flow of resources into the school.

In more recent work, Skilbeck (1984b:5) has placed SBCD in a broader, national context — the 'national curriculum framework' — emphasising that:

It is the interrelationship, including the quest for better communication, a more concrete kind of partnership and shared decision making, between the school and the larger educational environment that has to be the focus of our efforts in future.

This is a point which we shall re-emphasise in relation to the location of responsibility for curriculum decisions. Here, in connection with curriculum design in general, its relevance is the need to bring to an end any lingering sterile opposition set up between SBCD and other, wider contexts of curriculum development. There are clear implications for the role of educative leaders:

Educative leaders should take a lead in building a partnership between the schools and the wider educational environment which facilitates frank communication and shared decision making.

Indeed, there are good reasons to extend the scope of situational analysis so as to recognise that the situation relevant to curriculum development goes beyond the national to the international level. We might also note that there may be relevant levels *in between* the school and the national levels. In Australia, for example, there is a need to recognise regional and state levels. We can apply situational analysis to *any* of these levels. Consequently, it becomes a possibility that aspects of curriculum design can be handled at international, national, state, regional, local and school levels.

For Australian purposes, this means that certain levels at which, hitherto, action has been restricted to the administration and servicing of the educational system, might also be used for elements of curriculum design. This will depend on our *overall* situational analysis, interrelating problems arising at one or another level of generality in the society. For example (as has been observed in contexts other than education), the problems faced by a group of people frequently have much more to do with social relations and action at a regional level than at the state level. But it is an empirical question which can be answered only by analysis of the concrete situation.

This procedure for establishing criteria for curriculum design and content, obviously, has a political dimension. The proposal to think in terms of levels of generality of individual and social problems also captures the point that when people share problems or have varying problems, they also share or differ in their *interest* in the action taken at whatever level is appropriate for addressing those problems. An interest, here, is identified pragmatically. An individual or group has an interest in action taken at a given level when that individual or group has problems which are caused by, or might be solved by, action taken at that level. Some problems are pretty well local in character, and so are the shared or conflicting interests; others extend across regions, states and nations; while at the international level the whole of humanity, facing the problems of peace and war, but divided into various political alignments, has both shared and unshared problems.

We may now return to the question of what constitutes a relevant theoretical view about the curriculum raised earlier, where two claims were made about the plurality of views. First, it was claimed that any approach to curriculum development which failed to take into account the plurality of views is doomed to founder. Second, however, it was not insisted that any and every view should be reflected in the curricula developed; rather, it was proposed that educative leaders should be in a position to take all relevant views into account. Now all sorts of people may have views about the local, regional, state or national determination of curriculum design. But they might not all address the problems of people arising at that given level in that locality or region.

A relevant view is defined as a view which addresses the problems arising in a particular situation at a particular level, and therefore has some bearing on the solution of those problems.

It is worth pointing out that *problems may be graded according to severity*, and this will affect the curricular weighting of the content eventually chosen as relevant to the educational aspects of their solutions. Degrees of severity will occur both horizontally, across any one level (within the relevant situation: i.e. region, or state, etc.) and vertically, as between levels. Severity adds another dimension to relevance: greater severity heightens relevance. Severity is, of course, analysed situationally and empirically, by assessing the causes of our interrelated problems and the greater effect that some of them have on our capacity to solve the others. For example, national problems can become more severe in times of war or economic crisis, and arguably should be given greater weight in the curriculum. If so, then it is possible that at the present juncture in Australian education there should be greater national input in curriculum development.

A more precise specification may now be made of the role of educative leaders in fostering an educational environment of partnership:

Educative leaders should be aware of and capable of responding to the changing balance of relevant considerations, in both their horizontal and vertical relationships in the educational framework.

This is clearly tied to their role as leaders in educational change and innovation, an issue discussed below.

The pragmatism underpinning this problem-solving approach accepts, *as starting points* in curriculum development, that individuals and groups will bring to the development situation preformulated goals, values and perspectives. These are all acknowledged at the outset, but through the problem-posing approach, their legitimacy and practical viability may be reassessed insofar as they cause problems for other individuals and groups. Unlike certain other traditional approaches to curriculum development (e.g. Tyler, 1949) the pragmatic approach does not see goal setting as the first and fundamental step in curriculum development. Goals are analysed in relation to practical problems, so curriculum development commences with concrete situations at various levels. To set goals beforehand and make curriculum development a process of achieving them tends to result in abstract statements of aims and objectives which are then interpreted in different and often conflicting ways by people responsible for educational practice. This means that, in fact, different and divergent goals are pursued as people face up to the practical realities and problems of educational situations.

Pragmatism recognises that people will have different goals. It seeks unity of action in addressing the shared practical problems in pursuing their goals, and only then considers whether common goals are possible. Centralised goal setting is authoritarian to the extent that it works. To the extent that it doesn't work, it is idealist and impractical. Thus, the focus on problems is justified pragmatically, because it gives us the chance to develop curricula that will work in practice. It does not deny the importance of goals, values and perspectives, nor of course of the theoretical views in which these are located; rather, it gives each of these elements a practical focus. It judges them from the point of view of the problem-solving, and problem-causing power.

Here let us pick up again the holistic point about the unity of knowledge and practical reasoning. The problem-solving approach provides us, not just with decisions about what we will teach and how it will be organised, but also (which amounts to the same thing) with *knowledge* of what the curriculum ought to be. As we saw when comparing the work of scientists with that of school principals, there need be no fundamental difference in kind between the learning (research) of the disciplines, of those cultural activities usually described as 'science', or 'theory', and the learning (decision making) of practitioners, of those whose cultural activities are usually described as 'action', or practice. The problem-solving, holistic approach applies to both. When applied to curriculum theorising and development, it provides us with *normative* and *practical* curricular knowledge; knowledge of what we *ought to do*. Curriculum development is therefore covered by the same points of holistic epistemology outlined above.

Curriculum knowledge, or the knowledge produced in curriculum development, is produced through a search for coherent proposals for action to solve problems. It works through theory competition and touchstone, as does the process of research in any sphere.

Thus another way of saying that we look for shared problems in a situation at any particular level is to say that we look for *touchstone* in curriculum development. This is what imposes the theoretical discipline on our decision-making processes. It is what tells us which decisions will achieve the greatest coherence. We move from shared problems through shared standards of inquiry and justification to, hopefully, shared solutions.

Procedures

These points may be summarised in a pragmatic, holistic model of curriculum development. There are five practical steps to be taken by the educative leader in curriculum development:

1 Find out, through situational analysis, what the relevant people in the situation regard as their problems. The leader's own problems are of course part of this. Identification of perceived problems can be done explicitly, by obtaining written or verbal accounts from people of what is preventing them from obtaining their goals, or implicitly, by observing and interpreting their responses to situations and their more settled practices.

2 Given their explicit or implicit understanding of what their problems are, how do they see their options for dealing with them? How are these related to their theories and values, their views of learning and knowledge? Can the educative leader find out what participants in the situation think are available and practicable solutions to their problems?

3 Analyse each account of perceived problems and solutions (or each theory of the situation) and assess the degree of internal coherence in each account. Are there inconsistencies or very loose internal connections in the set of views and practices of the people whose account it is? Our assumption, of course, is that the greater the coherence, the greater the practical efficacy of the account.

4 Analyse the relations between these accounts, the different problems-solutions frameworks of participants in the situation, to determine the degree of mutual coherence between them. How do the perceived problems and solutions of one individual or group match up with the perceived problems and solutions of other individuals and groups? Where is the overlap (touchstone) and where is the conflict (theory competition)? How much of each is there and how significant, practically speaking, are they? Since, of course, these are rooted in the practical situation, the analysis for coherence means addressing the issue of culture, harmony, diversity or divergence between the ways of life present in the situation.

5 Work out what options may be available, either derived from or negotiated through touchstone, for tackling the shared and unshared problems of the participants in the situation. To maximise touchstone, it is possible that through further learning and negotiation some participants may come to see hitherto unperceived solutions to their problems or revise their ideas of what their problems are. If so, competition and touchstone will have been reconstructed.

Each step concerns problems which can be addressed through curriculum development (and therefore the learning of children and young people in educational institutions) by reorganising, through the generations, the content and distribution of a society or social group's culture, especially its knowledge.

This procedure also enables us to distinguish those curriculum experiences which should be common to all members of a particular group of students — e.g. in a school, a region, a state or the country as a whole, or to groups with special needs. The common curriculum in each case will consist of learning which addresses shared problems through the transmission and construction of curriculum touchstone. Other curriculum experiences will provide optional learning designed to meet unshared, specific problems and interests. Insofar as there is variation between situations (local, regional, etc.) in shared problems, the common curriculum will be specific to those situations and common to all students in them. It will be common for those who share the problems of the situation or whose actions might have some bearing on the causation or solution of them.

For any given school, the common curriculum may be represented as a cone within a potential cylinder (see Figure 3.1). Situational analysis through the five step model generates, through touchstone, common content at international, national, state, regional and school levels. At each level there needs to be some democratically based input into the analysis — a set of layered horizontal inputs into curriculum development reflecting educationally relevant problems pertaining to that level. To achieve vertical coherence, there needs to be genuine, and therefore two-way negotiation between educative leaders at each level, to ensure that the learning solutions cohere in the school. Thus the level of SBCD, since it is the situation of curriculum implementation and enactment, remains particularly vital, and without the creative leadership of principals the scheme will not work. By the same token, principals cannot do it on their own. Unless there is genuine negotiated support from other levels, the principal's task is next to impossible. Educative leadership is therefore essential at school, regional, state, national and, ideally, international levels.

It remains to say something of the very matter with which so many discussions of curriculum content actually begin: the fields of knowledge as we have them, however we describe their divisions and structure. The natural and social sciences, mathematics and the humanities, and so on, may not, according to the pragmatist, be necessarily and eternally divided according to the current categories, as is maintained by traditional epistemological partitionists, but knowledge *is*, as a matter of current social fact, organised into academic disciplines to a considerable extent.

The question of which of these disciplines, in what structure and with what weighting, should become part of the curriculum and at what stage of schooling, is, according to the present account, a question to be answered through problem-solving. It is not our purpose to argue at length in this chapter for our own views of what should be the substantive content of the curriculum. The point of this chapter is to present a view of curriculum theorising and development as a social process and to indicate some roles for educative leaders within that process. Nevertheless, two points are worth making.

First, there will be many possible organisations of knowledge within the proposed approach, and this is as it should be given our recognition that people's problems are likely to vary horizontally and vertically, as well as through time. Indeed, if they did not vary at all, something would be wrong with

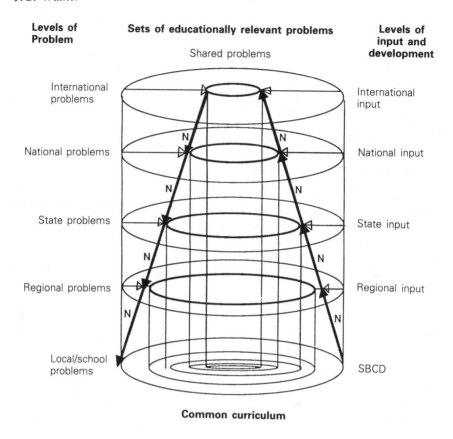

Levels of Problem	Sets of educationally relevant problems	Levels of input and development

Shared problems

Common curriculum

(N – negotiation)

Figure 3.1: Problem-solving model of negotiated multi-level curriculum development

our curriculum development process, or at least it would not be achieving much, since no variation in problems means that no problems are being solved. Curriculum development should be open and experimental, dynamic not static, as of course is the process of the growth of knowledge itself, whether in professional scientific research or in everyday life.

Second, the emphasis on identification of problems, and development of curricula to solve them through educational action, assumes a scientific view of society. We are dealing with cause and effect. What caused this problem? What interaction does it (causally) have with other problems? What will bring about (cause) a solution? How will that solution affect the possibility of our solving other problems? And so on. To take part in a decision-making process involving this kind of thinking, or at least to maximise one's effectiveness in it, one would be well advised to become familiar with scientific method, and in particular, the contributions of social science.

To take a lead in decision making, educative leaders could well keep aware of and receptive to economic, political and sociological studies of the kinds of social situation to be represented in their curriculum deliberations or contributions.

Now of course the pragmatist proposal requires that all genuinely interested parties, or makers of relevant contributions, should be able, through participatory or representative democratic procedures, to make some input into curriculum development. This is itself, then, an important educational goal. Education is an ongoing process which must itself maintain and secure the conditions for its continuation by educating each new generation in democratic procedures, especially reflexive inquiry into the social situation of education and one's own role and power within it.

Social science, then, conceived pragmatically, would be an important part of the curriculum. A similar case could be made for natural science and mathematics, given their causal importance in the conduct and development of modern society, and the great power which possession of such knowledge confers. But these are illustrations rather than definitive answers.

Judging Competing Views

What we have been calling 'theoretical views' may differ from each other on all sorts of scores. The theoretical perspectives of academic educationists may give conflicting accounts of the causes of teaching-learning phenomena and of the personal and social problems relevant to curriculum development. These differences will underpin differences of professional interest in curriculum development insofar as views adopted in practice become more powerful than those ignored.

But as we have said, theoretical views come from a wider range of possibilities than the academic. Anyone with an interest in a curriculum situation has a theoretical view, and if that interest clashes with other interests, it is likely that the theoretical views will clash too, and consequently the view of what ought to be done. There is, however, no neat one-to-one connection of differences of theoretical view with differences of personal or social interest. This is one of the complexities of the curriculum field alluded to earlier, and needs to be recognised lest crude distortions (as have, unfortunately, been advanced by academics among others) get in the way of practically effective decisions. Labelling all psychologists conservative, all sociologists radical, all philosophers irrelevant, or all practitioners vulgar and blinkered helps no one.

Educative leaders have a role to play in combating crude and prejudiced representations of competing views.

Nevertheless, it must be noted that in practice not all views can be dominant or even represented in the curriculum. Here we would like to recall the point made earlier about the conceptual looseness and theoretical fragmentation of much current curriculum theory and also the point about its lack of philosophical sophistication. We have introduced one strand of philosophical work, drawn largely from the Popperian (Popper, 1972) and Quinean (Quine, 1975) traditions and reflecting the pragmatism of Dewey (1948). The pragmatism of all these sources also fits well with Skilbeck's emphasis on SBCD within a wider regional, state, national and international context.

The major proposals drawn from this philosophical position — the emphasis on holism, problem-solving, theory competition and the identification, extension and reconstruction of touchstone — are all applicable to the problem of judging between competing theories in curriculum development.

The existence of competing views already indicates a degree of incoherence in curriculum theory, which, given our requirement that all relevant views be considered, has the potential to introduce incoherence into curriculum development. To deal with this we do not ban some of the competitors, we look for the common ground from which we can develop touchstone and make rational judgments between competitors.

At a very general level, the acceptance of any theoretical view involves a certain amount of logic and mathematics as well as semantic assumptions about terminology. Within the academic context of contributors to curriculum theory, touchstone between clashing theories of child development may involve case studies and cohort analysis, and divergent sociological theories may agree on the relevance to their claims of social survey statistics or ethnographic data (Walker and Evers, 1984). Touchstone, then, will always be specific to the particular theories competing in any given problem situation. Touchstone can never be a final and absolute 'foundation' for curriculum development. Touchstone is simply that shifting and changing body of claims, methods and findings shared by competing theories and is therefore entirely relative to those theories as they stand at any given historical moment.

The development of touchstone and of procedures for identifying starting points is necessary for communication, cooperation and progress. If the point were taken seriously, educationists would give a very high priority to identifying and clearly stating their points of agreement and disagreement on matters of substance and method, and would address themselves to improving and devising techniques, based on their agreements, for frank and rigorous examination of their differences. Openness is pleasant but ineffectual without hard-headed sophistication in inquiry; rigour is of limited benefit practised in private. We see the conduct of educational theorising and practice as being a process of open and *open-minded* theory competition. This would mean ceasing to hide behind disciplinary or professional boundaries, or simply 'doing one's own thing' (Walker and Evers, 1984:28).

Touchstone is more, though, than a set of assumptions and procedures for communication and cooperation. It is a way of making judgments between incompatible theoretical views and practical options. Once touchstone standards have been established, the very point of open-mindedness is that people are prepared to change their minds as well as frankly defend their own views and criticise those of others. The application of touchstone tests is aimed at determining which of the competitors is the best available solution of the shared problems.

Educative leaders have to be prepared to make judgments between competing theoretical views and to take responsibility for those practical options which are best suited to the problems within their brief.

Openness and the defence of fair competition do not preclude the need, under practical circumstances, to take sides. Leadership which is both democratic and efficient will manage to combine these values in decision making situations. Another way of putting the same point is to say that someone, and usually a leader, has to take responsibility for putting the competing theories, or at least one of them, to an experimental test.

Educative leadership means scientific research in action. This is a fundamental contribution to the development of curricular knowledge, which like all knowledge, proceeds and grows by the elimination of error through the trials of practical action. Leadership needs to be experimental. To admit you are wrong and change your mind does not mean you are a failure.

We cannot assume, of course, that all interested parties will agree with the decision taken as between competing views and their associated practical options, whether the decision-making mechanism is a vote or a choice by a representative or appointed individual or body, or a decision by a leader. Disagreements will remain and the conversation must go on. The assumption is that participants will continue the open-minded procedure whether they are, on occasions, winners or losers, whether they change their minds in the light of experimental evidence or further argument. The alternative is social breakdown. Educative leaders with a democratic commitment to the interests of all parties, as well as a preparedness to take action, also need the will and the capacity to keep the conversation going, to make touchstone continue to work as the basis for decision making on curriculum design, development, implementation and evaluation. In this process they are expected to be as open to criticism and revision as the next person and should welcome such scrutiny.

Laissez-Faire, Intervention or Collaboration?

From the above account of the nature and principles of organisation of curriculum knowledge, it is apparent that there will need to be decisions about curriculum design, implementation and evaluation taken at various levels, ranging from the national (ideally the international) to local and classroom levels. Thus our curriculum theory is part and parcel of our approach to the politics and administration of curriculum. We need a negotiated curriculum (Boomer, 1982) but the negotiations must transcend the SBCD/local level. Administratively, they need to be vertical as well as horizontal.

In order to achieve this, we need a holistic rather than a piecemeal approach. Now it is important not to identify holism with centralised intervention and piecemealism with decentralised *laissez-faire*. Skilbeck (1984a:92) has addressed the problem in the context of curriculum evaluation in the UK. His comments, however, apply as much to curriculum development as they do to evaluation, and to a federal system such as Australia's, with Commonwealth, state, and regional and/or local levels, as well as they do for the UK's national and local system.

It remains a matter of dispute ... whether the varied and numerous agencies with curriculum roles are best left to evolve their own patterns or whether vigorous intervention leading to greater coherence — and control — should be undertaken. The issue is: piecemeal change or holistic intervention. It is an issue which cannot be reduced to central-ism versus a decentralised model since intervention at the national level is not simply a matter of greater concentration of power in central government, nor does a holistic approach preclude substantial local initiatives.

This is a basically sound position, we think, but there are some qualifica-tions we would make. First, control can be exercised from and at any level: the issue is one of a satisfactory balance or distribution of power. If there is to be coherence, the question is what distribution of control/power across levels best serves democracy, equity and efficiency in tackling curriculum problems?

We need not assume that democracy is best served by control at the local level and efficiency best served by centralised control.

Thus it should not be assumed without argument that, in the words of a Victorian Ministerial Paper, 'as many decisions as possible should be made at school level and among various groupings of schools' (Fordham, 1983:3). The Ministerial Paper sees the primary role of central bodies as giving back-up in curriculum materials as required in view of local or regional decisions. The point we would make, however, is that the most important policy question is not about the *number* of decisions made at any particular level, but about the *quality* of decisions made at *appropriate* levels.

Second, in view of this, not only does a holistic approach not *preclude* local initiatives, but given our analysis of curriculum as a problem-solving enterprise, it will require local initiatives to deal with those problems which are most effectively dealt with at the local level.

In Australia over recent years we have seen some examples of curriculum development tending towards this kind of rationale (Marsh and Stafford, 1984; Musgrave, 1972). National curriculum development initiatives started in a sys-tematic fashion with the work of the Commonwealth Schools Commission (from 1973) and the Curriculum Development Centre (from 1975). For most of the 1970's these bodies strongly supported local curriculum development, especially SBCD, though more recently their activities have been politically restrained and confined to a more national emphasis.

A distinction needs to be drawn here between the principle of a national body endeavouring to take a lead in stimulating and promoting local initiatives — when state bodies might have varying opinions about those initiatives — and the kind of mixed vertical and horizontal negotiative-representative process suggested by our analysis of curriculum knowledge. In the search for coherence what is important is a *convergence of action taken* at the various levels — a convergence which is especially apparent at the level of implementation, at the point of student learning, the classroom — rather than strong but relatively isolated leadership at one particular level.

For the convergence of curriculum action from all levels actually to apply at the school and classroom levels, there needs to be not only scope for teachers and students to take prominent roles in the development of curriculum, which will include thorough situational analysis (Skilbeck, 1984a), but also systematic preservice and in-service training of teachers in curriculum development. From research done into SBCD, it would seem, also, that teacher education could well strive to undermine the consensus detected by Marsh (1986:98) citing studies by House (1974) and Lortie (1975):

> a consensus among a large number of teachers who argue that their major task is to be a skilful classroom teacher and not to be involved in sharing and planning activities.

Nevertheless, the picture here is not clear-cut, and there is evidence that under the right conditions and sometimes even under difficult conditions, teachers will work hard to adapt their practices and undertake their own curriculum development initiatives (Crump, 1984). The degree of success and coherence achieved is going to depend on the *overall* situational analysis (including all levels, not just the local) and vertical and horizontal negotiation at and between all levels (not just the local). There is an important role here for educative leaders:

> *People with a grasp of the theory, politics and administration of curriculum are required who can stimulate and foster convergence of action at and between levels, which means promoting overall situational analysis as well as horizontal and vertical negotiation.*

Educative leadership aiming at both democracy and efficiency will try to maximise the strengths which emerge from a variety of views at a number of levels of administrative and political complexity as well as smoothing the channels which enable individuals and groups to pursue their interests. Given the most coherent set of solutions, and given our intellectually open and experimental methodology, the interests of democracy and efficiency can be expected to coalesce.

Here we must part company with the proponents of the 'socially critical school' to the extent that they assume that democracy is necessarily participative and therefore more readily achievable in SBCD, and that efficiency is a bureaucratic value more likely of achievement in centralised decision making. Our pragmatism cuts right across this dichotomy, and makes the issue of *where* to locate power, to promote both democracy and efficiency, an open, empirical question. For us the issues of educative leadership will arise at all levels, and they will be basically the same in kind at all levels. The epistemology and pragmatic values outlined in this chapter underscore the general, but nevertheless clear, set of procedural steps and values outlined above for all educative leaders.

Continuity and Change

The holistic, pragmatic notion of curriculum development advanced here makes no sense unless the possibility of experimental change is built into our procedures. But possibility is not enough; obstacles will lie in the way and some people are more attuned to change than others. In keeping with the open-mindedness of our curricular epistemology, we should, however, avoid making hasty judgments about who will be the innovators and who will retard progressive change.

For educative leadership to flourish, encouragement of creative innovation at all levels and in all situations should be the norm.

Empirical evidence from past experience and situational analysis may suggest hypotheses about likely sources of change, and we should not be worried about acting upon them when practical circumstances require. But equally, we should guard against self-fulfilling prophecies that turn people into opponents of change just because of labelling or negative views held of their problems, goals and potentials. Classroom teachers are particularly susceptible to damage by self-fulfilling prophecies.

The potential of different kinds of participant in innovative problem-solving curriculum development is something for the pooled wisdom of practitioners at all levels to determine: it is not up to theorists to proffer abstract opinions. The task is a big one. In a genuinely educative, educational community, we need to remember good lessons and keep open communication between curriculum bodies at all levels, the Commonwealth and State Departments of Education, Boards of Studies, teachers' professional groups and associations, school councils, the inspectorate and other advisory services as they exist from system to system, teacher education and educational research institutions, principals and classroom teachers, students and parents.

Fundamental to all rational change is learning. The conditions for constructive change, in a very general sense, are equivalent to the conditions for learning about the causes of problems and considering options for their solution.

The basic model for change strategies, then, will be a problem-solving model. This, however, is compatible, depending on the development situation, with other models. For example, of the change models presented by Marsh (1986, Ch. 9), our holistic pragmatism is generally compatible with other interactionist views, with action research, and in organisational theory more generally with the account of organisational learning developed by Argyris and Schon (1978), and Simon's basically pragmatist theory of administrative behaviour (Simon, 1960), all of which can be interpreted in terms of cultural interaction (Reynolds and Skilbeck, 1976).

It is less compatible with the Research, Development and Diffusion model, except where it functions as a back-up to horizontally and vertically negotiated problem-solving, and with the centre-periphery model. As with the question of judging between competing theories, pragmatism suggests that we start with an empirical analysis of the social situations to which educational action is relevant, rather than with a choice between abstractly developed models and strategies. Curriculum development is a part of, not distinct from, social research.

Here, basic learning would seem to be vital. The education and training of teachers, administrators, consultants and curriculum specialists is the obvious place to begin. The fact that past evidence is not enormously encouraging about the capacity of pre-service training alone to develop innovative and experimental approaches among classroom teachers, for instance, does not mean that we should not work on it and set up closer ties between pre-service, in-service and ongoing educational practice. Our upward and outward negotiation model, of course, suggests greater input than is currently the case from people at all levels of the educational community into teacher education institutions.

But change, in and of itself, is no more an absolute value than anything else. It is justified pragmatically. The decision to innovate, indeed, presupposes continuity if it is part of a problem-solving process. We extend and adopt our best cultural resources, grafting new practices onto them where appropriate. The key is an *ongoing* process of *development*, rather than periodic upheavals punctuating a basically static curricular situation. The process of curriculum development occurs through a basically sound cultural community, sound in its open-ended, democratic and negotiative processes and realistically responsive to practical situations at all levels. It is the collective learning process of an *educative* community, whose leaders are charged with the creative maintenance and rational reconstruction of an educative culture, a way of life which enables individuals and groups to pursue their legitimate goals and interests by helping them solve the problems which get in their way. In the process of reconstruction, new goals and interests will no doubt be formed as people learn new ways of living in their changing environment. In a democratic society, a shared but not immutable core of shared values is essential to maintain responsibility, predictability and trust. Securing touchstone requires both cultural continuity and innovative educative leadership.

Conclusion

In this chapter we have proposed a philosophically justified and practicable approach to educative leadership in curriculum development. The educative leader is both a careful thinker and theorist and a practically effective problem solver. The leader, whatever the level at which he or she works, carries out a role requiring cooperation and negotiation, openness to the views of others and the capacity to make confident but revisable decisions. Pragmatism opens up rather than precludes opportunities for serious consideration of values, related to learning and the growth of knowledge. The creation of a genuinely educative cultural community, rooted in but transcending the school context, is a challenge for people of vision as well as hard-headed commonsense. The measure of both will be the quality of the curricula developed and implemented in our schools.

Summary of Main Points

1   Any approach to curriculum development which fails genuinely to acknowledge the plurality of views is doomed to founder.
2   For reasons of both efficiency and democracy, educative leaders might well be expected to be familiar with the current scope and content of curriculum theory, or at least confident that they can take relevant views into account.

3 As with the plurality of views, any approach to curriculum development and theorising which fails to acknowledge the complexity of the issues is unlikely to succeed.

4 Neither eclecticism nor compartmentalisation is satisfactory, on either efficiency or democratic grounds.

5 The interests of educative leadership in curriculum development can be advanced by increasing theoretical sophistication, which enhances rather than conflicts with practicality.

6 What counts as educative is itself dependent on the theoretical view taken.

7 Rather than a set of criteria for 'education' we need a set of procedures for judging between competing views.

8 Because of the practical nature of curriculum theory we cannot separate two apparently distinct questions:
> What criteria should be used in planning curriculum, selecting content, and in evaluation?
> Who should make decisions about curriculum, using what procedures and in what social structures?

9 Both the justification and the practicality of value judgments requires us to render them coherent with, or at least check them out against, our psychological and sociological knowledge, particularly our knowledge of learning.

10 Given the variety of value-orientations and the differences of opinion about how to justify particular value judgments as they arise in curriculum development, we need an approach which achieves the most coherent value package possible within a democratic framework.

11 The curriculum cannot but start with the cultural context as it is; what should be conserved and what should be changed has to be sorted out by cultural action, in which educative leaders, as learners themselves, discover the problems and possibilities of educational action through curriculum development.

12 The pragmatist holist epistemology is superior to its competitors as an account of the nature of knowledge, methodology and values.

13 Nevertheless, it is not necessary to accept the epistemology in its entirety to see merit in some of the practical research, development and decision-making principles it generates. These may be found useful by people of various epistemological persuasions.

14 To discover what are the shared and unshared problems in any given situation, we need to conduct a situational analysis.

15 Educative leaders should take a lead in building a partnership between the schools and the wider educational environment which facilitates frank communication and shared decision making.

16 A relevant view is defined as a view which addresses the problems arising in a particular situation at a particular level, and therefore has some bearing on the solution of those problems.

17 Educative leaders should be aware of, and capable of responding to, the changing balance of relevant considerations, in both their horizontal and vertical relationships in the educational framework.

18 Curriculum knowledge, or the knowledge produced in curriculum development, is produced through a search for coherent proposals for action to

solve problems. It works through theory-competition and touchstone, as does the process of research in any sphere.

19 To take a lead in decision making, educative leaders could well keep aware of, and receptive to, economic, political and sociological studies of the kinds of social situation to be represented in their curriculum deliberations or contributions.

20 Educative leaders have a role to play in combating crude and prejudiced representations of competing views.

21 Educative leaders have to be prepared to make judgments between competing theoretical views and to take responsibility for those practical options which are best suited to the problems within their brief.

22 Educative leadership means scientific research in action. This is a fundamental contribution to the development of curriculum knowledge, which, like all knowledge, proceeds and grows by the elimination of error through the trials of practical action. Leadership needs to be experimental. To admit you are wrong and change your mind does not mean you are a failure.

23 We need not assume that democracy is best served by control at the local level and efficiency best served by centralised control.

24 People with a grasp of the theory, politics and administration of curriculum are required who can stimulate and foster convergence of action at and between levels, which means promoting overall situational analysis as well as horizontal and vertical negotiation.

25 For educative leadership to flourish, encouragement of creative innovation at all levels and in all situations should be the norm.

26 Fundamental to all rational change is learning. The conditions for constructive change, in a very general sense, are equivalent to the conditions for learning about the causes of problems and considering options for their solution.

Note

1 According to this theory, it is just that there should be rewards in economic competition because this is necessary for overall economic prosperity, and as a result the *absolute* level of economic prosperity of lower income earners will rise. Social welfare, therefore, is also served, and to a higher degree than would be achieved through a distribution of wealth based on relative or even absolute equality. The wealth initially acquired by the most successful competitors creates more wealth, which trickles down the socioeconomic hierarchy.

References

ARGYRIS, C. and SCHON, D.A. (1978) *Organizational Learning: A Theory of Action Perspective*, Reading, MA: Addison-Wesley.

AUSUBEL, D.P. (1963) *The Psychology of Meaningful Verbal Learning*, New York: Grune and Stratton.

AUSUBEL, D.P. (1968) *Educational Psychology: A Cognitive View*, New York: Holt, Rinehart and Winston.

BANDURA, A. (1977) *Social Learning Theory*, Englewood Cliffs: Prentice-Hall.

BOOMER, G. (1982) (Ed.) *Negotiating the Curriculum: A Teacher-Student Partnership*, Sydney: Ashton Scholastic.

BOWER, G.H. and HILGARD, E.R. (1981) *Theories of Learning*, Englewood Cliffs, NJ: Prentice-Hall.

BRUNER, J.S. (1961) *The Process of Education*, Cambridge, MA: Harvard University Press.

BRUNER, J.S. (1966) *Towards a Theory of Instruction*, Cambridge, MA: Harvard University Press.

CRUMP, S. (1984) *Teachers after Wyndham: A Cultural Study of a Group of Secondary School Teachers*, unpublished MEd. thesis, Department of Education, The University of Sydney.

DEWEY, J. (1916) *Democracy and Education*, New York: Macmillan.

DEWEY, J. (1948) *Reconstruction in Philosophy*, Boston: Beacon Press.

DEWEY, J. (1963) *Experience and Education*, London: Collier-Macmillan.

EDEL, A. (1972) 'Analytic philosophy of education at the crossroads', *Educational Theory*, **22**, 131–52; reprinted in DOYLE, J.F. (Ed.) (1973) *Educational Judgments*, London: Routledge and Kegan Paul.

EVERS, C.W. (1979) 'Analytic philosophy of education: From a logical point of view', *Educational Philosophy and Theory*, **11**, 2, 1–16.

EVERS, C.W. (1984) 'Naturalised epistemology and neural principles of learning: Towards a congruence', in EVERS, C.W. and WALKER, J.C. (Eds) *Epistemology, Semantics and Educational Theory*, Sydney: University of Sydney Department of Education.

EVERS, C.W. and WALKER, J.C. (1983) 'Knowledge, partitioned sets, and extensionality', *Journal of Philosophy of Education*, **17**, 2, 155–70.

FORDHAM, R. (1983) *Decision Making in Victorian Education*, Ministerial Paper 1, Melbourne: Victorian Ministry of Education.

GROSSBERG, S. (1982) *Studies of Mind and Brain*, Boston Studies in the Philosophy of Science, 70, Dordrecht: Reidel.

HABERMAS, J. (1972) *Knowledge and Human Interests*, London: Heinemann.

HIRST, P.H. (1974) *Knowledge and the Curriculum*, London: Routledge and Kegan Paul.

HIRST, P.H. (1983) 'Educational theory', in HIRST, P.H. (Ed.) *Educational Theory and the Foundational Disciplines*, London: Routledge and Kegan Paul.

HIRST, P.H. and PETERS, R.S. (1970) *The Logic of Education*, London: Routledge and Kegan Paul.

HOUSE, E.R. (1974) *The Politics of Educational Innovation*, Berkeley: McCutchan.

KEMMIS, S., COLE, P. and SUGGETT, D. (1983) *Towards the Socially Critical School*, Melbourne: Victorian Institute of Secondary Education.

LAWTON, D. (1983) *Curriculum Studies and Educational Planning*, London: Hodder and Stoughton.

LAWTON, D. (1984) 'Cultural analysis and curriculum evaluation', in SKILBECK, M. (Ed.) *Evaluating the Curriculum in the Eighties*, London: Hodder and Stoughton.

LEVIN, K. (1935) *A Dynamic Theory of Personality*, New York: McGraw-Hill.

LEVIN, K. (1951) *Field Theory in Social Science*, New York: Harper and Row.

LINDSAY, P.H. and NORMAN, D.A. (1972) *Human Information Processing*, New York: Academic Press.

LORTIE, D.E. (1975) *School Teacher: A Sociological Study*, Chicago: University of Chicago Press.

MARSH, C. (1986) *Curriculum: An Analytical Introduction*, Sydney: Novak.

MARSH, C. and STAFFORD, K. (1984) *Curriculum: Australian Practices and Issues*, Sydney: McGraw-Hill.

MUSGRAVE, P.W. (1979) *Society and Curriculum in Australia*, Sydney: Allen and Unwin.

PETERS, R.S. (1967) (Ed.) *The Concept of Education*, London: Routledge and Kegan Paul.

PHENIX, P.H. (1964) *Realms of Meaning: A Philosophy of the Curriculum for General Education*, New York: Harcourt, Brace and World.

PIAGET, J. (1929) *The Child's Conception of the World*, New York: Harcourt, Brace and World.

PIAGET, J. (1971) *Biology and Knowledge*, Chicago: University of Chicago Press.

PIAGET, J. (1978) *Behaviour and Evolution*, New York: Pantheon.

PINAR, W.F. (1975) (Ed.) *Curriculum Theorising: The Reconceptualists*, Berkeley: McCutcheon.

PINAR, W.F. (1979) 'What is reconceptualisation?' *Journal of Curriculum Theorising*, **1**, 1.

POPPER, K.R. (1972) *Objective Knowledge: An Evolutionary Approach*, Oxford: Oxford University Press.

QUINE, W.V.O. (1975) 'The nature of natural knowledge', in GUTTENPLAN, S. (Ed.) *Mind and Language*, Oxford: Oxford University Press.

QUINE, W.V.O. and ULLIAN, J.S. (1978) *The Web of Belief*, second, revised edition; New York: Random House.

REYNOLDS, J. and SKILBECK, M. (1976) *Culture and the Classroom*, London: Open Books.

SCHWAB, J.J. (1964) 'Structure of the disciplines: Meanings and significances', in FORD, G.W. and PUGNO, L. (Eds) *The Structure of Knowledge and the Curriculum*, Chicago: Rand McNally.

SCHWAB, J.J. (1969) 'The practical: A language for curriculum', *School Review*, **78**, 1.

SCHWAB, J.J. (1973) 'The practical 3: Translation into curriculum', *School Review*, **81**, 1.

SCHWAB, J.J. (1983) 'The practical 4: Something for curriculum professors to do', *Curriculum Inquiry*, **13**, 3.

SIMON, H.A. (1960) *The New Science of Management Decision*, New York: Harper and Row.

SKILBECK, M. (1976) 'School-based curriculum development and teacher education policy', in *Teachers as Innovators*, Paris: OECD Publications.

SKILBECK, M. (1982) *A Core Curriculum for the Common School*, London: University of London Institute of Education.

SKILBECK, M. (1984a) 'Curriculum evaluation at the national level', in SKILBECK, M. (Ed.) *Evaluating the Curriculum in the Eighties*, London: Hodder and Stoughton.

SKILBECK, M. (1984b) *School-Based Curriculum Development*, London: Harper and Row.

SKILBECK, M. (1984c) *Readings in School-Based Curriculum Development*, London: Harper and Row.

SKINNER, B.F. (1968) *The Technology of Teaching*, New York: Appleton-Century-Crofts.

TURNEY, C. (1981) (Ed.) *The Anatomy of Teaching*, Sydney: Ian Novak.

TYLER, R.W. (1949) *Basic Principles of Curriculum and Instruction*, Chicago: University of Chicago Press.

WALKER, J.C. (1984) 'The evolution of the APE: Analytic philosophy of education in retrospect', *Access*, **3**, 1, 1–16.

WALKER, J.C. (1985a) 'Philosophy and the study of education: A critique of the commonsense consensus', *The Australian Journal of Education*, **29**, 2, 101–14.

WALKER, J.C. (1985b) 'The philosopher's touchstone: Towards pragmatic unity in educational studies', *Journal of Philosophy of Education*, **19**, 2, 181–98.

WALKER, J.C. (1988) 'Knowledge, culture and the curriculum', in SMYTH, W.J. (Ed.) *Educating Teachers: Changing the Nature of Professional Knowledge*, London: Falmer Press.

WALKER, J.C. and EVERS, C.W. (1982) 'Epistemology and justifying the curriculum of educational studies', *British Journal of Educational Studies*, **30**, 2, 312–29.

WALKER, J.C. (1984) 'Towards a materialist pragmatist philosophy of education', *Education Research and Perspectives*, **11**, 1, 23–33.

WEIL, M. and JOYCE, B. (1978) *Information Processing Models of Teaching*, Englewood Cliffs: Prentice-Hall.

WERTHEIMER, M. (1959) *Productive Thinking*, New York: Harper and Row.

YOUNG, M.F.D. (1971) (Ed.) *Knowledge and Control*, London: Collier-Macmillan.

Educative Leadership for Quality Teaching: A Synthesis and a Commentary

P.A. Duignan and R.J.S. Macpherson

A recent and important issue throughout the Western world is the encouragement of excellence through high quality teaching. It is our view that the professional service of teachers can only be enhanced if a complex process of in-service education and supportive services are planned, developed and sustained by leaders in education.

We presume that the quality of school life is greatly dependent on the quality of students' experience in the classroom. It follows that educative leadership will be central to the negotiations of what is to be regarded as valuable in the curriculum and what is believed to be excellent in teaching methods. This approach to leadership will nurture and protect these ideas of exemplary practice. To achieve this condition means defining excellence in specific terms. It also means planning in sophisticated ways to achieve desired outcomes. Educative leaders should, therefore, take responsible leadership actions to create organisational cultures that enhance the growth and development of all involved in teaching and learning.

The task is to identify the nature of leadership that creates and sustains quality teaching. Such leadership takes place in a rapidly changing societal and institutional context. Educative leadership, therefore, has to cope with many demands for change coming from such diverse sources as governments, government agencies, teachers, parents as well as students. As Northfield *et al.* point out in Chapter 4, educative leaders need a process to respond to plural demands, and change what exists so that institutional life can be improved.

This view of change emphasises that any educational change, such as the introduction of a new teaching strategy, is dependent on individuals changing. Changing people implies the use of a learning process which depends heavily on each individual's capacity and willingness to reflect on practice, to critically analyse it, and to experiment with new ways of thinking and acting. In other words, the change process is essentially a learning process and it is through this learning process that improvement occurs.

In the whole of this learning process there is a need for individuals to make personal sense of what is happening. Unless they can connect the proposed new ideas or practice with their basic assumptions, beliefs and experiences they are likely to reject the change outright. One of the challenges for the educative leader is to make proposed changes understandable and meaningful for those who are expected to implement the changes. They must also be actively involved in these change processes if they are to be committed to them and to the change itself. Such an approach to learning is referred to by Northfield *et al.* as a *constructivist approach.*

Northfield *et al.* argue that such improvement in teaching and learning is not accidental. The day-to-day requirements of teaching, and the isolated nature of the role, are two conditions not conducive to reflection on practice. Teachers need encouragement and support if they are to risk being involved in trying new ideas in the classroom. Educative leaders can play a crucial role by establishing and maintaining the conditions necessary for reflection, critical analysis and experimentation.

The educative leader is one who takes the initiative to facilitate the following conditions for implementing change in teaching and learning. The educative leader:

1 Creates opportunities to allow participants in any change process to reflect on their practice and to develop personal understandings of the nature and implications of the change for themselves;
2 Encourages those involved in the implementation of an improvement to form social groups to provide for mutual support during the change process;
3 Provides opportunities for positive feedback for all involved in the change; and
4 Must be sensitive to the possible outcomes of any development process and provide the conditions necessary for feedback and follow-up so that those involved have the opportunity to discuss and rethink their ideas and practice.

Northfield *et al.* highlight many other important aspects of educative leadership. For example, people learn best when they are actively involved in their own learning. This applies to student learning, to staff development and to leadership in education. In essence, the educative leader is a learner. Hence, to improve the quality of school leadership there is a need to:

assess the present strengths of leaders, their existing concerns and current practices;
utilise and build on existing skills and understandings;
provide leaders with opportunities to continually reflect on practice and make personal meaning of their practice; and
be sensitive to the range of possible outcomes in any change process which attempts to bring about improvement in leaders' practices — leaders' responses can vary from full acceptance to outright rejection of the ideas and or practices.

In summary, valuable innovation, such as the development of quality teaching, is not accidental. The concurrent reform of pedagogy and leadership can be accelerated if deliberate and systematic strategies are used to establish the conditions in which learning about leading and teaching can occur. Leadership development involves a process analogous to teacher development and student learning — a key theme developed by Northfield *et al.* in Chapter 4.

Leadership to Promote Quality in Learning

J. Northfield

in collaboration with Ken Craze, Pat Duignan, Mac Macpherson, Elizabeth McKenzie, and Anne Pegum

As a student teacher, I learned that students waste time during class. Two years later, I learned that teachers waste more time in class than most disruptive students could imagine. Learning about the extent of student time-wasting was a blow to the ideal that led me to teaching. Learning about teacher time-wasting was a shock; had I learned it in my fifteenth year of teaching rather than my second, I imagine that I would have been shattered. (A teacher, Mick Dunne, in Mitchell and Baird, 1986:190)

Introduction

This chapter begins by reviewing some promising lines of development in areas of teaching and learning. Several important perspectives need to be outlined to enable an understanding of the arguments presented. A fundamental perspective is a view of learning which can be described as a constructivist or generative model (Osborne and Wittrock, 1985).[1]

This is a particular view of learning which seeks to understand how ideas are processed and structured by learners. The term 'constructivist' emphasizes the importance of pre-existing views held by the learner. It also highlights the personal meaning that is acquired as new ideas and information are presented to the learner. This approach will be used to interpret developments in teaching and learning within the classroom and also the teacher development process occurring when teachers consider new information and ideas. This approach will be extended to present a view of leaders as learners in the leadership process. Teachers and leaders are, therefore, considered as 'constructivists' continually reconciling new ideas to gain more satisfactory explanations of classroom and school change efforts.

The Australia-wide emphasis on fostering school autonomy and school-based curriculum development (SBCD) would appear to be compatible with greater teacher involvement in curriculum research and development. The rhetoric for SBCD is strong and consistent, although there is widespread scepticism about commitment to implementing policies related to school autonomy. Doubts exist about the approaches to educational change that are employed in implementing SBCD ideas. There is also evidence that SBCD is not being implemented widely in Australian schools (Cohen and Harrison, 1982). This chapter is intended to contribute to a view of change which will support schools as they attempt to respond to SBCD. It begins with the lessons of a case study.

Teaching that Begins with Learning: The Peel Project

This section outlines a case in one school where a group of teachers undertook the task of improving the quality of teaching and learning. The effort is analyzed and implications for further developments will be made.

The case study began in late 1984 with a unique set of circumstances. A group of teachers was expressing concern about students being too passive in classroom learning situations. A teacher (Ian Mitchell) was able to connect the problem to some recent research on learning. Baird (1984) had conducted research to identify poor learning habits in students and then explored interventions in the classroom designed to assist students to improve their approach to learning.

This research served as a reminder that failure in learning in classrooms can be due to persistent poor learning strategies as well as students' limited intellectual ability and lack of motivation. Other related research that influenced Mitchell's thinking was the study of the effect of students' prior views on what happened in their learning (for example, Osborne and Freyberg, 1985).

These ideas reinforced Baird's belief that a group of teachers could do something positive to affect the quality of student learning. He had also reflected on the process of educational change and was sensitive to the problems of implementing ideas at the school level. Almost two years later, the first part of the case study activity had been documented by the participants (Baird and Mitchell, 1986). An analysis of what the teachers had attempted is set out in Table 4.1.

The teachers in the case study were concerned with the learning process as well as the learning outcomes of knowledge about new content and ideas about learning. The desired outcomes therefore included the development of more active learning strategies. There was also the realization that the results for students could vary from teachers' expectations. The teachers anticipated that outcomes might be disappointing (see Stage D in Table 4.1).

Earlier reports (Northfield and Gunstone, 1985) had highlighted the difficulties associated with implementing an approach to teaching and learning which differed from the classroom experiences of the students. Students have expectations of how the classroom operates and, in the case study, they became uncomfortable when new values and approaches were introduced. Altering the teaching-learning situation created issues that affected student learning; assessment, student negotiation and curriculum content selection. It was therefore necessary for teachers to understand students' expectations and build on these expectations rather than ignore them (see Stage B in Table 4.1).

The case study provided evidence of significant teacher development as the participants reflected on their practice and described the range of teaching

Table 4.1:   Improving student's classroom learning

To improve student classroom learning there is a need for the teacher to:	Stages in Student Learning
A. identify, and be familiar with, children's present views about the topic and their existing learning approaches;	The initial perspective.
B. design curricula which build on, rather than ignore children's views on the topic and existing learning approaches;	The plan for the learning program.
C. provide challenges and encouragement for children to change their views on content and to adopt more active learning approaches; and	The learning process for students.
D. be sensitive to the possible results of teaching according to the above principles. The range of outcomes for students could include: • the new content and learning approaches are rejected; • the new content and learning approaches are misinterpreted by students; • the new content and learning approaches are accepted but in isolation from other teaching-learning situations; • the new content and learning approaches are accepted but lead to confusion for students; or • the new content and learning approaches are accepted and form a coherent view of the world.	The learning outcomes.
E. Support children's attempts to rethink their ideas in more active ways.	Summary of a 'constructivist' approach to student learning.

strategies that had been developed and used to create new learning situations. The results for students were less clear and constitute a major challenge for future evaluations of the case study.

The Concepts of Quality and Leadership

In this section the concepts of quality and leadership will be developed and linked to the case study. The goal of quality in teaching and learning is a high priority for all educators. The term quality can mean many things and therefore needs to be defined in practical terms. In the context of this chapter, the term quality has two components: one related to the value of learning outcomes, and the other related to the process by which the outcomes are achieved. In the case study, each teacher sought:

> to exercise his or her authority in ways which continually promote the educational development and psychological well-being of children. (NSW Department of Education, cited by Sharpe, 1985:56)

More generally:

> When the teacher's concern is demonstrated through the preparation, development, implementation and evaluation of educational programs geared to student needs and which maximize student achievement, quality education is likely to result. (Sharpe, 1985:6)

The situation in the case study is also related to leadership. The leadership tended to be subtle but crucial in establishing and maintaining the conditions for teacher development. Leadership was expressed when the group was able to obtain:

> information and ideas about student learning;
> reassurance when there were doubts about the value of the time and effort being put into the project;
> time and limited resources; and
> some understanding of educational change.

Leadership had been provided by a variety of people, including the teacher participants, often in unplanned ways. The teachers had accepted a large amount of responsibility for the leadership required to maintain the project. The change effort in the classroom was therefore closely related to the quality of leadership. The concept of quality was defined in terms of teacher development outcomes and how well teachers were supported in the change effort.

In reviewing the case study as an example of teacher development, it is useful to consider the process of teacher change as analogous to the process of facilitating student learning as presented in Table 4.1. Table 4.2 illustrates the analogy and the next section develops these ideas in terms of our knowledge of educational change.

A View of Change Drawn From the Case Study

Table 4.2 illustrates a particular view of educational change as it relates to teacher development. The stages in teacher development can now be clarified. The initial assertion is that *there is no educational change without individual change*. This assertion is supported in particular models of educational change (Hall and Hord, 1987) and emerges from reviews of change research (Fullan, 1982).

In the case study, the teachers identified an area of concern and came to the

Table 4.2:   An analysis of the case study: Fostering teacher development

To foster teacher development there is a need to:	Stages in Teacher Development
A. assess teachers' present strengths and find out what really happens in classrooms;	The initial perspective.
B. utilize and build on existing teacher strengths, extending their present skills, rather than neglecting or undermining them;	The plan for teacher change.
C. assess which aspects of the content and format of any new ideas will be likely to appeal to teachers and to find ways of encouraging teachers to reflect on practice; and	The learning process for teachers.
D. be sensitive to the possible outcomes of any teacher development. The range of outcomes could include: • the new ideas are simply rejected; • the new ideas are misinterpreted to fit in with, or even support, existing ideas; • the new ideas are accepted, but the teacher cannot apply them in other situations; • the new ideas are accepted but lead to confusion; or • the new ideas are accepted and form part of a coherent long-term personal view of teaching.	The development outcomes.
E. Provide feedback and follow-up activities to allow teachers to rethink and discuss their ideas.	Summary of a 'constructivist' approach to development.

realization that individual change was essential. The teacher's statement that introduced this chapter clearly acknowledges that educational change will involve change in the individual.

When the change originates outside the school, such as new government policies and guidelines, the first challenge for leaders is to help teachers explore the implications it has for themselves. Having done this it will then be necessary to explore the implications it has for the school (Stages B and C in Table 4.2).

The second stage presumes that *effective change will be more likely when participants' values, skills, present practices and capabilities are identified.* This assertion is also a fundamental assumption of the Concerns-Based Adoption Model (CBAM, Hall and Hord, 1987). Information about the present concerns of the participants, and what is presently happening, is crucial in planning for change. In the case study, the teachers spent a great deal of time discussing their concerns and teaching practice so that activities and ideas were considered and used by individual teachers as these seemed appropriate.

A fundamental principle in any school improvement effort is that *change is a process, not an event*. However, this principle is frequently ignored in a general underestimation of what is required to bring about significant educational change. The case study involved a group of teachers who volunteered to review their teaching approaches to achieve more active student learning.

The first three months of the project were marked by a decrease in morale as the participants developed personal understandings of the issues involved. Many ideas were introduced into the group. These ideas were related to teaching techniques and views about student learning and educational change. However, the ideas had to be considered, tried, adapted or rejected by each teacher in each classroom (see the range of possible outcomes for teachers in Table 4.2). This development of personal meaning requires adequate time as a major condition for real change at the classroom level. Indeed, *the making of personal meaning is essential for participants*.

The case study also indicated that there were four related requirements to gain the commitment of teachers in the initial stages of the change effort.[2] The change must be perceived as intelligible, beneficial, plausible and feasible.

Part of reason for the tendency to underestimate the time taken for educational change is an overestimation of leaders' ability to make the change *intelligible* to participants in the early stages. The change should be understood sufficiently by participants to be seen as potentially *beneficial* to them. Changes in teaching and learning approaches should be seen by teachers as having more satisfying outcomes for themselves and their students. Any proposals will also need to be seen as *plausible* approaches to achieving the intended outcomes. The participants have to feel that the ideas might work and that the overall plan is *feasible*. The feasibility condition is particularly relevant for teachers in a time when there are expectations that teachers will take on enlarged roles as curriculum developers, and as participants in increased school decision-making. Many changes are being proposed for teachers and schools, but what is being satisfactorily accomplished is disappointing to many people. Teachers are tending to ask questions about priorities and are increasingly seeking the conditions in which planning for specific change is feasible.

In the later sections of this chapter, it will be argued that quality in leadership, which promotes improvement in teaching and learning, is associated with the ability to influence teachers' perceptions that a proposed change is intelligible, plausible, feasible and beneficial.

The third stage (see Stage C in Table 4.2) assumes that *improvement in teaching and learning requires teacher change and this in turn can be equated with teacher learning*. To begin a consideration of the process of teacher learning, a teacher's description of a classroom event is presented below and then interpreted to develop some general ideas. The teacher wrote that:

The turning point came on 27th February. After encouraging students to ask questions, think about what they are doing, show initiative etc., I was still getting passive or negative results. I wrote notes on the board which students mechanically copied down. I held a geography book in my hand and pretended to copy the two paragraphs shown below from the text:

Water
The degree of rainfall for each half year and the annual seasonal deficit are the systems which determine which areas will receive rain and which won't.
However, in planning where to plant crops it is not enough to know the system, one must also take account of the different levels within each seasonal system.
We must also know how much of the soil will be lost by evaporation.

Length of the daylight period
Plants depend on light. The daylight hours vary from town to town depending on altitudes. Towns in low lying areas depend largely on the degree of photosynthesis and rainfall — clouds create shade which affects people's vision.
Melbourne's hygration can vary by 20 cm from Sydney's at any particular time.

This procedure was a spur of the moment decision. I made the nonsense notes up on the spot. My instructions were to 'copy the notes down from the board'. The topic under study was 'Agriculture', where students could be expected to use technical terms and definitions. I waited until all students had copied the notes and then asked if anyone had any questions — I asked this a number of times and, to my recollection, out of two Year 10 classes, only one student per class had a question. One asked the meaning of a term used, the other hesitantly questioned whether soil could evaporate. I guess it was from this point on that I realized three things.

First, I thought I had been teaching in a fashion that encouraged student involvement and initiative. I now realized that I had not been challenging the students enough. My reaction to these two classes was one of concern about my teaching methods.

Second, I was surprised to see to what extent students expect teachers to dictate and dominate class situations. Students either believe that teachers should not be questioned or believe that it is much easier not to get involved in class discussion.

Third, that as a teacher I had an obligation to alter my teaching strategies. Even though I believed that I was using strategies that the PEEL[3] program professed, I had to have a much closer look at the program and adapt it to my classroom methods. (A teacher, Damien Hynes, in Baird and Mitchell, 1986:30–31)

This classroom incident can be interpreted as a teacher showing a willingness to 'reflect on practice' (Schon, 1983). Effective changes in teaching and learning situations follow reflection on practice. There are conditions necessary to facilitate such a process.

In the extract, the teacher was prepared to examine a common teaching practice (notetaking by students) in terms of an expressed value for active learning on the part of the students. The teacher's spur of the moment decision represented a willingness to examine this taken-for-granted teaching practice

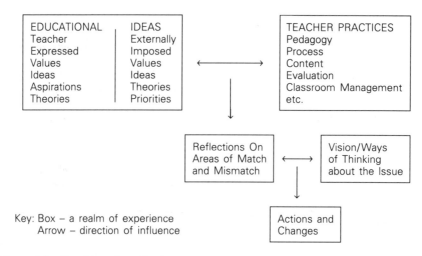

Key: Box – a realm of experience
Arrow – direction of influence

Figure 4.1: Conditions for reflection

(see Figure 4.1). It is crucial to be able to think about an aspect of teaching in a new way before change can occur. In this example, the teacher became aware of a mismatch between practice and aspirations, and this realization was summed up in the three points made at the end of the extract. The third point outlined the proposed actions and changes that the teacher subsequently attempted in the classroom.

The extract provided a good example of a teacher reflecting on practice, but did not deal with the conditions necessary to facilitate the process (see Figure 4.1). The day-to-day requirements of teaching, and the isolated nature of the role, are not conducive to reflection on practice. The teacher was in a school where a group of colleagues had expressed similar concerns about the nature of learning at the classroom level. These teachers had agreed to try some new teaching ideas and were providing mutual support when the outcomes generally fell below expectations. The teacher could easily have become depressed, but was part of a group wherein the experience could be shared. This became a positive contribution to the project and a turning point for the teacher.

The process of reflection occurred when teachers considered classroom practices in relation to their aspirations for students. This process may appear straightforward but one should not underestimate the challenge of establishing the conditions necessary for teachers to be reflective in this way. One role of leadership is to establish and maintain the conditions necessary for reflection on practice, thereby fostering quality teaching.

It can be assumed that *improvement in teaching and learning is not accidental*. Participants require a common understanding of how change occurs. At a system level, it would be desirable to have an expressed view of educational change as part of the set of educational policies. It is also rare for schools to have policies about educational change. Such policies could include statements about the importance of individuals establishing personal meaning, about the

Table 4.3:   Planning for change: Areas where actions have to be taken to support change

Areas for Action	Description of Area for Action	Examples of Action
Developing Support Arrangements	Actions taken to develop policies, establish responsibilities, restructure roles, provide resources and manage staff.	Have a staff member coordinate the purchase of materials.
Teacher Development	Actions taken to develop knowledge, skills and resolve any problems that arise.	Plan workshops for staff.
Consultation and Reinforcement	Actions taken to encourage implementation, identify and resolve any problems that arise.	Hold staff meetings to review progress
Monitoring and Evaluation	Actions taken to gather information about the change effort and impact on students and staff.	Administer questionnaire at the end of the year to students and staff.
External Communication	Actions taken to inform and/or gain support of individuals.	Hold parent-teacher meeting.
Dissemination	Actions taken to encourage others to see the value of the change.	Have teachers present ideas at workshop.

expectation that changes will take time and require support, about procedures for establishing priorities, and about a commitment to plan activities in each of the areas set out in Table 4.3.

The six areas for planning set out in Table 4.3 provide a set of activities regarded as essential for any successful improvement (Northfield, 1985). Such a framework implies the range of support mechanisms that need to be provided for schools and teachers involved in change.

Another related issue is that of understanding the process of change. To begin:

the source of genuine improvement is in the school itself and even more particularly in the classroom. I am suggesting that it is primarily teachers and school administrators who will give us the kind of schools we need. It is only through what they create that any view of the school we need will have any chance, whatsoever, of being realized. (Eisner, 1984:11)

An innovation should be designed primarily with the participants in mind rather than focusing solely on details of the change. The Concerns-Based Adoption Model (Hall and Hord, 1987) emphasises the concerns that participants have when considering an educational change (see Table 4.4).

Table 4.4: *Stages of concern about the innovation (Hall and Hord (1987:60).*

Impact	6 REFOCUSING: The focus is on exploration of more universal benefits from the innovation, including the possibility of major changes or replacement with a more powerful alternative. Individual has definite ideas about alternatives to the proposed or existing form of the innovation.
	5 COLLABORATION: The focus is on coordination and cooperation with others regarding use of the innovation.
	4 CONSEQUENCE: Attention focuses on impact of the innovation on student in his/her immediate sphere of influence. The focus is on relevance of the innovation for students, evaluation of student outcomes, including performance and competencies, and changes needed to increase student outcomes.
Task	3 MANAGEMENT: Attention is focused on the processes and tasks of using the innovation and the best use of information and resources. Issues related to efficiency, organizing, managing, scheduling, and time demands are utmost.
Self	2 PERSONAL: Individual is uncertain about the demands of the innovation, his/her inadequacy to meet those demands, and his/her role with the innovation. This includes analysis of his/her role in relation to the reward structure of the organization, decision making, and consideration of potential conflicts with existing structures or personal commitment. Financial or status implications of the program for self and colleagues may also be reflected.
	1 INFORMATIONAL: A general awareness of the innovation and interest in learning more detail about it is indicated. The person seems to be unworried about himself/herself in relation to the innovation. She/he is interested in substantive aspects of the innovation in a selfless manner such as general characteristics, effects, and requirements for use.
Unrelated	0 AWARENESS: Little concern about or involvement with the innovation is indicated.

The initial concerns for more details of the change and personal reservations about the change require different interventions from those that might be provided for teachers at later stages when task and impact concerns may be more important. The concerns that teachers have at each stage in the change process need to be satisfied, and it must be realised that different interventions will be necessary as teachers develop their understanding and confidence.

Peters and Waterman (1982) have identified a range of human needs which are too often neglected in educational change. They discuss a participant's need for meaning which can be interpreted as a need to understand the change itself as well as a need to appreciate how the process of change is likely to occur. In the case study, the teachers achieved a personal meaning of the change over a period of several months. Initial sessions, discussing concepts such as metacognition and learning theories, were seen to have little impact on the teachers, although similar ideas were later developed by teachers and expressed in terms of their own experiences. The point was that the teachers' actions and behaviors shaped their attitudes, beliefs and understandings — a significant observation when we think of the way most changes are introduced to teachers. Too often, we concentrate efforts on lectures and papers to persuade teachers to see a point of view, hoping they will then change their practices.

The development of the participants' understanding of the change process was unplanned in the PEEL project. At a point when morale was low and there were grave doubts about the future of the project, a discussion of the Concerns-Based Adoption Model ideas was introduced (see Table 4.4). This reassured teachers that personal concerns were a normal part of any change process and that they were likely to pass through a number of different stages of concern. This simple description of the change process was the first time that the teachers involved had considered what happens in educational change. Later comments from the teachers indicated how important this idea of change was in giving them some understanding of what was likely to happen.

From Ideas to the Classroom

Major efforts at change in teaching and classroom learning appear to require the establishment of a social group in which the participants can interact. This concept of a social group is similar to improvement models which emphasize the 'creation of a culture' (Sackney, 1985:5).

In the case study, a sub-group of teachers within the school developed 'a common mission, an emphasis on learning, and a climate conducive to learning' (Sackney, 1985:5). The climate was developed to foster learning for both teachers and their students. However, before such a group could form it was essential that any proposal be regarded as plausible (likely to lead to improvement) and feasible (some possibility of being achieved in the existing work context). Teachers had to understand the proposal sufficiently to feel that the outcomes would be beneficial to themselves and/or their students.

In the project, the social group was formed and maintained through regular meetings of participants. These required timetable arrangements to free teachers at the same time and a commitment by teachers to use these periods for discussing the project.

It appears that the formation of a social group around the change provides a focus for maintaining the effort. Information and ideas can then be introduced and discussed. Participants can gain support from colleagues and from external sources. Teachers can also form networks with colleagues in other schools. Such groups can meet in their own time, or arrangements can be made between schools to allow teachers to meet in school time.

Sources of Support and Leadership

Leadership occurs when people find ways of facilitating the types of conditions outlined above. Leadership can occur at the senior levels of an education system with the production of policies on change and commitment. It is also necessary to organise resources to support such policies. At the school level, the principal and senior administration must at least sanction any proposals for change. More active support would entail the promotion of a school policy on change and, within constraints, the taking of steps to arrange the conditions set out above. Such system and school leadership is important in creating the climate and opportunities for change. However, the project highlighted less obvious sources of leadership and support.

Establishing and maintaining the project group required many subtle forms of leadership and support. Teachers were encouraged to raise the issue of passive learning and at least one teacher had a vision of what could be attempted. The ideas were allowed to be discussed at a staff meeting and the person responsible for the timetable was prepared to schedule a meeting time.

The participants took on leadership roles when they placed their classroom experiences before the social group. This implied that leadership required the confidence and commitment of participants to take risks. This form of leadership must be accepted if there is to be change in the quality of teaching and learning by the participants. In terms of the research on effective schools, the teachers in the project:

> adopted a pedagogical style designed to match the preferred learning style of pupils. They were in effect operating their own 'grounded theory' — they had developed a plan of attack jointly, which while being accepted as the best possible approach for the moment, was being constantly revised in the light of emerging data. (Ramsey *et al.*, 1983:297)

The project was an example of a successful improvement in teaching and classroom learning. In Fullan's (1985) terms, improvement has occurred because the participants were able to explain what happened in their own terms and why the change was an improvement.

Implications for Leadership

The most obvious implications from the ideas above is that the leader is a learner. Another is that leadership is defined as occurring when someone takes the initiative to facilitate the following conditions for implementing change in teaching and learning. There must be:

> opportunities to allow participants to develop personal understandings;
> opportunities to form social groups to allow for mutual support during the change process; and
> encouragement to reflect on practice.

These conditions also apply to the professional development of leaders in education. The view of learning originally presented for students, and then applied to teacher development, can be extended to leader development. A leader is, therefore, anyone who takes initiative in a change effort. Table 4.5 elaborates this idea of leader-as-learner.

In summary, leadership involves a process analogous to the view of teacher development advocated, and to the view of student learning proposed above. Leadership involves the performance of specific functions necessary to create

Table 4.5: Fostering leadership in education

Stages in Learning	To improve the quality of school leadership there is a need to:
A. The initial perspective	assess the present strengths of leaders and their existing concerns and relevant practices;
B. The plan for leaders change	utilise and build on existing leader strengths extending their present skills;
C. The learning process for leaders	make personal meaning of and assess current practice. The crucial requirements are *to reflect continually on the practice of leadership*; and
D. The outcome of reflection on practice	be sensitive to the range of possible outcomes in any change effort which might include that: • the change is rejected; • the change is misinterpreted; • the change is accepted but not applied widely; • the change leads to confusion; or • the change is accepted and widely regarded as an improvement

conditions for change. Table 4.6 identifies the functions that must be addressed when leaders begin to initiate the conditions that foster change.

In keeping with the approach in this chapter, leaders should not regard the functions set out in Table 4.6 as being exhaustive. These functions should be considered as a contribution from the literature and an invitation to leaders to reflect on their leadership practice. These lists might help to stimulate discussion and lead to clarification and modification of the functions presented. In the next section, they are developed into a typology of critical leadership functions.

The Principal as a Leader

An important point to be emphasized is that *many expectations to do with leadership focus on the principal*. While leadership can be found at all levels of the education system, the principal occupies a key leadership position. The responsibilities and functions of the position are now addressed to conclude this chapter.

A number of critical leadership functions of the principal are suggested in Table 4.7. These functions are derived from extensive research into the principal's role in the change process. A major implication of the ideas presented in Table 4.7 is that principals are likely to be most effective when they concentrate their leadership efforts in relatively few areas. Hall and Hord (1986) argue that nine functions need to be addressed during any change effort. From their experi-

Table 4.6:   Functions for Effective Leadership: as Identified by Selected Researchers*

Instructional Support Functions (Gersten and Carnine, 1981)	Instructional Leadership (Gall *et al.*, 1984)	Team Functions for Facilitating Change (Hall and Hord, 1986)
visible commitment	priority setting	sanctioning/ continued back-up
monitoring	resource acquisition	providing resources
technical assistance	monitoring	technical coaching
incentive systems	compliance training	monitoring/follow-up
explicit strategies	instructional policy-making	training reinforcing
	assessment	pushing/nudging
	external relations	telling others
	maintenance	approving adaptations

* Derived from Hall, G.E. and Hord, S.M. (1986) *Configurations of School-Based Leadership Teams*, R & D Report 3223.

Table 4.7:   Critical leadership functions of the school principal (Hall et al., 1982)

	Leadership function	Involvement in the change
Principal must —	Sanction	Permits change to occur.
Principal or someone else must	Push	Makes priorities clear. Ensures some action.
Not to be done by the Principal —	Day-to-day details. Technical assistance.	Indirect faciliation. Principals might not have the time nor the personal understanding of those directly involved in the change process.

ence in studying school change, and from reviews of the change literature, they have shown the relationship between the leadership functions of key participants in a change process (see Table 4.8). The *degree of importance* explicit in Table 4.8 provides a stimulus for discussion.

Principals may wish to reflect on a particular change effort and discuss the distribution and relative weightings they would give to each of the leadership functions in Table 4.8. Other leadership functions could also be identified from Table 4.6 above and assessments made of the importance of the various

Table 48:   Leadership functions of significant participants in the change process (HAll and Hord, 1986)

Leadership Functions	The Principal External	Other Leaders in the School	Support Staff
1. Sanctioning/Continued Support	++++	++	++
2. Providing Resources	+++	++	+
3. Technical Coaching	+	++	+
4. Monitoring/Follow up	++	++	
5. Training	+	+	++
6. Reinforcement/ Encouragement	++	+++	+
	++	++	+
7. Pushing/Nudging			
	++	+	+
8. Telling others			
	++	+	+
9. Approving adaptations			

++++very important
+minimal importance

leadership contributions made during the change process. Some examples of strategies and tactics that principals can use to influence the change process are now listed:

1 Sanctioning/Continued Support (Item 1 in Table 4.8)

The Principal:

— approves the project at concept stage. He/she supports the original idea however 'rough';
— approves the project proceeding through each stage;
— approves the re-arrangement of times, the purchase and use of resources, visitors, meetings, use of buildings, and the rearrangement of classes;
— demonstrates willingness to take whatever role is required of him or her;
— demonstrates support with presence — at meetings, with parents and with community;
— demonstrates interest — willing to talk, encourage, willing to listen;
— is accessible to participants;
— meets regularly, as appropriate, with participants, offers encouragement, support and ideas;
— provides input, direction, if appropriate, or encourages others to do this;
— acts as trouble-shooter or encourages another to do this, if appropriate; and
— gives recognition to participants by giving credit, encouragement, provid-

ing visibility and status for participants and protects participants, if appropriate.

2 Providing Resources (Item 2 in Table 4.8)

The Principal:

— assists with the establishment of priorities for resources;
— keeps reserve fund as an emergency resource;
— arranges for resources from external sources to be regularly identified;
— organises submissions for extra funds, if appropriate; and
— rearranges fund allocations to meet project needs; and identifies human resources for projects of various kinds.

3 Reinforcement/Encouragement (Item 6 in Table 4.8)

The Principal:

— provides necessary time and structure for meetings;
— acts as link person with external agencies, if appropriate, or encourages teachers to link, if appropriate;
— actively fosters arrangements for meetings;
— 'irons out' human relations problems, if appropriate, or encourages others to do this;
— provide opportunities for reporting on progress of the project; and
— sees the project through to its conclusion.

4 Pushing/Nudging (Item 7 in Table 4.8)

The Principal:

— identifies necessary tasks, and persons who should be involved;
— identifies persons needing development and seeks ideas;
— helps identify areas for improvement; and
— identifies persons causing concern and offers incentives for change.

Concluding Statement

The role of principal has been used to exemplify some of the ways this important leader might arrange the conditions for the development of quality in teaching and learning. For the principal, as for any educative leader, the key features are the leader (as a learner) providing opportunities for participants to develop personal understanding and encouraging the conditions for reflection on practice.

Notes

1 Osborne and Wittrock use the term 'generative' to describe their view of the constructivist model of learning.
2 These four requirements are derived from Hewson (1981) where the author identifies conditions for student learning, but it is argued here that they apply equally to teachers learning about teaching and learning.
3 Project to Enhance Effective Learning (PEEL). This name was given to the project by the teachers involved.

References

BAIRD, J.R. (1984) 'Improving Learning through Enhanced Metacognition', unpublished PhD thesis, Monash University.
BAIRD, J.R. and MITCHELL, I.J. (Eds) (1986) *Improving the Quality of Teaching and Learning: An Australian Case Study — The PEEL Project*, Melbourne: Monash University.
COHEN, D. and HARRISON, M. (1982) *Curriculum Action Project*, Sydney: Macquarie University.
EISNER, E.W. (1982) 'The kind of schools we need', *Interchange*, **15**, 2, 1–12.
FULLAN, M. (1982) *The Meaning of Educational Change*, New York: Teachers College Press.
FULLAN, M. (1985) 'Integrating theory and practice', in HOPKINS, M. and REID, K. (Eds) *Rethinking Teacher Education*, London: Croom Helm.
GALL, M.D., FIELDING, G., SCHALOCK, D., CHARTERS, W.W. and WILCZYNSKI, J.M. (1984) *Involving the Principal in Teachers' Staff Development: Effects on the Quality of Mathematics Instruction in Elementary Schools*, Eugene: Center for Educational Policy and Management, University of Oregon.
GERSTEN, R. and CARNINE, D. (1981) *Administrative and Supervisory Support Functions for the Implementation of Effective Educational Programs for Low Income Students*, Eugene: Center for Educational Policy and Management, University of Oregon.
HALL, G.E. and HORD, S.M. (1986) *Configurations of School-Based Leadership Teams*, R & D Report 3223.
HALL, G.E. and HORD, S.M. (1987) *Change in Schools: Facilitating the Process*, New York: State University of New York Press.
HALL, G.E., HORD, S.M., GOLDSTEIN, M.L., RUTHERFORD, W.L., NEWLOVE, B.W., HULING, L.L. and GRIFFIN, T.H. (1982) 'Principals as Change Facilitators: Their Interventions', paper given to an American Educational Research Association Conference symposium, New York.
HEWSON, P.W. (1981) 'The conceptual change approach to learning science', *European Journal of Science Education*, **3**, 383–396.
NORTHFIELD, J.R. (1985) 'Assisting Schools to Respond to Change: An Outline of One Approach to Supporting Schools', paper presented at Australian Curriculum Studies Association Conference, Latrobe University.
NORTHFIELD, J.R. and GUNSTONE, R.F. (1985) 'Understanding learning at the classroom level', *Research in Science Education*, 1985, **15**, 18–27.
OSBORNE, R. and FREYBERG, P. (1985) *Learning in Science: The Implications of Children's Science*, Auckland: Heinemann.
OSBORNE, R. and WITTROCK, M.C. (1985) 'The generative learning model and its implications for science education', *Studies in Science Education*, **12**, 59–87.

PETERS, T.J. and WATERMAN, R.H. (1982) *In Search of Excellence*, New York: Harper Row.

RAMSEY, P., SNEDDON, D., GRENFELL, J. and FORD, I. (1983) 'Successful and unsuccessful schools: A study in southern Auckland', *The Australian and New Zealand Journal of Sociology*, **19**, 2, 272–304.

SACKNEY, L.E. (1985) *School District Imperatives for Effective Schools*, Saskatoon: University of Saskatchewan.

SCHON, D.A. (1983) *The Reflective Practitioner: How Professionals Think in Action*, New York: Basic Books.

SHARPE, F.G. (1986) 'Quality Leadership — Quality Education', paper presented to the Western Region Primary Principals Council, Parkes, NSW, March.

Introduction to Chapter 5

Educative Leadership and Rationalisation: A Synthesis and a Commentary

P.A. Duignan and R.J.S. Macpherson

The services of many education systems and institutions have been subjected to dramatic and traumatic reforms in recent years. These changes have been attributed to the 'oil shocks', the difficulty of relating expenditure on education to economic or political outcomes, the emergence of neo-conservative ideologies and new technologies, the need for greater responsiveness in the delivery of social services, and the fresh willingness by governments to use education as a vehicle for social, industrial and economic policies.

While the merits of these explanations can be debated, a key point made in Chapter 5 is that educative leaders have a proactive role to play in helping communities make sense of changes in ways that help reform social, political and economic relations. The chapter by Pettit *et al.* takes up this point by focusing on how educative leaders can take an appropriate role in reorganising educational services. Note that rationalisation is given to mean the situation where incremental adjustments to structures and practices can no longer cope with demands for reform, and where fundamental reorganisation is considered the only possible option.

Another point made in Chapter 5 is that while any person can offer educative leadership, some administrators have both a mandated responsibility and a strategic vantage point to offer particular services. In this regard, Pettit *et al.* recommend that educative leaders accept three major responsibilities when involved in reorganising the delivery of education services.

First, they should provide the processes whereby educators can begin double loop learning about being re-organised. Briefly, where single loop learning in an organisation monitors activity to detect any deviation from the norm, double loop learning also regularly questions the appropriateness of operational norms.

Second, educative leaders should provide the support services that help ameliorate the grief and bereavement associated with radical change. It is a common feature of reorganisation that people have to adjust to the partial loss of a valued professional self while they are developing a new persona in a dimly perceived emergent organisation.

Third, educative leaders must provide appropriate leadership services at each stage of reorganisation. In general, since the structure and practices of organisations are reinforced by the social forces of dynamic conservatism and the type of technology in use, any intervention, to be effective, has to be cultural in form.

Pettit *et al.* begin with a managerial analysis of reorganisation in a public policy context, and identify the large extent to which changes are determined by political theories in use. They, therefore, call for the interconnected use of rational and comprehensive planning techniques and participatory democracy in rationalisation processes.

They also advise that inevitable conflict can best be managed by adopting a step-by-step phasing approach, by consulting and bargaining, and by coupling gains with losses. What is often unavoidable is the destablisation of cherished meanings of self, organisation and service. The loss of legitimation can be personally devastating to professionals and this can trigger a range of deflection techniques.

Pettit *et al.* therefore suggest particular roles for educative leaders during each of the six major stages of reorganisation. The first stage is when the reasons for change and its likely nature become manifest. It is typically marked by a high degree of confusion and ambiguity, attempts to defend the status quo, and by threats of withdrawal. An educative leader would act as a catalyst by timing appropriate mechanisms to define the fundamental problems within the parameters of system policy, and to identify those with legitimate interests, especially key influentials.

The second stage is where purposes, goals, participation, responsibilities, authority, alliances and key issues are clarified. Pettit *et al.* recommend that an educative leader help with this process of clarification, assess needs in human, financial and physical terms, determine time scales, create compromises and devise creative solutions to blockages.

The third stage is where the planning and consultative process proceeds within an agreed negotiating framework. Collegial or confrontationist in nature, the process continues. An educative leader would help those involved to develop feasibility tests for proposals, generate a degree of consensus before seeking wider affirmation, and create confidence that the system can and will deliver on the agreement.

The fourth stage is the implementation stage. An educative leader would help to determine phases, timescales, objectives, indicators and the role of the implementation steering group. As with all previous stages, the educative leader needs to serve in a variety of roles; as an individual to serve personal interests, as a representative of the school community to serve institutional interests, and as a representative of the Department and Minister to serve the wider community's interests.

Chapter 5 highlights the need for and value of particular understandings: that a stable state in not inevitable; emotions rather than rationality will prevail in disruptive periods; personal loss is a major feature of change; anger directed at authority figures is often symbolic; conflict over status and power is normal when their distribution is disturbed; educational priorities are inevitably linked to macro-political and economic matters; change can be shaped to achieve educational ends; an educational rationale has to underpin the change; and that new visions are exciting and can raise commitment. Since educative leadership has such a key role in shaping change, Pettit *et al.* stress the need for directed support for leaders.

Like all participants, educative leaders need accurate information and adequate lead times. They need an informal peer support group. They need professional development to build their understandings and skills. They need quick access to resources so they can offer responsive leadership. Finally, it is recommended in the coming chapter that educative leaders need to think in wider realms, and have opportunities to reflect on trends and purposes, if they are to see the whole spectrum of possibilities.

Chapter 5

Reorganising the Delivery of Educational Services and Educative Leadership

D. Pettit and Ian Hind

in association with Maureen Boyle, Pat Duignan, Mac Macpherson, Margaret Mitchell, Wal Payne and Therese Reilly

Introduction

This chapter is about understanding and managing radical change in organisations and systems. It aims to provide a synthesis of useful theories that can be used by those who are experiencing the rationalisation of services and resources. It focuses on those leaders in schools and systems who are expected to represent the interests of both the learning community and the state in responding to a major form of change — reorganisation. The complexity of such a role and the pressures brought about by reorganisation are not to be underestimated.

School, college or agency reorganisation involves major changes to the existing way that the institution operates. It could mean closure, consolidation, amalgamation, clustering or restructuring (the creation of middle schools, the setting up of senior high schools, etc.). Although not the specific focus of this chapter, reorganisation also encompasses internal changes, such as major reform to the curriculum involving the creation of new departments and the demise of others, major changes in teacher's roles or very different and more direct forms of accountability, for example, to a governing body.

There is a voluminous literature on declining enrolments, institutional closures, reorganisation of schools, optimum size and the management of decline. Some of this is in the nature of a quest for an over-arching theory or paradigm. Much of the literature deals with case studies. There is much advice for system-level administrators on 'what works' and 'what doesn't work'. Part of the literature questions the legitimacy of reorganisation when it is driven by public policy.

Whether people favour small schools or large schools, change or no change, centralised or devolved decisions about change, there are research findings available that will buttress the view of every proponent.

Our reading, understanding and interpretation of the literature have been shaped by our experiences as school administrators, consultants, researchers and system-level administrators in programs of reorganisation and rationalisation of schools over the last five years. Such sources could not be referenced. We also drew on research in other Australian states and many international settings.

We made a number of assumptions. First, we presumed that those involved in reorganisation will be knowledgeable about (or become *au fait* with) macro-changes in Australia's economic position, the nature of the labour market and the effects of technology, Second, we assumed that they will keep up-to-date with industrial policies, major educational initiatives and government policy changes at state and federal levels. We also assumed that the leadership role in institutions and systems is important, and further, that it will be 'educative'.

Such assumptions imply that institutions and their members are part of an open 'learning system' (Schon, 1973) that is capable of facing a problem (the need for rationalisation), inventing a solution involving reorganisation, producing the solution, evaluating the outcome, and discovering new problems, and is open to outside influences throughout the process. The basic premise is that leadership in an institution dedicated to education must itself be educative.

The exercise of educative leadership is multi-faceted. It requires institutional leaders who are able to set clear goals, command attention, inspire respect and motivate teachers, students and the community.

Principals, for example, can play a crucial role in the process, especially if they recognise that they cannot succeed alone. Effective educational leaders must have a sense of imagination that sparks the vision and wins the trust and commitment of students, teachers and the parent community, and unites them in a shared dedication to excellence. It involves continually reinforcing superior performance, encouraging innovation and risk-taking. We hold that educative leadership is a key element in creating schools which are responsive to the challenges of today's society and which give their clients optimum skills to live productive lives in the future.

This chapter is divided into two different but fully related parts. The first part takes a 'distanced', analytical, somewhat technical and management view of reorganisation. The second is an analysis of the local and institutional issues in the management of change. Joining the two parts are two basic concepts. One, already discussed, is that of educative leadership. The other is double loop learning (Argyris and Schon, 1974; Argyris, 1977) and what it involves in human terms. The concepts of educative leadership and double loop learning are themselves linked, the latter being essential to educative leadership and for the comprehension and management of change in its conceptual and human dimensions.

The local perspective on reorganisation focuses on understanding issues such as the conflict, anger, loss, grief and bereavement which accompany major change. These issues are not a standard feature of change literature. Yet we believe that they are central to understanding and coping with the cultural disorientation that reorganisation brings in different degrees to everybody involved. Finally, the chapter addresses the need for positive approaches to educational opportunities that reorganisation offers. We note in passing that the two-part Korean character representing 'crisis' is a combination of two concepts; danger and opportunity.

Part A: Public Policy and the Reorganisation of Educational Services

We take the view that reorganisation is a matter of public policy; public policy with a high profile born of destabilisation. Public policy is an outcome of competing ideologies, demands for new services and the review of existing policies and provisions. Policy analysis involves finding out what is being done now, why and to what effect.

Reorganisation, we believe, is the subject of public policy for several reasons:

> it is one way a system can respond to fiscal restraint by, for example, responding to demands for lower taxation, for lower expenditure in the public sector, for the leaner operation of state instrumentalities and for increased efficiency and accountability as evidenced through program budgeting and economies of scale;
>
> it is a way of responding to public demand for more equity in the distribution of services. It may involve the relocation or expansion of facilities to give spatial equity.
>
> An example of this is the creation of new tertiary institutions in the western suburbs of Sydney and Melbourne and relocating inner metropolitan hospitals. It can also cause the reallocation of resources across portfolios (e.g. to meet the health needs of an aging population) and within portfolios (e.g. responding to falling enrolments in schools by transferring resources to a tertiary sector faced with expanding demand);
>
> there is a belief that reorganisation involves indepth reviews of services and stimulates improvements.
>
> For example, increased retention of students, reconceptualisation of curricula, alternative structures for the delivery of curriculum, community use and involvement, technology studies and welfare liaison have all been consequences of rationalisation exercises; and
>
> it is a necessary response to large-scale demographic change.

The politics of policy creation can be partially explained by systems theory. Figure 5.1 is a useful way of conceptualising what are often complex political and social phenomena and how they are studied and understood. It highlights the all-pervasive influence of the environment in which political decisions are made.

There is, however, a need to be aware of the limitations of overly simplistic systems theory. It can ignore much of the dynamics of decision making, particularly the role of professionals and bureaucrats. Processes are rarely neat, orderly, logical and linear. Politicians and policy makers do not just respond to demands or inputs; they can and do initiate and generate change. The rhetoric of policy makers is important because it can set the context to which institutions have to respond. It is sometimes the case that systems thinking fails to consider the human trauma which results from precipitate changes to policy or bureaucratic decisions. Bureaucrats can play a number of roles in a reorganisation. Some of these possible roles and their theoretical underpinnings are now discussed.

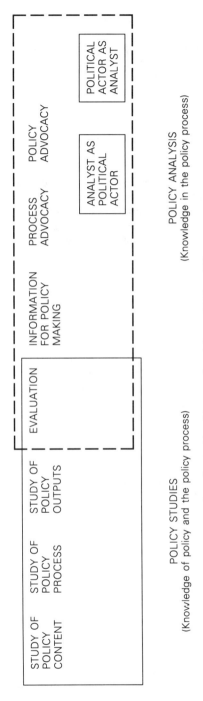

Figure 5.1: Types of study and public policy-making (Hogwood and Gunn, 1981 p. 29)

Political Theories and Reorganisation

Political actions are not random; they are guided by political theories, however well disguised these may appear to be on occasions. Four political theories are useful in illuminating the role and functions of bureaucrats in promoting change and the role that those involved in reorganisation come to play.

Pluralist or Liberal Democratic Theory

This perspective emphasises the constraints imposed by a wide range of groups. Policy is largely a reflection of the preferences of these groups. Power is widely distributed. No group is without power but no group is dominant. An example of the operation of liberal democratic theory was the federal government's back-down on the Australia Card legislation. Another is a local school community using political channels to amend bureaucrats' plans for institutional reorganisation.

Elitism

This perspective emphasises the power of a small number of well-organised pressure groups for particular interests. One example was the Queensland Government's banning of Secondary Education Materials Project (SEMP) and Man, A Course of Study (MACOS) programs in government schools at the instigation of a small group of people. Another is a decision of a Minister using executive power to close or to relocate a school.

Marxist Perspective

This view assumes that the state maintains the dominance of a particular class by, for example, using selection procedures to create an elite. On the other hand, this perspective suggests that the state can use mass education to lessen the economic and social advantages of citizens that are distributed by education.

Corporatist or Galbraithian Perspective

This perspective emphasises the importance of the changing structure of the economy and the state's dominant role in determining the public versus private relationships, for example, in the balance of government and non-government schooling. It is evident in the way that the Corporate Management Group developed for the Schools Division in Victoria mirrors business structures and business criteria. It is also reflected in the instrumentalism pervading Commonwealth approaches to education that is reinforced by the close links created between training and employment.

Implications

Political theories in use also have implications for the nature of decision making and the role of the stakeholders in decision making. Similarly, the role of the bureaucrat will vary with the approach taken. For example, the implementation of democratic theory would be participative in nature whereas an elitist approach to reorganisation would be at best consultative, at worst, dictatorial.

Different stages in change can be marked by the predominance of various theories. The initial decision to reorganise may be taken arbitrarily, whereas reshaping the reorganisation could be participative or involve extensive consultation. Some theorists distinguish between meta-policy making, systemic policy making, and institutional policy making and implementation.

The four theories above also provide insights into the nature and cause of conflict related to reorganisation; whether or not, for instance, it is class or interest-based. We believe that conflict associated with rationalisation and the reorganisation of educational services in Australia tends not to be class-based but to be an outcome of much more complex and conflicted political and economic relations.

In our experience and research it also appears that a great deal of the conflict is found among professionals, bureaucrats and parents who act as individuals and interest groups at local and central levels. Most of the tension revolves around the nature and extent of influence at the local level.

An understanding of these various political theories will help highlight the dominant ideologies and basic assumptions underlying the actions of those involved in a particular reorganisation attempt. They are apparent in the actions of those who attempt to manage rationalisation.

Strategies for Managing Rationalisation

Strategies for change in education systems with a degree of devolved power will differ from those in centralised systems. Issues such as the industrial climate, agreed working conditions and effective career structures, may encourage or lessen the degree of confrontation. It is, therefore, not surprising that a major role in effective planning and management of demographic decline is geared to generating strategies that will minimise or at least contain conflict to an acceptable level.

The cultural and political environments, to a large extent, determine the balance between the two major reorganisation strategies now to be discussed — rational planning and participation. The two basic strategies, which are outlined below, are widely evident in the research literature and in the experience of the authors.

Those with local responsibilities are unlikely to determine, and indeed may not be consulted about, the strategy used. Nevertheless, understanding the basic strategy in use is important in making local processes and administrative decisions more effective. They are referred to as the PLAN and AGREE strategies (Sargent and Hardy, 1974; Boyd, 1983).

Strategy 1: PLAN. Use rational, comprehensive planning techniques.

Overall, this strategy means:

— collecting and analysing data; and
— planning ahead since the data will be necessary in the implementation phase.

Planning involves deciding:

— the extent to which the public accepts the professional planning expertise of the bureaucrats (it may not);
— whether consultation with communities occurs after the bureaucracy has developed its plans (or at all); and
— whether to have a local planning group, its membership (representative or otherwise) and the extent to which it has participative responsibility for making recommendations.

Strategy 2: AGREE. Encourage participation.

It is considered desirable to:

— involve people in decisions that affect them so that less resistance to change is likely to occur; and
— help them find a basis for agreement so that informed and committed support for the adopted solution is generated.

Encouraging participation has political and organisational implications. Politicians are understandably nervous about public brawls concerning state instrumentalities. They look for compromises that will lower the level of conflict whilst achieving desirable aims. It is also more effective, in organisational terms, for all involved to have agreed to the need for and to the nature of any proposed change. Goodwill is an important factor in effective change, but an issue that is not nearly as headline-catching as overt conflict. It follows that there are many organisationally and politically favourable aspects to participation.

Nevertheless, the term participation is often misused. It can be used incorrectly as an synonym for involvement or consultation. Participation means that all concerned have an equal capacity to affect the outcome. These conditions do not often, if ever, apply. Why?

In the first place, reorganisation is normally bureaucratically initiated and proposals professionally shaped (see the PLAN Strategy above) prior to the release of plans for consultation with those affected. Consultation is not participation; the power to make policy decisions is reserved elsewhere, normally with politician or a bureaucrat. While devolutionists resent centralism, it is a fact of life that the democratic structures of our society give Ministers reserve powers to ensure that what they deem to be the 'general good' outweighs what is seen as the 'local good'.

The conditions for participation are extremely important. Full participation implies that the criteria for change are clearly determined and fixed, ordered and/or weighted, and known to all involved. It also implies that the process reflects genuine intent. For example, a consensus decision, by definition, cannot be subject to arbitrary veto.

Determining the conditions of participation does not always happen in a systematic manner. It is often the case that not all factors can be predicted and pre-determined. Who can, for example, anticipate the effects of the climate of change. In the destabilised environment of reorganisation, people can easily feel that they have been subjected to confidence tricks. Everybody is suspected of having hidden agendas, especially bureaucrats who appear to have considerable reserve power and are able to escape the effects of their intervention. The suspicions may be accurate, and in such circumstances, the process is better described as cooption rather than participation.

There are also differences in people's capacity to affect outcomes. Communities are not homogeneous. Some people are politically efficacious, skilled in manipulation and manoeuvering; others are not.

There are other difficulties. Participation and consultation raise expectations concerning influence. People rarely agree on solutions unless all lose or gain equally, a circumstance that rarely occurs. Participation is time-consuming. Bureaucrats, as well as politicians, often have specific fears such as the loss of control or a public exposure at having failed to get agreements. Both outcomes can be detrimental to the administrator's and the politician's status and ego.

For these reasons, participation can exacerbate rather than obviate conflict. And in this matter, the AGREE strategy has a dual function. It is the mechanism for releasing as well as for resolving the conflict and aggression that change generates. This point is discussed further in the next section.

In summary, while managers and administrators may get by with ad hoc approaches in times of growth, it is essential to plan for the management of decline. The PLAN and AGREE strategies together form a basic change management approach. However, it would be misleading to imply that there are purely technocratic solutions that can be used to achieve institutional or systemic reorganisations or that conflict is avoidable.

Conflict in Context

Conflict generated by closing or reorganising institutions stems from the type of policy decision involved and the nature of the public goods being allocated or distributed. This is because the public goods delivered through the political system, as against the market system, are judged on two basic dimensions:

the extent to which the impact of the public good is uniformly or differentially distributed; and
whether the public good involves a gain or a loss as perceived by interest groups.

School closure or rationalisation is commonly regarded as very difficult to 'win' or 'sell' in a political sense, because it is usually perceived as a loss that has been differentially distributed. Closing a school is usually judged as having an immediate and separable harm in which some will be more disadvantaged than others. This is why resistance and conflict are almost unavoidable.

In an amalgamation, it is virtually impossible for the institutions involved to be equally advantaged or disadvantaged. Opposition can be expected from the interest groups so threatened, but little support if any may come from the general public which might benefit. Yet the public, and particularly the interested parties, usually and often naively expect the outcomes of any reorganisation to be positive in both political and educational terms.

Education cannot be dissociated from the political context because it is intimately concerned with the relative distribution of benefits and losses. Schooling helps distribute life chances. School reorganisations are inherently political and so are the criteria by which they are judged. Decisions can depend as much upon such things as the balance of seats in Parliament, the electoral majority, or the time to the next election as they can on an educational rationale. Most change has to be well timed in a political sense. Examples of timing include moving soon after an election when a mandate is fresh and there is ample time to cope with the less pleasant aspects of change, or when opinion polls favour urgent reform.

The complexity of any reorganisation is compounded by the economic ramifications of educational decisions. Almost inevitably these have political implications. Most people can recognise when a nation or state faces times of economic restraint. On the other hand, not all understand the significance of governments' changing attitudes to market forces. For example, Galbraithian policies that value private and public open market competition (deregulation), have implications for the balance of enrolments of government and non-government schools. People may 'vote with their feet' or voice their dissent. And as the New Zealand government has recently demonstrated, governments do not necessarily bring or expect quick savings when they encourage rationalisation in education.

There is no one proven recipe for the successful management of conflict. Our experience and reorganisations overseas seem to indicate that the following approaches can be helpful for administrators who have to create gains out of the management of decline.

Adopt a step-by-step phasing approach dealing first with crisis or near crisis situations, rather than proposing a comprehensive 'grand' plan.

A grand plan can precipitate a backlash from the institutions not requiring or desiring reorganisation immediately, and so deflect bureaucrats' attention from the sites that are critically in need of change.

Use bargaining strategies.

This means being prepared to come back to a 'bottom line' which might be less than the original 'ideal' public position first expressed. This has the added advantage of allowing institutions scope to shape their futures.

Couple gains with losses to create a more positive environment and to compensate for the disruption.

Gains can be of three kinds:

> monetary incentives, for example, returning a proportion of savings achieved by reorganisation to the 'new' institution;
>
> planning benefits, for example, upgrading technological services and the integration of human services, such as health clinics, welfare centres or neighbourhood houses, on the site being developed; and
>
> develop a new vision through the creative reworking, remoulding and reorganisation of available resources to produce improved environments and expanded opportunities for young people in a time of declining enrolments.

All three approaches have been used to varying degrees in reorganisation, although the emphasis in the recent decade in Australia has been predominantly on institutional reorganisation rather than on systemic or regional rationalisation. A consideration of the leadership challenges involved in managing decline follows.

Part B: Educative Leadership in the Local Context

The Scope of Change

Institutional reorganisation, like marriage, is not something to be entered into lightly. Unlike marriage, there is often no choice for the partners. The pressure for macro-change such as reorganisation can come from:

> a crisis precipitated by outside events — examples could include falling enrolments, rising costs, a policy decision to dezone, declining youth labour market;
>
> a crisis arising within — an example is where an institution becomes too small to offer acceptable/adequate curriculum. Another is where major changes occur in student preferences; or
>
> a crisis deliberately created to destabilise an over-conservative, unresponsive system — an example was the Australian Commonwealth Government's decision to make all tertiary institutions bid for development funds. Another is the New Zealand Government's recent decision (Macpherson, 1989; 1990) to locate most management decisions, resources, powers and accountability with institutional leaders.

Reorganisation is not usually a matter of adjustment or minor adaptation to change initiated within an institution that can be controlled. It tends to be macro-scale change involving substantial alterations in personnel, operations, facilities, assumptions and relationships. The complexity of the change at the institutional level is often compounded by other contemporaneous and related policy shifts in education. Examples might include devolution, curriculum change, integration of disabled students, changes in the dole for teenagers and industrial relations agreements.

It is important to realise that many public organisations, such as schools, colleges and universities, only have to confront dysfunctions developed over time when what might be termed 'the public worm' turns and fiscal restraints have to be imposed. Since this has not been the general experience of administrators, who have tended to cope with incremental adjustments in expansionary contexts, it is not surprising that the general knowledge system of administrators requires elaboration.

Incremental adjustment involves relatively simple but nevertheless demanding 'single loop' learning (Argyris, 1977). Single loop learning occurs when an individual (such as a teacher or a principal) or a group (such as the school staff or a college or university council) reviews and reflects on the shortcomings of the present operation and takes corrective actions *without* having to change radically the relationships, operations, structure or assumptions of the institution. There is no need to violate institutional values and goals. People learn within the confines of their existing mindset and organisational norms.

In this context, the role of the educative leader (e.g. principal) is largely one of keeping abreast of organisational and curriculum change, feeding information into the school and presiding over or delegating the processes by which adaption occurs.

Reorganisation, on the other hand, involves an additional loop, the means of questioning underlying values, assumptions, policies and goals, stated and unstated; all of which are exposed by pressure for macro-change. This type of comprehensive change to learning necessitates what has been termed 'double loop learning' (Argyris, 1977) by all those involved, but particularly by those responsible for delivering the educational service — principals and teachers.

Figure 5.2 sets out the experiences people go through in unfreezing their values and norms and developing new ones.

Double loop learning involves discarding the existing taken-for-granted assumptions and meanings that have become inappropriate over time or have been undermined by structural or environmental change. An example of obsolete structures was that based on the presumption that schooling to year 12 is appropriate for only a minority of more able students. Examples of rapid environmental change were experienced when the ACT adopted year 11–12 college systems and when sharply declining enrolments in Victoria led to the evaporation of staff employment opportunities in schools and severely curtailed the development of curricula.

Double loop learning also involves those in an organisation reassessing the framework of assumptions underpinning their work practices. 'Work' has to be reviewed as both individual actions and as the aggregate of institutional practices. This form of 'organisational learning' is most effective when the members of an organisation — system or institutional — can detect and correct organisational dysfunctions on a regular basis.

This brings us to the responsibilities this implies for educative leaders. In essence, we argue that they have to create and maintain the conditions for 'double loop learning'. These conditions usually have to be destabilising because it means changing from single loop to double loop learning, and this involves adopting a new set of governing values or norms. This is often difficult for a leader because it can involve his or her own assumptions being challenged, and

Governing variables for action	Action strategies for actor	Consequences on actor and his associates	Consequences on learning	Effectiveness
I	II	III	IV	V
Model I				
1 Achieve the purposes as I perceive them.	1 Design and manage environment so that actor is in control over factors relevant to me.	1 Actor seen as defensive.	1 Self-sealing.	Decreased.
2 Maximise winning and minimise losing.	2 Own and control task.	2 Defensive interpersonal and group relationships.	2 Single loop learning.	
3 Minimise eliciting negative feelings.	3 Unilaterally protect self.	3 Defensive norms.	3 Little testing of theories publicly.	
4 Be rational and minimise emotionality.	4 Unilaterally protect others from being hurt.	4 Low freedom of choice, internal commitment, and risk taking.		
Model II				
1 Valid information.	1 Design situations or encounters where participants can be original and high personal experience causation.	1 Actor seen as minimally defensive.	1 Testable processes.	Increased.
2 Free and informed choice.	2 Task is controlled jointly.	2 Minimally defensive interpersonal relations and group dynamics.	2 Double loop learning.	
3 Internal commitment to the choice and constant monitoring of the implementation.	3 Protection of self is a joint enterprise and oriented toward growth.	3 Learning-oriented norms.	3 Frequent testing of theories publicly.	
	4 Bilateral protection of others.	4 High freedom of choice, internal commitment, and risk taking.		

Figure 5.2: Exhibit I: Theories of Action (Argyris and Schon, 1974.)

enduring resistance by others. Further, to implement double loop learning involves a leader in:

helping those involved to produce data that demonstrate the scope of the required change;

knowing that relationships will be disrupted, and that this will be accompanied by anger, loss and conflict;

offering support to others while managing the change towards an outcome only vaguely delineated;

understanding the significance of 'invisible' assumptions about relationships, behaviour and ethos disturbed by the change; and

drawing upon support from within and without the organisation in order to map the process and offer distanced, more objective views in what is, from time to time, a highly charged atmosphere.

Ironically, while rationalisation can be initiated by political and bureaucratic intervention, it is not often realised how supportive a system's bureaucracy can be.

Bureaucracy, Reorganisation and Conflict

The expectations and attitudes directed towards 'the bureaucracy' in education systems are extremely diverse. Some, especially principals, look to the bureaucracy for support and legitimation. At the other end of the scale are those who always see the bureaucracy as 'the enemy' whose heavy-handed, ill-conceived or ignorant interventions are to be resisted at all times.

There is often a mismatch between what schools expect bureaucrats to do and what they are in fact capable of doing. Bureaucracies are complex. Bureaucrats are not homogeneous. Many of their activities do not appear to cohere and their aims seem ambiguous. The information that bureaucrats provide is sometimes confusing. They are often unable to deliver what schools expect — resources, information, support. Some bureaucrats appear to expect change to occur because they want it to, and view it as a rational process, capable of being implemented by planning alone.

Originally conceived as ideal types, bureaucratic organisations and structures tend not to depend on familiar relationships but on the coordination of functions in impersonal and distanced ways. Such explicit assumptions about how people should be organised often offends, stimulates hostility and conflict, and can help generate the 'them and us' syndrome.

So common are the pejorative meanings of the term 'bureaucracy', it is relatively easy for those confronted with the need for double loop learning to express opposition to any reorganisation proposal on the grounds that it is 'bureaucratic'. While the use of the descriptor can be challenged, usually on technical grounds and be shown to be inaccurate, such claims are better understood as symbolising a reactive defence. Double loop learning involves destabilising long-shared and cherished notions such as 'the school', 'the college' or 'the university' and means reconstructing deeply held views of 'valued professional self'. It is small wonder that the initial reactions to such fundamental change tend to be emotional and defensive.

Stability, Conservatism and the Effects of Change Initiated from Outside

Educational institutions are complex and sensitive organisations. They are as complex and as sensitive as the people who take the organisational culture for granted as both important and valuable.

Educational institutions need stable patterns and predictability to offer learning. They typically favour predictability of behaviour, or norms, as a convention for the expression of meaning in order to establish, among their members of all ages, a shared sense of significance and rightness (Macpherson, 1987). Such meanings are elaborated in the particular institutional setting to express purposes. Thus, change strategies which ignore the specific cultural context do so at the risk of creating massive conflict.

Change not only threatens the previous meanings people give to institutions, it also threatens an individual's confidence in his or her views on work, professional self, and more broadly, valued life. To disturb the patterns of teaching and learning is to demand a crucial transition of all involved. The destabilisation is:

a critical break in the pattern of relationships between people, which in turn;
threatens the structure and continuity of meanings, the interpretation of experience and the taken-for-granted assumptions; and
is accompanied by people experiencing a deep personal sense of loss and wishing to revert to the familiar or to search for a new sense of balance and well-being.
As radical as this might seem, this crucial transition is a necessary part of the substantial personal change required for effective double loop learning. It needs to be understood and catered for by educative leaders.

The transition phase is often characterised by a sense of powerlessness and resentment at the institutional level. Certain beliefs become common; events are being orchestrated by others — the faceless 'them' from 'the Department', 'the Ministry' or 'the Authority' and that the change is too big to stop or adjust.

For some, the transition experience may lead to a deterioration in self concept and a lack of confidence in presentation of self. Other common symptoms include anger, illness, apathy, disengagement, and hostility. In contrast, some can be quick to grasp the potential for improvement and the excitement that change brings. Overall, transition requires those involved to reconstruct and reinterpret their ways of seeing life and seeing themselves at work in an educational organisation. This is the double loop learning referred to above.

The transition involves personal loss. It is accompanied by a form of bereavement that embraces all members of the learning community, albeit in different degrees. Bereavement is the result of the irretrievable loss of familiar

> relationships, meanings and conventions. It is an inevitable part of reorganisa-
> tion. It involves grief and mourning.

Curiously, although individual and group grief is a normal part of reorganisation, there is virtually no reference to it in reorganisation literature. As
O'Connor (1981:54) put it:

> we tend to think of grief only as a reaction to death [but] such a tendency
> detracts from a broader understanding of this emotion.... Equally so is
> grief the reaction to the loss or passing of everything — event, person or
> whatever — that we value.

Why, then, is grief associated with reorganisation so hurtful? O'Connor
(1981:54) went on to explain that:

> unlike the mourning that accompanies the death of a relative or friend, the
> grief accompanying change is not supported by custom, is not rendered
> accessible. Whilst to mourn for one's deceased relatives is socially accept-
> able and indeed a clearly articulated and spelt out form of behaviour, to
> mourn for the loss of oneself is an alien, unsupported grief.

Individual grief results from the disruption or suspension of meanings, beliefs
and actions that have become habitual. Grief often suspends and sometimes
changes the capacity of individuals to accommodate change. It involves loss of
meaning. The intensity of the grief is normally related to the intensity of the
prior involvement and the degree of change that has to be accommodated.

It can be devastating for those already reshaping their personal lives in
middle age (O'Connor, 1981). Educative leaders need to empower people in
such circumstances by helping them create a sense of vision to replace lost
purposes.

It is crucial to realise that grieving has to take place for a continuity of understanding to occur.

As Marris (1974:31) pointed out:

> Grief is the expression of profound conflict between contradictory impulses
> — to consolidate all that is still valuable and important in the past and
> preserve it from loss: and then at the same time, to establish a meaningful
> pattern of relationships in which the loss is accepted.

It is important to note that the resolution of grief occurs as a person or a
group abstracts what is fundamentally important in previous relationships, structures and meanings, and then grafts them onto a new situation, or, more
accurately, into the new shared interpretation of the situation.

The working through of a bereavement, caused by institutional reorganisation, basically involves adaptation to changed circumstances. The stages are
uneven and discontinuous and involve many manifestations of emotion. As well
as making individual accommodations, there is a collective aspect to working

through bereavement as members renegotiate with one another, or with other groups, the emerging basis for new roles and practices.

Opposition and anger is likely and can be expressed in a variety of ways. Even as it occurs it allows people to clarify their stance. As people express their position, the issues can become more comprehensible and manageable and the process more acceptable.

The point is that a supportive setting for open communication has to be provided as a way of legitimating the change and creating a framework for new relationships, meanings and experiences.

Many problems can be encountered and should be anticipated with responsive and responsible leadership. Defensiveness about change is not necessarily resistance to learning. Even confident learners can behave defensively in the service of learning (Argyris, 1982:8). Not all the points of conflict will be fully resolved for everybody. There may be only partial catharsis. Having an educative leader who arranges the conditions for addressing these issues, however, restores continuity and a sense of purpose and this, in turn, helps to promote the accommodation of change. If loss is not or cannot be articulated, its suppressed tensions may, in the end, prove more profoundly disruptive than the social conflicts which relieve them.

Unfortunately, politicians and bureaucrats are not generally tolerant of open conflict because it is seen as politically damaging and disruptive. Both groups become more vulnerable because of this attitude. Bureaucrats and their masters demand change and yet find it difficult to accept its emotional and social manifestations.

The demands on regional and local leaders for a quick, tidy resolution can be unrealistic. Leaders state the doubts of their community, yet, have to try to suspend their own perspectives in order to move on. Leaders have to help people through the grieving phase and 'out the other side' where visions are glimpsed and built upon as touchstone. Yet they are as loath as anyone to let go of the finest qualities they see in 'their' institution.

The conservative reaction to change is predictable and understandable. Engagement in the process lessens the sense of powerlessness. It does not preclude conflict and grief.

Dynamic Conservatism: Resistance Strategies in Social Systems

Conservatism, whether expressed individually or collectively, seeks to protect familiar things which give meaning to or make sense out of life. Dynamic conservatism is the expenditure of great energy to resist change. Social systems, such as Departments of Education, schools, faculties and mothers' clubs, develop and maintain a cultural equilibrium, and are unlikely to change from this stable state, voluntarily, for the sake of change.

As social systems, such as schools, change, they move from a relatively stable state through a 'zone of disruption' (reorganisation) to a new zone of relative stability. Initially the focus of individuals' attention is on the loss of the stable state, with its attendant conflict, anger and grief. This is most evident in recollection behaviours at a time when the next stable state (of relationships, structures, meanings) is not yet, or even becoming, clear.

Reorganisation involves extended and extensive disruption. It is an essential part of double loop learning. People in institutions may not welcome this disruption to their stable state. It puts individual and group self concepts at risk in the public arena where they are most vulnerable and where uncertainty is more intolerable.

As a result, deflection techniques (Schon, 1973) become a common 'counter-strategy'. They are used by members of the school community, often initially subconsciously, to stop or limit change and disorientation. The deflection techniques listed below demonstrate an increasing recognition of the pressure for change. At their most basic, they are an initial 'gut reaction' against double loop learning:

> *Ignore.* People give selective inattention to the promoters and topic of rationalisation. There are, typically, claims that 'there is no problem here'.
> *Counter-Attack, Preventative Attack or Denial.* There is a tendency for people to claim that 'the facts are wrong; we are gaining numbers' or 'we are doing well; they aren't'.
> *Containment/Isolation.* Attempts are made to compartmentalise the issue. For example, 'if you close that school, there will be enough children to go round'.
> *Cooption.* The idea here is to involve or coopt others in order to defuse or dilute the problem. For example, 'we want an extended participative process' or 'if the region can't help us with the survey then we can't proceed' or 'we are all agreed that we can do no more without extra assistance'.
> *Nominal/Token Change.* This is a minimal compliance deflection technique. For example, 'If we cluster or have a consortium of schools and specialise, there will be enough children at the upper levels to be able to offer a larger range of subjects. We will have reorganised. And overall, that's better than closing a school'.

Negotiations and bargaining used as deflection techniques are classic forms of dynamic conservatism. Staged negotiations are not often really about the purported blockages to change or about removing them, though this may happen, but about delaying or frustrating the change. They have to be understood as strategies for buying time in order to influence or control the pressures for and the extent of change.

The activities of teachers' unions can provide an example. Reorganisation rarely poses a threat to teachers' economic security. It is not usually about being laid off, forced into early retirement or being made redundant. Yet teachers and their unions often tend to employ deflection techniques; they commonly call for a renegotiation of teachers' transfer priorities or the maintenance of seniority and privileges.

While this is a legitimate activity in support of teachers' career opportunities, it is also a technique for delaying implementation in the larger scene. It tends to be supported uncritically because from the outset, reorganisation threatens teachers' structures of meaning. Such fears are easily transformed into demands for both a guarantee of no reduction in privileges *and* breathing space.

Teachers' unions may also encourage delay in a responsible way to develop administrative policy where none exists. On the other hand, delays can also serve to cushion repercussions on the organisation's leadership from members threatened by the disruption. The shared perception of an external enemy can help avoid a damaging drift into internal scapegoating. More broadly, however, given the increasing need for teachers unions to adjust their own organisations to cope with the restructured management of entire education systems, union leaders need time and breathing space to adjust strategically. In such circumstances, the overt bargaining for resources can also be seen as a deflection technique.

The loss, the anger, the grief, the apathy, the deflection techniques are all features of what Schon (1973) calls the 'zone of disruption' that lies between the stable state that is lost and the emerging state as reorganisation is accomplished. This zone deserves special attention.

The Zone of Disruption

Destabilising the stable state of institutional culture is initially marked by confusion and then a degree of order as more double loop learning becomes normal with some instability remaining. A staged analysis (after Davies, 1982) suggests a way of moving towards a new stable state where relationships and roles and new taken-for-granted assumptions become clearer. In some cases of major reorganisation, a regular progression through the stages occurred but in others there was reversion to earlier stages. Some stages were by-passed altogether.

At every stage those involved at the institutional level had to recognise the system's role and power in agenda creation, time setting, defining the role and power of local committees and the responsibility for implementing industrial agreements. In each of the major restructurings examined, the Minister was the only person who could decide, although worked-through and agreed-upon proposals from local levels carried heavy political weight. We also noted that Ministers preferred to 'get in front of' an emerging consensus within the policy guidelines they had helped generate, rather than trying to 'redirect the mob'.

The responsibility for managing the process of reorganisation in a 'zone of disruption' fell upon different people depending upon both the political culture and the nature of the tasks. Nevertheless, we advise that there is a need for participants to work through the stages, outlined below, although there is always differentiated understandings amongst participants and a desire to move at different speeds.

The First Stage

As noted above, the first stage is normally marked by a high degree of confusion and ambiguity. The problem and the need for change are presented in overview terms. Possible solutions are quickly developed and canvassed. A high degree of tension is often coupled with strong attempts to maintain the status quo and with threats of withdrawal from the process. An educative leader would act as a catalyst by picking the right time and the appropriate mechanisms to:

define the problem within the parameters of system policy; and
identify people or groups with interest in and capacity to contribute, especially key influentials.

The Second Stage

The second stage is the political stage. There are the initial negotiations, the clarification of the purposes and goals, the formalisation of the participants — those to be included in the negotiations — and their responsibilities, authority structures have to be determined, the initial building of alliances and the early analysis of the issues occur. An educative leader would help those involved to:

clarify the authority and power of the participants, the dimensions of problems and goals, and the perceptions of participants of the problem;
assess needs generated in human, financial and physical terms;
determine the time scale of the operation;
strike bargains, reach compromises; and
devise new ideas and creative solutions to blockages and provide stimulation.

The Third Stage

In the third stage, the negotiation process is legitimated by the engagement of the parties within an agreed framework. Although a collegial style of decision making is preferable, because of the desirability of agreed outcomes, it may not necessarily develop. Confrontation may be the norm. It is important to note that confrontation does not stop the process. It merely makes it more unpleasant.

The scope of the decisions to be made are clarified. Bargains are restruck as solutions are tested against the problem. An educative leader would help those involved to:

develop feasibility tests for their proposals;
obtain a degree of consensus before seeking public affirmation; and
create confidence that the system can and will ratify, resource and generally, deliver on the agreement.

The Fourth Stage

The fourth stage is the implementation stage. It includes modifications to meet administrative norms and the adjustment of plans as the initial stages of implementation occur. The planning group may or may not be the implementation group. The implementation group's role is different from that of the planning group, although it is desirable to have a degree of continuity of membership across these two groups to maintain the spirit as well as the purpose of the reorganisation. An educative leader would help to:

determine the implementation phases and the timescale;
determine the specific goals for each phase;
achieve early tangible indicators of commitment to the new state; and
clarify the role of the implementation group.

Most people find it very difficult to cope with the uncertainty about individual and group futures that occurs in the zone of disruption. There is often a search for quick solutions or cries for imposed resolution by, for example, the bureaucracy or the Minister. Our findings were counter-intuitive.

> *Limiting the period of disruption may lessen the conflict and the bereavement at the expense of the commitment of those who have to implement the change. Not all the participants will be at the same stage of the process at the same time. In some cases, elements in the community may request more system direction to speed up the process and deflect the criticisms that local participation engenders. The price of this may be conflict later at the implementation stage.*

Attempts to move social systems beyond the stable state can have two possible outcomes. The first is the triumph of dynamic conservatism and, at best, cosmetic change to the social system. The success of conservatism, through whatever strategy, is likely to lead to an increasing mismatch between the institution and its proper functions — this will result in either a loss of clients or the increasing irrelevance of its functions. Trenchant conservatism leaves an institution vulnerable to unnegotiated executive action. The Minister can act.

The second outcome is the transformation of the social system which will involve a period of disruption marked by crises, instability and individual and group bereavement. This period is a stage in the move toward the establishment of a new, relatively improved stable state. We can now discuss and summarise the role of educative leadership in the process.

The Institutional Leader as Educative Leader

Institutional leaders have a central role in promoting educative change. Research into their role suggests that it has two dimensions — the containment or reactive role of crisis management, of keeping small problems from becoming big ones, and the proactive or promotional role. Another way of perceiving the dimensions is in terms of management and leadership where management functions focus on organisational maintenance and leadership involves a proactive, visionary role (Sergiovanni, 1987; Duignan, 1986).

An emphasis on the containment role means that the potential of the institutional leader to become an agent of change is extremely limited. This aspect of the role is marked by a variety of tasks and fragmentation of time through attendance at meetings, sporadic conversations with people about a variety of matters, response to official correspondence and ad hoc data gathering.

The promotional and visionary role can provoke tension with the norms of containment favoured by those committed to maintenance and driven by dynamic conservatism. In school or college reorganisation, the principal needs to adopt a proactive role of educative leadership to obtain effective change. It means directing planning and managing for longer term goals and negotiating with a range of interested parties who may not be convinced, initially, of the need for change.

In these circumstances, a basic challenge exists for the principal. As a result of experience, the principal may have adopted a set of values and philosophies which often come into conflict with those of people who also have a strong vested interest in the future of their school. Unless guarded against, this can gradually place a principal into a reactive role.

Yet the same principal has to try to achieve a sensitive balance between the reactive containment and the proactive promotional roles. Within the zone of disruption, there is a need, too, for times of maintenance or reflection, without losing the impetus and commitment to the change process.

Previous experience, formal training and the process of selection have not, necessarily, prepared the principal for the requirements of leadership in reorganisation and the inevitable associated conflicts. New understandings and skills are required, such as those to do with encouraging double loop learning and the capacity to empathise with the disorientation of colleagues, students and parents, while holding to and understanding the stages, patterns and required timescales, often cruelly extended, of change.

We believe that many principals, long protected by a Departmental culture of maintenance, are recognising, or are being forced to recognise, that the context of education has changed. Historically, the 'servants of the crown' were protected from the local community by 'the system'. This is no longer so. Even in centralised systems there are expectations that schooling will be more responsive to and more involved with the community.

Reorganisation poses a fundamental threat to all members of a learning community. It is even more challenging for the principal. Principals suffer role 'loneliness'. Their self concept is even more publicly tied to 'their' school than other members of the school community. Loss is perceived as more overt and their vulnerability is therefore higher.

Self concept is strongly associated with public status. The typical absence of threat to livelihood and economic security from reorganisation may not be a major consideration; it may even encourage disengagement, apathy and non-commitment within the security of tenure. Further, a principal's normal peer group support may be undermined by the potential threat of a regional re-organisation of service delivery. Colleagues can become competitors overnight. There have been instances where peer principals have become resource-raiders.

The perspectives and desires of the local community and the education system may also be in conflict. This places the principal in a difficult position in terms of allegiance to employer and community. The principal may appreciate the prior democratic legitimacy of the Ministry or Departmental view, but could also recognise that support for the view would bring opposition from the local community or the ancillary staff and the teachers and their unions. Supporting the local view may bring Ministerial odium to a local leader. Relatively few principals have the tangible means to offset the loss or to implement damage control.

There are expectations that principals will act ethically and morally in support of the best interest of students even though the best interests of students are rarely clear-cut in either the short or long term. Parents may act in what they see to be the best interest of students by 'voting with their feet' and transferring their allegiance elsewhere. We found a number of cases where, once the initial hostility to proposed change had abated, well-informed parents and their children saw that their best interests were better served by making new arrangements, and so anticipated what others later came to see as inevitable.

For institutional leaders, the randomness of the pressure for reorganisation itself can be personally undermining and it may produce bitterness. A 'good' school, for example, may be undermined by the vagaries of its location rather than the quality of its operations. To seek help (to lessen stress) from the welfare units in 'the system' (if such exist) is still too often seen as displaying weakness, and held as possibly detrimental to career options. The assurance of salary maintenance cannot compensate for the loss of status and the personal trauma of losing position and self respect. Exiting through early retirement is not a viable option for all.

In assuming a position on reorganisation, the chief executive is constantly made aware of the multiple stakeholders in public schooling and the different values espoused by them. The leader's position is likely to be closer to that of the teachers, parents and students than to that of the system administrators. This is particularly so in a devolved organisation with local selection of principals. The catch is that system administrators tend to work through the principals.

In centralised systems, a school principal could be expected to advise the system of the likely effects of any proposed reorganisation of the schools' students and community. He or she could be expected to take into account the global — economic, social, political — environment in which the system is making decisions. This involves political awareness and sensitivity. In a devolved system, the extent to which the loyalty of the principal appointed by local selection to report 'neutrally' or objectively on perceived educational benefits and decrements of proposed changes should be assumed to be problematic.

To summarise, in situations of change the institutional leader acts in a variety of roles. The major ones are as an individual, which involves self interest, as a representative of the Department and Minister, and as a representative of the school community. There is a need to recognise the complexity and conflict inherent in the trinity of roles.

While we have emphasised the problems, it must be emphasised that reorganisation also offers opportunities for new and improved approaches to teaching and learning. It is a time when the professional educator has the opportunity to offer creative, proactive and educative leadership.

The next section discusses the difficulties and the potential inherent in a situation where the delivery of education services is being reorganised. It emphasises the need for self awareness and the need for specific skills, knowledge and understanding on the part of involved administrators. The need for support and the opportunities available are also highlighted. The focus is on the productive management of change in a climate of instability and conflict which will become more commonplace as external demands on educational institutions increase.

Personal Skills, Knowledge and Understanding

Given the present economic and demographic realities, reorganisation is unavoidable. Double loop learning is essential for positive adaptive change and personal growth in institutions affected by reorganisation. Reorganisation poses a threat to the self concept of professionals and offers a

> *temptation to opt out, to withdraw or resist change on behalf of the institution and self.*

To adapt positively requires an honest appraisal of one's personal skills, strengths, and style of leadership. It means being aware of those things that one does well and those best delegated. Reorganisation cannot be 'fixed' by one person working in isolation. It is too substantial to be kept private, too big to be 'controlled' and too complex to be achieved without help.

An important personal skill is the capacity to keep an emotional distance from the reorganisation. It means becoming reflective and parenthetical. It involves learning to see oneself in action in the institution's change programs. Without this perspective, it is difficult to get and maintain an overview and to make a reasonably objective analysis of the situation and the personality traits of those involved, including oneself.

Reorganisation requires a lot of the educative leader, especially knowledge and understanding of colleagues and their possible reaction to change. It is our view that wise educative leaders draw on the strengths, and support the growth, of others. This empowers both the leader and the followers. This approach will not shield those involved from their loss, disorientation and grief, but it can help create the circumstances for coping, responding and growth.

Reorganisation requires the institutional leader to have negotiating skills and the capacity to resolve conflict and to determine a clear 'bottom line'. It requires sensitivity to the different values and leadership styles of other participants.

Reorganisation assumes a knowledge by the institution's chief executive of intended outcomes, bureaucratic and political processes and relevant industrial agreements covering all staff. It involves understanding that:

a stable organisational state is neither inevitable nor, in the longer term, educationally justifiable;
emotions rather than rationality will often prevail in disruptive periods;
loss, with all its attendant manifestations, is a major feature of change;
anger directed at authority figures is not necessarily personal but often symbolic;
conflict is the norm during periods of change and uncertainty;
educational matters are inextricably linked to macro-political/economic matters;
change can often be shaped to extremely positive and productive ends;
the principal has a key role in shaping change;
an educational rationale should underpin the change; and
'new visions' are exciting and can raise commitment.

Above all, the leader needs to have the confidence to exploit the situation and achieve improved outcomes without becoming disoriented and embroiled.

Support for the Institutional Leader

Considering the expectations detailed in the preceding sections, it may come as a shock to realise that the leading administrators of institutions and agencies are both human and not over-rewarded for their endeavours. They are rarely left to live the common life 'undisturbed, indifferent and without disquiet', as Oscar Wilde described it. Reorganisation is usually not of their making and not in their control in an absolute sense. Leaders need support. Wise leaders admit and anticipate their own needs; some follow.

Information

The institutional leader needs early information of any change initiated from 'outside', on a confidential basis if necessary. The information needs to make his or her role clear, what is considered negotiable and non-negotiable, and the parameters for the institution *vis-à-vis* the region's and the centre's power. This is a sign of respect for the operational role of the leading administrator. It also maximises the time available for the issue to be considered, its initial implications to be reviewed and can be redeployed as lead time for consciousness-raising.

The leader will be expected to be up-to-date with information about any matter of reorganisation which involves the destabilisation of the stable state. People — parents, teachers, students, employers — will expect support and wish to consult with the institutional leader.

Personal Support and Professional Development

The chief administrator needs key people within the formal system who can act as confidants, give advice and encouragement and up-to-date, reliable information. There is a need for informal peer group support.

Professional development must be provided to the leader (and staff) on an on-going and specific basis. This should promote understanding of and ways to manage change constructively. This is particularly necessary for those administrators entering reorganisation, since it presents challenges not previously experienced.

Resources

Macro-scale change creates additional work. Additional personnel and financial support is needed for an extended period. If more than one site is involved, administrative and clerical work is expanded and requires resourcing. Finance is required for the inevitable costs of meetings and publications. Public information, such as advertisements, has to be paid for. Indeed, many with experience speak of the value of quick, tangible change at the early stage of implementation. The symbolism of successful change is one important matter to attend to, another is that it helps justify the use of scarce resources.

Some Positive Aspects

Reorganisation offers opportunities if those involved spend energy on bargaining to retain the positive features of the institutions and help improve education rather than resisting the inevitable.

Focusing on the curriculum and the quality of teaching that the clients experience is more important than the mechanics of rationalisation and justification of the change in general terms. This appeals to teachers' professional values, a central aspect of teacher satisfaction. This is also true for the school community.

The challenge of generating creative solutions that include shaping the future destiny of the institution with vision is attractive to the whole community. It complements the resolution of grief and is a subtle form of educative deflection. Since it is central to the process, educative leadership is at a premium. Looked at positively, reorganisation can be a form of professional development for an entire learning community.

Conclusion

Reorganisation initiated from outside initially has little to recommend it to those who find themselves embroiled. It is a common enough experience for managers — administration and principals — yet little attention has been paid to how they can at least cope or, more positively, reshape their organisation to creative and educative ends.

Bureaucrats, spurred by political or administrative pressure, and using a variety of more or less plausible rationales, tend to be technocratic. They gather data, plan and usually seek to 'impose' their solutions. The initial response of those at institutional level is typically very emotional. Change is a threat to professional self-esteem. Dynamic conservatism and deflection techniques abound. As reorganisation proceeds, the loss, the grief, the anger, and the apathy typical of the zone of disruption predominate. Disorientation and low morale are endemic.

The institutional manager has to deal with a situation that is largely defined in emotional terms. There is often an irrational disjunction between the management of the human problems involved or perceived and the rationality of planning.

The administrator who is unaware of the macro-political pressures, unable to discriminate between likely bureaucratic approaches and, more particularly, becomes subject to the emotional nature and pattern of change and the personal conflicts that reorganisation causes, can not expect to stand apart, assess the whole picture and offer sophisticated leadership. The capacity to distance oneself and to maintain a rational, yet sensitive analysis is essential for personal and organisational health.

Reorganisation also provides an opportunity for the educative and the visionary elements of leadership. Like the skipper of the surf boat, the leader has to encourage and stimulate the crew, read the seas, catch the waves and maintain direction. It is our view that no one can do all that, and row too.

References

ARGYRIS, C. (1977) 'Double loop learning in organisations', *Harvard Business Review*, September–October, 115–117.

ARGYRIS, C. (1982) *Reasoning, Learning and Action*, New York: Jossey-Bass

BOYD, W.L. (1983) 'Rethinking educational policy and management: Political science and educational administration', *American Journal of Education*, **92**, 1, 1–29.

DAVIES, H. (1982) 'Declining school enrolments', *Journal of Educational Administration*, **20**, 2, Summer.

DIVOKY, D. (1979) 'Burden of the seventies: The management of decline', *Phi Delta Kappan*, October, 87–91.

DUIGNAN, P. (1986) 'The culture of school effectiveness', in SIMPKINS, W.S., THOMAS, E.B. and THOMAS, A.R. (Eds) *Principal and Change: The Australian Experience*, Armidale: UNE Press.

EDUCATION AND URBAN SOCIETY (1983) *The Politics of School Closings*, **15**, 2, February.

EASTON, D. (1965) *A Systems Analysis of Political Life*, New York: Wiley.

GRAHAM, J. (1987) *Declining Enrolments and Reorganisation — A Schools Perspective*, Melbourne: Participation and Equity Program.

HAM, C. and HILL, M. (1984) *The Policy Process in the Modern Capitalist State*, Brighton: Wheatsheaf.

LENAHAN, R. (1983) *School Size and Cost*, Canberra: Commonwealth Schools Commission.

MACPHERSON, R.J.S. (1987) 'Talking up organisation: The creation and control of knowledge about being organised, *Studies in Educational Administration*, **41**, Armidale: CCEA.

MACPHERSON, R.J.S. (1989) 'Radical administrative reforms in New Zealand education: The implications of the Picot Report for institutional managers', *Journal of Educational Administration*, **27**, 1, 29–44.

MACPHERSON, R.J.S. (1992) 'The reconstruction of New Zealand education: Devolution and counter-pressures to effective school governance', in BEARE, H. and BOYD, W.L. (Eds) *Restructuring Schools: An International Perspective on the Movement to Transform the Control and Performance of Schools*, New York: Falmer Press, forthcoming.

MARRIS, P. (1974) *Loss and Change*, London: Routledge Kegan Paul.

O'CONNOR, P. (1981) *Understanding the Mid-life Crises*, Melbourne: Sun.

SARGENT, A. and HARDY, B. (1974) *Fewer Pupils/Surplus Space: A Report*, New York: Educational Facilities Laboratory.

SCHON, D.A. (1973) *Beyond the Stable State*, New York: Norton.

ZERCHYKOV, R. (1982) *A Review of the Literature and an Annotated Bibliography on Managing Decline in School Systems*, Boston: Institute of Responsive Education.

Introduction to Chapter 6

Educative Leadership in a Multicultural Community: A Synthesis and a Commentary

P.A. Duignan and R.J.S. Macpherson

The monocultural concept of the Australian way of life has been questioned for decades and yet it is notable that multiculturalism has become a major policy in most Australian education systems in comparatively recent years. In Australia, as in most Western democracies, the formal and belated recognition of multi-culturalism has led to many recent attempts to devise reformist curricula (Rizvi, 1985).

The approach taken in the coming chapter by Rizvi *et al.* draws on an international literature and presumes that educative leaders should recognise the moral, social, planning and political complexities of the multicultural context of educational policy making, and should value the potential this context has for enriching society through the agency of teaching, learning and administering. This implies the need to explore and explain the value bases of educative leadership in a multicultural context, to identify the major dilemmas that attend to these understandings, and to describe, by exemplars, appropriate strategies and practices.

The position developed by Rizvi *et al.* criticises the ideology of assimilation that underpinned the 'White Australia' policy, notes the culturally destructive nature of integration policies, and then points to the limitations of a policy of liberal multiculturalism spelled out first in the Galbally Report (1978). This analysis is informed by experiences in North American and British settings.

The rationale behind liberal multiculturalism is shown to be conceptually flawed. One reason is that the celebration of ethnicity, as a static concept, has deterministic consequences and acts against the interests of migrants. It does this by reifying the cultural experiences of ethnic groups as fixed traits and disposi-tions, rather than seeing these experiences as part of their on-going economic and political relations with others.

Another flaw to liberal multiculturalism is that it creates the illusion that the maintenance of ethnic identity leads to greater equality of opportunity. By also ignoring other factors such as social class and gender, liberal multiculturalism leaves unquestioned the distribution of power in societies.

A third flaw to the policy of liberal multiculturalism is how it tends to explain racism in terms of individual behaviours. This approach sets aside the origins of institutional and societal prejudice which can have their origins in social, political and economic histories and structures.

It is therefore argued below, by Rizvi *et al.* that educative leaders will have to be far more aware of the major structures in society that impede educational reforms and, therefore, celebrate cultural exchange and participative democracy in the governance of education.

At both the institutional and systemic level, this will mean challenging those features of organisation that suppress critical and creative education or that are dismissive of cultural traditions. It will also mean reforming any practices that help reproduce patterns of inequality. This can be most easily achieved by democratising the processes used to negotiate the organisational culture.

Central to such reform will be the review of communications and social relations; are they effective, fair, transparent and able to recognise the rights of all stakeholders? It will mean developing processes that can help resolve the problems emerging with representative school councils; central powers can provide overly restrictive guidelines and they can be dominated by groups that excel at committee work and representative politics.

Rizvi *et al.* recommend participative democracy. In essence they call for educative relationships that are continuous and reciprocal, and that involve all members of a school community. They assume democracy to be a way of life that needs to be defended and strengthened, not just a set of activities that produce decisions. They develop a case for engaging the school community in direct participation whenever and wherever possible.

In such circumstances, a policy of critical interculturalism would become a principle to be explored, negotiated and tested for meaning and significance at the institutional community level. Instead of the principles of justice and equality of educational opportunity remaining abstract policies, Rizvi *et al.* argue that learning, teaching and administering should respond to local experiences of injustice and disadvantage.

While educative leadership could come from any community member, Rizvi *et al.* argue that school principals have both a mandated responsibility and a strategic vantage point to anticipate needs and to create the conditions that enable school communities to collaboratively understand and reform inappropriate policies evident in their rituals, myths, traditions and practices. Similarly, system administrators have a responsibility to redress injustices by questioning the norms implicit in the rationale of governance and resource allocation.

In Chapter 6, Rizvi *et al.* set out how schools can help by educating citizens who are capable of clarifying misconceptions, challenging entrenched attitudes and devising new paths towards socially just societies. While they make Australian problems the case in point, the argument has international applications. Educative leadership in a multicultural setting, it follows, should bring people together in ways to help increase intercultural understandings that will, in turn, help reform social, political and economic relations. It would, therefore, help develop a critical interculturalism.

Chapter 6

Educative Leadership in a Multicultural Society

F. Rizvi

in association with Pat Duignan, Colin Gaut, Barbara Hall, Mal Lee, Mac Macpherson and Ken Murray

Introduction

The term 'multiculturalism' has had a rapid rise in prominence in Australian policy discourse. For more than a decade now, it has been widely used in most of the public policy documents which governments have produced. It has become a catch-cry, a political metaphor, by which Australians of all backgrounds have been asked to think about their society. It has invited us all to celebrate the fact that Australia is a culturally diverse nation. In more specific terms, multi-culturalism has meant the allocation of funds for a variety of services to enable the participation of Australians of non-English-speaking background (NESB) in the mainstream institutions of this country and to give them a greater and more equitable chance of obtaining the social and economic goods Australia has to offer.

It has, perhaps, been in the area of education that multiculturalism has been most seriously promoted. Between 1978 and 1986, it was promoted through the Commonwealth Schools Commission's Multicultural Education Program (MEP). Governments attempted to get all schools and education systems to initiate reforms so that they would more accurately reflect Australia's demographic composition — that is, one of the most polyethnic societies in the world. And while the MEP ended in 1986, the rhetoric of multiculturalism has not diminished. State education departments have been asked to take up the challenge of ensuring the further promotion of multiculturalism by 'mainstreaming' reform initiatives begun under the MEP. So, even without the levels of funding that were once available, the Federal Government's commitment to multiculturalism remains as strong as ever. Schools are to continue to work towards the realisation of the principle of 'education in and for a multicultural society'. This chapter addresses the issue of the implications of multiculturalism for leadership in schools.

Multiculturalism

How should leadership be conceived in schools committed to multiculturalism? In approaching this question, we face the immediate difficulty of confronting competing definitions of what multiculturalism is and what implications it has for educational practice. Multiculturalism remains a highly contested notion. Over the years, these contests have resulted in the notion of multiculturalism undergoing substantive changes. A review of official documents (such as the reports and program outlines) reveals the extent to which formulations of the policy of multiculturalism, its particular features and the scope of its emphasis from Grassby to Jayasuriya, have altered. Perhaps the best way of tackling the issue of multiculturalism and educational leadership might therefore be to review the short history of multiculturalism in Australia, to identify the substantive changes that have taken place and to explore what implications the emerging definitions have for the role of leadership in educational institutions.

The Liberal Theory of Multiculturalism

The liberal theory of multiculturalism, developed in the Galbally Report (1978), assumed in the early formulations of the MEP, and still implicit in the programs that many schools offer in the name of multicultural education, is fundamentally flawed. It is therefore an inadequate educational response to the problems of a culturally diverse society. It is referred to as the 'liberal' theory because it is based on the philosophical assumptions concerning the nature of the relationship between the individual and society traditionally associated with classical liberalism (Mill, 1859). In arguing against these assumptions, it will be suggested that the theoretical foundations upon which the liberal view of multiculturalism is based are flawed on a number of counts.

First, this formulation of multiculturalism incorporates a concept of ethnicity that is theoretically inadequate to explain the experiences of many NESB Australians in contemporary Australia. This is so because the view of ethnicity contained within the liberal theory tends to *reify* the cultural experiences of people and, thus, divorces them from issues of power and on-going economic and political relations. The 'reification process' locks cultural traits and dispositions into static states and treats them as if they are not subject to modification and development.

Second, the liberal view of multiculturalism rests on the mistaken belief that the maintenance of ethnic identity could somehow result in greater equality of opportunity. It assumes that ethnicity is the primary factor involved in understanding the problems of inequality facing NESB Australians, and thus minimises the importance of other factors such as social class and gender. The implicit belief seems to be that, if only we could enable non-English-speaking Australians to maintain their culture then we would have somehow gone a long way towards giving them equality of opportunity. Such a view, it will be argued, ignores the issue of the distribution of power in Australian society.

And third, the liberal view assumes an account of racism in Australian society that is, at best, incomplete. Resting as it does on the assumptions of individualism, it cannot satisfactorily tackle the problems of institutional prejudice since it involves ways of thinking which Syer (1982) has characterised as *pyschologistic* and *deterministic*. Psychologism rests on the assumption that human behaviour can be fully explained in terms of individual psychology. So, for example, instances of racism are thought to be fully explicable in terms of a person's mistaken attitudes, rather than in terms of society-wide relationships, the biases of the nation's social institutions and its political and economic order. Determinism suggests that some aspects of human behaviour and social phenomena will happen inevitably — they are assumed to be the given. An example of deterministic thinking might be that people belonging to a certain 'race' or 'ethnicity' will inevitably behave in certain ways.

Responses

Some of these criticisms of the liberal view of multiculturalism have been widely acknowledged in recent years. The writings of such academic critics of liberal multiculturalism as Jakubowicz (1981; 1986) and Kalantzis and Cope (1984; 1986), who have relentlessly argued that the liberal view of multiculturalism eschews issues of the intersection of ethnicity with class and gender in the reproduction of life-chances in schools and society, seem to be at last making some impact on the thinking of policy-makers and educational administrators. In an extensive report, which reviewed multicultural education initiatives in schools and was funded by the MEP, Cahill (1984) acknowledged that many MEP programs he encountered were informed by liberal assumptions. He argued that the program had failed to bring about any 'substantial and lasting change', and suggested that the initiatives remained confined to activities that mostly celebrated ethnicity in a piecemeal and *ad hoc* fashion. By and large, he suggested that schools did not confront the more complex issue of the social outcomes of schooling.

In a report for the National Advisory and Co-ordinating Committee on Multicultural Education (NACCME), Jayasuriya (1987) summed up some of the limitations of the liberal view of multicultural education which had been identified by a range of critics. In its place he advocated a revised conception of multiculturalism — 'equitable multiculturalism' which incorporated a critical and more dynamic notion of culture — and he stressed the principle of equity of outcomes for ethnic minorities in the changed demographic circumstances of the late 1980s. Interestingly, however, the suggestions Jayasuriya put forward were not new: many education departments had already moved along the directions proposed by NACCME. New South Wales and Victoria, for example, had during 1983 and 1984, substantially revised their policies to avoid some of the pitfalls of the liberal view of multicultural education. Of course, the extent to which these developments have had an impact on school practices still remains an open question.

Welcome though these developments are, it can be argued that the analysis upon which they are based still devotes insufficient attention to the way contemporary schools are structured, and how this structure makes the realisation of a more ambitious and a socially critical approach to multicultural education difficult to achieve. Of course, reforms are never easy to achieve in large and complex institutions like schools. But, more than this, our schools are currently not organised in ways that enable multicultural education to be practiced in anything but the most minimal liberal sense. The promise of the kind of multiculturalism NACCME proposes conflicts with the reality of contemporary Australian schools and school systems. For example, in hierarchically bureaucratised schools, powerful incentives, such as the chance of social mobility, exist for NESB children to assimilate into the dominant order. By and large, most schools and school systems are structured neither to facilitate pluralism nor to promote greater equality of educational opportunity and outcome.

Developing An Alternative

To arrive at a more adequate formulation of multicultural education we have to examine not only the problems inherent in the liberal theory of multiculturalism but also the structure of contemporary schools which makes attempts at social reform through education extremely difficult. Multicultural education needs to be reformulated around a more satisfactory account of the relationship between schools and society. Of course, it has to be admitted that schools are part of a broader economic and political context and cannot be expected to promote social reform on their own. However, they can have a crucial catalytic social effect by preparing children for life in a more just and democratic Australian society in which they have a critical understanding of the nature of their society and the issues of social and economic inequality.

For this to happen, fundamental changes are required in the way in which relationships are conceived and organised in schools. We need to challenge those features of schools which tend to suppress critical and creative education, and those which promote both deterministic and psychologistic thinking. For example, current practices in the area of assessment and accreditation need to be examined, as part of multicultural education, to assess the extent to which they are inimical to creative thinking, dismissive of cultural traditions and reproductive of patterns of social inequality. Reforms along these lines imply a political purpose, namely the *democratisation* of schools and the creation of those forms of social life in which all groups in Australia have an important and equal role in negotiating the nation's cultural values in a dynamic way.

The achievement of this political purpose requires *educative leadership*. Such leadership would not necessarily reside in particular persons or institutional positions, but in those *acts* which might help to create the conditions that permit genuine participatory democracy to emerge (Wood, 1984) and be practised inside and outside of schools. This requires attention to a range of *internal* conditions, such as the development of knowledge and skills, that would enable all members of school communities to analyse and challenge the ways in which present structures prevent them from exercising greater control of their collective destinies. Educative leadership also implies attending to a set of *external* conditions, such as the need for political action to ensure that funds for public education are equitably distributed and not reduced even further than they have been over the past few years.

From Assimilation to Multiculturalism

Multiculturalism as a public policy in Australia emerged during the 1970s. A number of writers (Jakubowicz, 1981; Rizvi, 1985; Foster and Stockley, 1984) have argued that it was a response to the failure of the policies of assimilation and integration to contain what successive governments saw as a developing crisis in ethnic relations in this country. There is certainly ample evidence for this view in the assumptions of the Galbally Report (1978) which rested on the assessment that in the mid-1970s ethnic relations in Australia were at 'a critical stage'. According to Galbally, such a situation required an urgent policy response to contain the growing social tensions caused by the 'migrant presence'. He noted that since the Second World War the number of migrants coming to Australia had risen dramatically, and that the country's social and economic institutions had become inadequate for dealing with the emerging problems. He pointed to a need for greater provision of resources for migrant services. Galbally also showed how the policy of assimilation had failed. He also went on to demonstrate (1978, p. 4) that the:

> needs of migrants should in general be met by programs and services available to the whole community but that special services and programs are necessary at present to ensure equality of access and provision.

Assimilation

The policy of assimilation was deceptively simple. It was couched in terms that stipulated that all Australians, regardless of their origin, were to gradually attain the same manner of living, to share a common culture, to live as members of a homogeneous Australian community, to enjoy the same rights and privileges, to accept the same responsibilities and to observe the same customs. All Australians were to be influenced by the same beliefs, hopes and loyalties. This effectively meant that the existing Anglo traditions were to dominate the social life of all Australians, regardless of their origin.

Between 1945 and the late sixties, more than a million non-English-speaking migrants settled in Australia. These migrants, who were mostly from Europe and who had significantly changed the cultural landscape of Australia, were expected to assimilate into the existing institutions. In the education systems, this meant that no special provisions were to be made for migrant children attending Australian schools. This logic was reflected in such phrases as 'sink or swim' and 'to pick up the Australian way of life by sitting next to Nelly'. Through osmosis, migrant children were to become assimilated into a supposedly homogeneous Australian culture. Not all migrants could, but it was expected that second-generation migrants would.

The policy of assimilation had the purpose of leaving unchallenged the structural features of the Australian nation. Instead of questioning the appropriateness of the educational services provided, the system branded the children who could not assimilate as 'difficult' or even 'slow'. They were believed to require compensatory treatment. In some cases, such treatment included referral to child psychologists', or even to speech therapists (Martin, 1978). So instead of the biculturalism of the migrant child being regarded as a positive attribute, it was condemned out of hand.

Towards the end of the 1960s it was clear, however, that assimilation was not as easily attainable as the policy-makers had hoped. Successive studies (e.g. Jupp, 1966; Martin, 1972) showed that not only was it difficult for migrants to shed their cultural traditions, but also many did not want to do so. A wide variety of professionals, who were expected to work with migrants, forcibly challenged the widespread assumption that assimilation was, in fact, feasible. Teachers, for example, who were now equipped with the rhetoric of child-centred education and greater community participation in education, saw a major contradiction between the policy of assimilation and their professional beliefs.

Contrary to the government's rhetoric, which claimed that all ethnic groups had an equal opportunity 'to take an equal and informed part' in the creation and maintenance of Australian society, many NESB Australians were not in a position to do so. Adult migrants, who had in general occupied a low status in Australian society, had hoped for social mobility for their children. And yet, for a variety of structural reasons, their children were unable to gain this social outcome. It was apparent that widespread racism and the xenophobic attitudes of many Anglo-Australians represented a major barrier to NESB Australians wishing to participate in the major institutions of their new country (Martin, 1972).

Integration

By the late 1960s, the ideology of assimilation was clearly exposed as being both impractical and morally bankrupt. Far from promoting liberal and egalitarian ideals, it denied significance to migrant cultures and life-styles. Frustrated by the lack of services and equal opportunities, some ethnic organisations such as the Greek Welfare Association began to organise themselves politically in order to question policies and practices. This constituted a serious challenge to the blunt instrument of assimilation. Governments faced the problem of obtaining the legitimation from many NESB Australians that they had once taken for granted. These difficulties were most evident in the area of industrial relations. In the early 1970s, for example, a series of bitter strikes, over among other things poor conditions, by workers representing a number of non-English-speaking ethnic groups at Ford's Broadmeadows plant in Melbourne, demonstrated to governments a high level of political volatility and awareness by groups who had, until that time, chosen to remain politically silent (Connell, 1979).

The initial policy response to this growing realisation of migrant discontent came in the form of an experiment with the policy of integration, imported to Australia from the USA. The Johnson presidency there had earlier rejected assimilationist ideas in favour of the concept of the 'nation as a melting pot' (Glazer and Moynihan, 1971). The purpose of the integration policy in Australia was to encourage the creation of a society in which different cultural groups, including the Anglos, participated and contributed fully and equally in the development of the nation's social, political and economic institutions. The rhetoric of integration suggested a view of inter-cultural relations in which all groups lived with each other in a climate of mutual accommodation. However, as far as ethnic organisations were concerned, this new policy remained bedevilled with a fundamental problem. They recognised that equal participation was still not possible in Australia because the nation's political and economic structures, the way individuals and groups interacted with the agencies of the state, continued to be dominated by the Anglo traditions.

Many leaders of ethnic organisations argued that the dice, so to speak, with which the integrationist game was being played, were already loaded in favour of the existing power structures. There was no real possibility of realigning power relations. While integration represented a shift in policy away from the emphasis on Anglo conformity in cultural terms, it nevertheless required the complete political integration of all ethnic groups into the existing system. Hence, the policy of integration could no more appease the increasingly militant minority ethnic leaders than had the assimilationist policy. The politicians continued to be troubled by what they increasingly saw as a crisis of significant and growing proportions.

Liberalism

It was from within this problematic context that the policy of multiculturalism emerged. It represented an attempt by the Fraser Government to contain discontent among NESB Australians, to overcome heightened social tensions and to restore their acquiescence to an Australian system dominated by Anglo traditions. Successive reports published in the 1970s, including the Galbally Report, made it clear that unless a more *liberal* policy, such as multiculturalism, was adopted Australia would face 'unacceptable alternatives' (Australian Ethnic Affairs Council, 1977:7). Implicit in this reference to unacceptable alternatives was the fear that increasingly volatile minority ethnic communities could no longer be expected to remain a docile workforce, especially in times of increasingly high levels of unemployment, which effectively meant that some ethnic groups were more at risk than others. The government also realised that for a new policy to be effective it had to accommodate some of the demands of NESB Australians and, at the same time, articulate the widespread sentiments of the general Anglo-Australian population. The Fraser Government could not afford to have a new policy which was not predominantly in line with the interests of the majority.

Releasing the Galbally Report, the Fraser Government claimed multiculturalism to be a significant departure from the policies of assimilation and integration. The new policy rejected the idea of cultural homogeneity as either possible or indeed desirable. It emphasised the right of all minority groups to maintain their culture. Ethnic diversity was encouraged. The academic proponents of multiculturalism, such as Smolicz (1974) and Zubrzycki (1979), argued that ethnicity was a natural primordial phenomenon in human society. It followed from this premise that a policy promoting cultural homogeneity could never have succeeded, even in modern industrial societies characterised by a preference for large and uniform institutions. Indeed, they argued that the need for cultural identification was even greater in modern industrial societies than in traditional communities.

These academic analyses of the role of ethnicity in modern industrial societies were adopted by the Liberal Government of Malcolm Fraser in its construction of the policy of multiculturalism around the set of principles enunciated in the Galbally Report. However, it is important to point out that the Galbally principles of multiculturalism differed somewhat from the political program for multiculturalism that Grassby had promoted when he was the Minister for Immigration under the Whitlam Government. It is worth noting this because Grassby is often credited with initiating the popular rhetoric of multiculturalism. While both Galbally and Grassby stressed the importance of according as much validity to minority cultures in Australia as to the claims of the Anglos, Grassby's program of 'a family of the nation' (1973) envisaged an integrated Australian nation developed around concerns of equity and fairness, as well as the maintenance of diverse cultural traditions. Grassby saw political and cultural issues of multiculturalism as inextricably linked.

In contrast, a convincing case can be mounted to suggest that the Galbally Report and the reports published by Australian Ethnic Affairs Council in the late 1970s sought to have these issues separated. While Grassby's program was a populist and reformist one, informed by social democratic principles, the Galbally agenda was informed by pragmatic considerations in a concern to contain minority unrest and create conditions for the continued acquiescence of NESB Australians to the existing system. Grassby's 'multiculturalism' was an expression of his welfare reformist agenda directed at eradicating forms of social injustice. Galbally's language, on the other hand, stressed difference, individualism and cultural pluralism — it was a conservative liberal orientation that emphasised the right of individuals and ethnic groups to live in Australia in any way they saw fit.

Galbally listed three key principles of multiculturalism. These were the maintenance of cultural identity, the promotion of equality of opportunity and the preservation of social cohesion. However, the Galbally Report itself was unclear as to how these principles related to each other within a coherent social theory. For devising programs or allocating funds around the new policy, Galbally provided no clear criteria to help determine the priority of any one principle over the others.

Reports that followed Galbally were however not so hesitant in asserting that the principle of the maintenance of cultural identity was to be supreme, and that therefore multiculturalism implied separating cultural from political issues. A report published by the Australian Ethnic Affairs Council (AEAC) in 1977 explicitly rejected the idea that there was a necessary connection between multiculturalism and 'the way in which or the degree to which ethnic minorities have access to decision-making and political power' (AEAC, Ethnicity was, moreover, regarded as something 'irrelevant to political access', p. 6).

Because of Fraser's political interest in dismantling Labor's welfare reformism, it was not surprising that of the three principles of multiculturalism, the programs his government devised, stressed the need to maintain cultural identity ahead of the principle of equality of opportunity which was only symbolically mentioned. Certainly, in education, the principle of cultural pluralism was taken up by state agencies with greater vigour than the other two principles. The Galbally Report singled out education as an institution fundamental to making Australia a truly multicultural society. For the Galbally Report, this implied the development of a 'multicultural attitude' in children. Schools were given the responsibility of 'fostering the retention of the cultural heritage of the different groups and promoting inter-cultural understanding' (Galbally Report, 1978:11–12).

To many working in schools, the emphasis placed on this strategy seemed to suggest the view that ultimately multiculturalism was concerned only with changing prejudiced attitudes and defusing inter-cultural conflict. As Foster (1981:364) points out, for Galbally, 'multiculturalism is not a fact with social consequences but simply an attitude to be encouraged'. It was not that the principles of equality and social cohesion were totally ignored by Galbally, or indeed by the educational institutions that attempted to implement the Galbally principles, it is just that relative priority was accorded to activities that aimed to promote cultural diversity and attitudes of inter-cultural tolerance.

In 1982, another major report of a committee chaired by Zubrzycki endorsed the Galbally principles. Zubrzycki (1982:13) insisted that, 'the means to achieve multiculturalism were to be found in two areas: public policy and community attitudes'. In the area of public policy, Zubrzycki argued, multiculturalism must be based on support for a common core of institutions, rights and obligations and that the principle of a national identity must be recognised. Social cohesion was thus regarded as a unifying political value around, and within the framework of which, diverse ethnic groups were encouraged to celebrate their cultural differences. Zubrzycki stressed the ideal of equality of opportunity, but in much the same way as Galbally had done a few years earlier, relegated it to secondary importance, and, in any case, presented an analysis of the notion of equality of opportunity in a very weak liberal sense as equality of treatment. In sum, between the Galbally and Zubrzycki reports, the liberal view of multiculturalism remained largely unaltered.

Multicultural Education

So far in this chapter, the origins of the liberal theory of multiculturalism, as it was articulated in the various reports presented to and accepted by the Fraser Government, have been discussed. But as most policy analysts know, principles contained in reports are one thing, their actual practice is quite another. The question we now need to ask is how were the Galbally principles, as refracted through the MEP, translated into concrete educational practices in schools. Answering this question is no simple task because, under the MEP, schools devised a wide range of practices which were informed by differing understandings and meanings of multicultural education. However, it is possible to make some general statements about how schools approached multicultural education by referring to accounts provided by Hannan (1983), Kalantzis and Cope (1984) and the Cahill Report (1984) which is perhaps the most comprehensive evaluation of the Commonwealth Schools Commission's Multicultural Education Program, and was sponsored by the Commission itself.

Victoria

Hannan (1983) argued that whatever meanings multiculturalism may have had for policy-makers, her research revealed that schools in Victoria had developed a range of meanings and practices of their own and that these varied a great deal. She identified six approaches.

> First, multicultural curriculum was seen as something that 'helped migrant children and the children of migrant families into the general society'. This version of multicultural education still incorporated assimilationist assumptions.
> Many schools did no more than continue with the teaching of English as a second language, as a compensatory measure.
> Second, a school program was thought to be multicultural if it planned a number of discrete activities, some of which were outside the curriculum, such as 'ethnic nights' and 'international days'. This view of multicultural education was very common and was based on the schools' wish to give different ethnic groups a chance to display a part of their culture.
> Third, some schools believed that a multicultural curriculum described an overall attitude to the subject matter. This approach, according to Hannan, led to the conclusion that as long as right attitudes were present then all that was required was a set of activities linked to these attitudes, no matter how disconnected or incoherent.
> Fourth, some schools saw the multicultural curriculum as 'a substitute for Community Language Programs, because it can reach everyone in English and provide them with an understanding of different cultures'.
> Fifth, though fewer in number, some schools saw multicultural education as a 'necessary support and complement to a Community Education Program'.
> And finally, only a handful of schools viewed multicultural education in a more comprehensive way as the introduction of a set of values that challenged the ethnocentricity implicit in the content of conventional curriculum and organisational practices.

Hannan's research indicated that for the large majority of schools the focus of multicultural education was thought largely to be a matter of developing appropriate attitudes of tolerance and inter-cultural understanding between all Australians through learning about the backgrounds of each other. This thinking rested on the assumption that maintaining and nurturing cultural and linguistic heritages in Australia would inevitably result in greater communication between diverse groups, leading to the eradication of mutual suspicion and racism. The maintenance of ethnic heritage, in its folkloric, religious and artistic aspects and customs, would serve to strengthen identity. Multicultural education would thus be a way of improving the self-concept of the NESB children by ensuring that they viewed their cultural traits positively.

New South Wales

There are considerable parallels between Hannan's analysis of Victorian schools and the descriptions of how five Sydney schools approached multicultural education provided by Kalantzis and Cope (1984). Kalantzis and Cope found that there was an overwhelming emphasis on multiculturalism as simply a matter of attitudes, feelings and personal development, at the expense of the requirements of intensive and specialised teaching. According to Kalantzis and Cope, there was a tendency in programs of multicultural education to view 'culture' in very narrow terms, to dwell on the 'traditional', to celebrate festivals and foods, even if these had little significance for NESB children in contemporary Australia. They argued that a 'curriculum consequence of this simplistic cultural pluralism is to trivialise culture and thereby to draw stereotyped peculiarities'. Culture was presented in an arbitrary way, removed from the concrete social relations that might confront NESB families. According to Kalantzis and Cope, when presented in a piecemeal fashion, multicultural education played a negative role in structuring social outcomes.

Australia

Five years after the Commonwealth Schools Commission first introduced the Multicultural Education Program, a team from the Philip Institute of Technology in Melbourne, led by Cahill, conducted a nation-wide review of the progress of multiculturalism in Australian classrooms. While acknowledging the MEP's many achievements, Cahill's assessment of the issues and problems confronting multicultural education confirmed in many ways the more academic analysis of Hannan, and Kalantzis and Cope. Cahill reported that 'the Program has in ways big and small touched the activities of many schools in Australia and has had a direct impact on the lives and outlooks of thousands of Australian teachers and the children they teach' (Cahill Report, 1984:320). The report listed a large range of initiatives sponsored by the Commonwealth Multicultural Education Program. These included classroom activities to improve inter-cultural understanding, major language curriculum projects, provision of ethnic liaison officers for schools, interpreter and translation services, and initiatives in bi-cultural and bilingual education. The Cahill Report also noted the significant impact of many school-based research activities into the problems that NESB children face. Despite these developments, the Cahill Report remained lukewarm in its endorsement of the Multicultural Education Program. It argued that multicultural education was, 'still very delicately poised ... we have found much evidence of shifts in perceptions, growth in expertise and development in programs. However, shifts do not mean substantial and enduring change but they can presage it' (Cahill Report, 1984:318).

Problems

Cahill remained troubled by the force of the implication of a distinction drawn by Bullivant (1981) between life styles and life chances. While endorsing many classroom developments, Cahill argued that these were largely aimed at the concerns of life style and did not address the issues of how they increased the educational opportunities and life-chances of NESB children. He also noted that teachers involved in multicultural education remained reluctant to address issues of ethnic politics. Implicit in this observation was the claim that while multi-cultural education might have provided all kinds of ways for minority ethnic groups to maintain their cultural identities, it was not clear how it could be instrumental in providing greater equality of opportunity and access for non-English-speaking Australians; and, in so far as issues of inequalities were linked to the issues of prejudice, how it might contribute to reducing levels of racism in Australian society.

It would be a mistake to regard these criticisms of multicultural education as the failure of individual teachers, who have, by and large, been highly diligent and committed to making Australia a fairer society. Even with very limited institutional support, most teachers have not been reluctant to experiment with new ideas. The problem lies with the formulation of the liberal theory of multiculturalism itself, since it is this theory that informs the popular school-based conceptions of what kind of activities it is appropriate for multicultural education to include. In what follows, it will be argued that it is not that multicultural education as it was practised under the MEP was entirely mis-taken, though elements of it were, but rather that it was an incomplete educa-tional response to the problems facing Australian society. Emphasis was placed mostly on the less important matters of life-style. And, in so far as it did not face up to the issue of the existing patterns of social and economic inequalities in Australia, its scope remained confined to celebrating cultural diversity. And consequently, whether by design or effect, multiculturalism has served as an ideology, because by portraying ethnicity as a reified static category, divorced from political concerns, it has become instrumental in defusing and masking the more fundamental political issues of class and gender inequalities and the cur-rent patterns of social and economic disadvantage in Australia.

This assessment of the liberal view of multiculturalism has been shared by a growing number of political and educational analysts. Increasingly, the assump-tions of both the liberal theory and practice of multiculturalism have been subjected to sustained scrutiny by both the right and left wings of Australian politics. The right, represented by such writers as Chipman (1980) and Knopfel-macher (1982), has wished public policy to return to the days of assimilation and a more uniform curriculum that stresses traditional values, while the left, represented by such sociologists as de Lepervanche (1984) and Jakobuwicz (1981), has viewed multiculturalism as yet another instrument of state control. The assumptions underlying the liberal theory and practice of multiculturalism will be discussed in the next three sections.

Liberal Multicultural Assumptions

The Idea of Ethnicity and the Maintenance of Cultural Identity

The liberal theory of multiculturalism stresses the importance of maintaining ethnicity and cultural identity. Through such public institutions as schooling, the maintenance of religion, language, kin ties, ethnic customs and folk life-styles is emphasised. In contrast with assimilationist ideas, a whole range of writers such as Isaacs (1975), Bostock (1981) and Smolicz (1979) have argued that the maintenance of ethnic cultures is a moral right, essential for a positive self-concept and human dignity. Within the educational sphere, great pressure has been placed on teachers and administrators to be aware of the distinct language and culture of 'ethnic' minorities, and to take these into consideration in curriculum planning and organisational decision-making. The notion of ethnicity has thus become a central focus for the development of the theory of multiculturalism. But how is the concept of 'ethnicity' understood?

Rizvi (1986a) examined three influential accounts of ethnicity and argued that while these accounts — of Barth (1969), Glazer and Moynihan (1971) and van den Berghe (1981) — are in response to different theoretical problems, they nevertheless share a common problematic and a similar set of assumptions. These assumptions are also shared by those who have stressed the importance of ethnicity in the development of the liberal theory of multiculturalism in Australia. Ethnicity has been viewed as a theoretically autonomous category that involves communal ways of thinking, feeling and acting in groups. Following the analyses of Barth, Glazer and Moynihan and van den Berghe, it has been treated as a category which has a theoretical capacity to explain social life independently of such considerations as class and gender.

While Barth views an ethnic group from an interpretivist perspective as consisting of those persons who self-ascribe and identify with a way of life which is shared with others and Glazer and Moynihan recognise it in terms of its having a distinct set of interests and needs which require collective organisation in order that they be pursued or defended, van den Berghe defines ethnicity in primordial terms, as something that results from the natural selection of our specifically human capabilities: the configurations we call 'culture'. The focuses of these definitions are clearly different. Yet, they each take culture at its face value, as something objectively given and therefore as something that can be abstracted from its historically contingent circumstances. Culture and cultural interests thus appear in each of these definitions as static, fixed and unchanging, dislocated from their political and historical contexts. Ethnic boundaries are presented as complete and clearly differentiable.

The liberal theory of multiculturalism assumes ethnicity to be a primary category of social analysis. Of course, it has to be acknowledged that people do conceive of themselves and others as belonging to certain ethnic groups and do describe certain sorts of situations and relations as being ethnically related. But this fact should not imply that social analysis must be restricted to the interpretive analysis of the actors themselves, for the categories of description used in everyday discourse can often provide a false and misleading explanation of activities. Thus, for example, the experience of migrants in Australia is not confined to matters of life-style, and is not entirely explicable in ethnic terms. Various minority ethnic groups occupy a particular position within the class structure of Australian society and play an important role in the production of economic relations. This is a role that actors cannot be assumed to be able to theorise. However, their inability to theorise about these economic and political relations cannot imply that these relations are not important, or even that they are unrelated to an analysis of ethnic relations. By focusing on the interpretive understanding of the actors themselves, we are always in danger of reifying ethnic identity, since ethnic and economic relations cannot be assumed to be entirely independent of each other. Yet, this is an assumption which appears implicit in the liberal theory and practice of multiculturalism. But such a theory fails to address questions of how certain cultural differences come to be regarded by various ethnic groups as more significant than others, and how particular ethnic traditions evolve in their specifically Australian contexts.

In opposition to the liberal theory of multiculturalism, it can be argued that we cannot regard ethnicity as a primordial 'objective' category, resistant to change. Ethnicity is socially constructed and ethnic traditions change continuously, especially when they become historically relocated through the process of migration and come in contact with other traditions. As individuals and groups need to solve new problems they form new networks and theorise about their traditions differently.

The consequences of defining ethnicity in terms of fixed cultural differences, divorced from their political and historical locations, are significant. It leads to a failure to identify class, gender and other divisions which exist within various ethnic groups. While the Greek-Australian shop-owner, for example, may have some cultural characteristics in common with other Greek-Australian workers, the differences between them, in respect of economic relations, are also extremely important. Similarly, the differences between Turkish-Australian males and females may be more significant than their similarities. Also, it is possible that the similarities between Greek-Australian and Chinese-Australian women may be more important in particular contexts than the differences that are attributable to their ethnicity. Thus, the emphasis on cultural differences may obscure the facts of commonality *across* ethnic divisions.

Moreover, it is a mistake to assume that any similarities in life-style are of primary importance equally to all members of an ethnic group. Economic circumstances always have, for example, the potential of 'bursting the ethnic bond' between employers and employees, if the mode of production necessitates the imposition of those conditions upon the employees which for material and political reasons they find unacceptable. So, it appears that it is a fundamental conceptual error to assume a degree of uniformity and homogeneity among members of ethnic groups. Such homogeneity often does not exist to anywhere near the degree which some proponents of liberal multiculturalism often suppose. This discussion also reveals that cultural and political issues cannot be so easily distinguished. An adequate grasp of ethnic experiences in Australia is impossible unless we also pay attention to the political nature of ethnic relations and the dynamics of change and conflict.

In teaching about cultural experiences in Australia, it is always a mistake, therefore, to assume uniformity in traditions, experiences and ways of thinking. People approach social and cultural problems differently and no a priori judgments are possible about the range of attitudes or problems children from various backgrounds might have. Nor are teachers likely to encounter problems in the same way in dealing with particular individuals from groups believed to share common origins.

The Nature of Prejudice and Multicultural Education

According to the liberal view of multiculturalism, we should aim to achieve an Australian society 'in which all people have the freedom to express their cultural identity' (Zubrzycki, 1982:17). Zubrzycki argues that the legacy of assimilation has meant that residual prejudice against minority ethnic groups continues to exist in this society. To overcome this prejudice, he suggests 'educational programs that promote intercultural tolerance of and respect for cultural patterns other than one's own' (Zubrzycki, 1982:17). A number of other authors, like Kaldor (1982) and Lippman (1984) have also spoken of 'the need for the encouragement of a multicultural attitude' through curricula offered in schools. These authors seem to put a great deal of faith in the schools' ability to promote inter-cultural tolerance, and thus minimise levels of racism in society.

However, these theorists seldom ask the questions of whether, and the extent to which, schools can in fact meet these expectations. Nor do they address the issue of the nature and causes of racism in Australian society in any satisfactory manner. Their view, widespread in schools and in society at large, appears to rest on the assumption that prejudices are simply a matter of mistaken and irrational attitudes that some individuals have towards other individuals and groups. A problem with this view is that it does not explain how individuals come to hold such irrational views in the first place. It presents an account of attitudes as something that individuals possess, not as the way certain kind of relationships may be described. The focus is on the individual, who is often assumed to be remote from history and social structure. No attempt is made to link the issue of racism to the issues of political and economic disadvantage or to the patterns of inequalities present in society. In other words, prejudiced attitudes are seen as irrational phenomena that are a function of an individual's inadequate personality. The individual is solely held responsible and is blamed implicitly for not 'knowing better'.

But arguably this analysis of the nature and causes of racism is excessively 'psychologistic'. That is, too much weight is being put on the individual's psychology and not enough on the social forces that produce irrational beliefs. Syer (1982:93) refers to this fallacy as involving 'a tendency to see the trees but not the wood'. The real causes of racism are not seen to be the wider social forces and the structures within which education systems are located, but the characteristics of the individual. Multicultural education thus emphasises attitudes, dispositions and respect for self and others, and avoids discussion of the politics and economics of racism.

Against the view that defines prejudice as an instance of an individual's irrational belief, a number of sociologists, like Miles (1982) and Castles and Kosack (1973), have argued that racism is a much more complicated phenomenon. They have demonstrated it can be located in the way social practices are structured in institutions. The reality of racism is often masked. Castles and Kosack have argued that racism is causally linked to conflict over economic and social interest.

Prejudice does not manifest itself only in the explicit racist attitudes or the use of deliberate emotive and inflammatory language, or even the playground fights. More insidiously, it consists in what Hall (1980) has referred to as 'inferential racism', a more pervasive and subtle form that is based on taken-for-granted assumptions that often pass as common sense. Not all forms of racism rest on conscious intentions, many are located in mistakenly held stereotypes, negative patronising attitudes and beliefs that hinder expectations and create misunderstanding. Moreover, racism, when located in policies and entrenched practices, goes beyond simple acts of discrimination such as direct abuse directed at one's background. According to Spears (1978), institutional racism is not always overt but structured into political and social institutions, arising not necessarily from the willful acts of prejudiced individuals but as covert acts of indifference and omission.

Syer (1982) points out that another very widespread form of racism in schools and society involves the holding and teaching of deterministic beliefs about people. Determinism is a theory which suggests the inevitability of characteristics ascribed to groups of people. It involves the assumption that if someone belongs to a particular group then he or she is bound to have a particular set of attributes. If a person's background is, for example, Chinese, then a determinist will assume that person's character, intelligence, food preferences and aptitudes for particular kinds of work are somehow pre-determined. Of course, determinist beliefs can exist independently of racism but when applied to predict inter-ethnic behaviour they become particularly obnoxious.

In education, racial determinism remains widespread. Deterministic thinking can be argued to be the basis of intelligence tests, especially when they are used to predict the educational outcomes of different racial or ethnic groups. Similarly, home background cannot be used to make any reliable predictions, and yet it could be argued that the theory of cultural deprivation involves precisely this mistake (see Keddie, 1974). Indeed, paradoxically, there is a always a danger that the multicultural educational programs that stress the need to maintain cultural identity by teaching about ethnic traditions may unintentionally promote deterministic thinking about various ethnic cultures.

It has been argued in this section that racism is not simply a matter of irrational, prejudiced attitudes and that it is often built into the social structures of a society. It is linked to conflict over social interests and is often produced by the economic conditions that prevail in society. Given this broader understanding of racism, that includes institutional racism, it would seem that it may be more widespread than the liberal view might allow one to admit.

Now if the analysis above of the nature of racism is correct, then the limited programs in multicultural education that stress celebrating life-styles cannot have any great capacity for achieving the goals of cultural tolerance and inter-cultural understanding. That is not to say that they may not be helpful in some cases in pointing out mistaken beliefs to students, but it would be a mistake to overstate schools' capacity for social transformation. As de Lepervanche (1984:194) points out, 'education per se will not lead to the removal of prejudice and discrimination or to the institution of equal opportunity'. If prejudice is a product of socio-economic conditions, then we cannot expect to change prejudiced attitudes simply by encouraging cultural tolerance in classrooms. Prejudice cannot be reduced unless we also attend to the broader social and economic factors that help produce it in the first place. What we can do in schools, however, is to institute those forms of study that enable all students to talk about Australian society openly, as it affects them, and develop a more adequate understanding of how racism works in society and how it is reproduced through various social and political institutions. And as teachers, we can also do something about avoiding the errors of determinism and psychologism identified by Syer.

Equality of Educational Opportunity

While the goal of promoting equality of opportunity did not feature all that prominently in the Galbally Report, the Zubrzycki Report (1982:21–22) stressed that

> equality of opportunity is an essential part of the concept of multiculturalism. Indeed cultural diversity by itself would be a hollow achievement if there were no equal opportunity for occupational advancement or for obtaining access to positions where important decisions affecting the Australian community are made.

It was clear that Zubrzycki viewed the notion of equality of opportunity in terms of providing greater access to migrants so that they were better placed to compete for occupational advancement and participation in Australian community life. However, Zubrzycki's notion of equality of opportunity remained wedded to the ideas of meritocracy. That is, he did not question the structural features of the existing ideological order in Australia. And it was within the framework of the status quo that he invited NESB Australians to maintain their cultural identity and compete for the social rewards available. So, what this view of equality of opportunity implied was that while minority groups were not prohibited from competing for the social goods Australia offered, they had to do so on the implicit terms of the dominant institutional values.

In the liberal theory of multiculturalism Zubryzcki proposed, it remained unclear how he thought the celebration of ethnicity could in fact lead to the realisation of equality of opportunity. Indeed, if meritocracy is taken seriously then there would appear to be little reason for members of those minority ethnic groups who are at the bottom of the social ladder to endorse the policy of pluralism. On the contrary, there would seem to be powerful incentives for the members of the disadvantaged ethnic groups interested in social mobility to assimilate into the mainstream dominant culture. As Steinberg (1983) argued, the history of polyethnic societies has shown that migrants who have succeeded in climbing the meritocratic ladder have been those who have been prepared to reject their ethnicity and compete essentially on the implicit terms of the dominant culture. Given that 'social cohesion' is one of the three main principles of liberal multiculturalism, the dominant structural institutions of Australian society are unlikely to change in any dramatic way. This much Zubrzycki has very clearly stated. Under these conditions, it would follow that equality of opportunity would be more likely to flow to those who are prepared to assimilate into the existing structures.

The conclusion that since structural inequalities exist in Australian society, equal opportunity in practice means social rewards only for those people whose ideas and values conform with those of the dominant Anglo-Australian culture can be demonstrated to have direct application to education. Since the provision of equal opportunity is already defined in terms of the goals and structure of Australian schools, for NESB children, equal opportunity can only be achieved by absorbing the values of the dominant culture as quickly as possible. This means accelerated mastery of the English language, learning the 'hidden curriculum' of the school culture and selecting those courses of study most directly linked to passing external examinations such as the HSC with a view to entering a higher education institution or getting jobs higher up the occupational ladder.

Given this understanding it is not surprising that, according to the liberal meritocratic view, equal opportunity is often viewed solely in terms of the provision of more services and resources (often compensatory instruction) so that Anglo and non-Anglo students alike have an 'equal' chance of achieving the competitive middle-class academic objectives already set by the school system. To view equal opportunity in this way is to confirm that, as Mullard (1982:128) suggests, 'those who desire social and academic achievement need foremost to conform, to accept, if only passively, the school ethos before they can usefully gain from the supposed equal opportunities provided'. Bullivant (1981) has noted the contradiction between the goal of equality of opportunity and pre-servation of cultural identity. He refers to this as the 'pluralist dilemma in education'. The dilemma has to do with promoting equality of opportunity as a political concern on the one hand, while at the same time advocating the maintenance of cultural differences in spite of the possibility that this may lead to some not achieving the former goal. Bullivant (1981:6) argued that the liberal theory of multiculturalism rests on a fundamental distinction between life styles and life chances: 'The latter has to do with access to power and equality of opportunity, but this fact is obscured by programs that stress life styles'. A limited educational approach that stresses aspects of ethnicity like food, dance, music, religion and cultural artefacts may promote ethnic self-identity and en-hance inter-ethnic curiosity, but it has little to do with migrants' life-chances since it skirts across the issues of the distribution of power and economic aspirations of most migrants. As Jayasuriya (1983:26) has pointed out, 'the legitimate aspirations of migrants as members of minority groups for a share of the resources and social rewards of society at large — the public domain of life — may be impeded by an excessive and exclusive concern with "privatised" aspects of social and cultural life'.

What seems evident is that the idea of equality of opportunity has become a part of the slogan system of the liberal view of multiculturalism. In education, it has come to be used in almost a platitudinous way to suggest that regardless of their background all children should have an equal chance to show what they can achieve in a competitive system. As such, the notion is predicated on the assumption that society will always be based on social differentiation. What is being suggested by the proponents of the liberal view is that the system should give all children an equal chance to be 'successful', first of all in education and then in society at large — that is, all children should have an equal opportunity to be successful. However, the logic of this view also implies that all children have an equal possibility of being a failure. The implicit assumption is, as Tierney (1982:35) has observed, that failure is a permanent possibility in educa-tional and social life. In a society where inequality exists everywhere, the concept of equality of opportunity implies that people should have an equal chance to be unequal. Tierney (1985:35) went on to ask:

If society is differentiated on the basis of power, wealth and education, then how can children coming into the education system from various parts of that differentiated society, ever, as it were, line up equally?

This is liberal multiculturalism's central dilemma. It is a dilemma that is a central theme in the more recent writings on ethnic relations in Australia. It is also central to attempts to reconstruct a new agenda for multiculturalism, both by academic writers and by various departments of education.

New Directions in Multicultural Education

So far in this chapter, some of the problems associated with the liberal theory of multiculturalism have been discussed. And as the Cahill Report found, to a large extent, it was the assumptions underlying this theory that informed much of the practice of multicultural education under the MEP.

However, it should be noted that in schools the commitment to these assumptions was never complete. By the time the Hawke Labor Government was elected in 1983, many schools and state education authorities were already beginning to take some of the criticisms of the liberal theory seriously. Victoria and New South Wales in particular had already set out to revise their multicultural education policies along lines that acknowledged the problematic nature of the notion of ethnicity and stressed equity ahead of issues of the maintenance of cultural traditions.

New Policies

In 1983, the New South Wales Department of Education published its revised Multicultural Education Policy (1983). It rejected the piecemeal incremental approach to multicultural education, which involved only a section of school life, and stressed the need for a *whole-school* response. The whole-school approach implied that multicultural education was relevant to all Australian students, and not just for those from minority ethnic backgrounds. It also meant that all aspects of school life — curriculum, pedagogy, evaluation and organisation — were involved. Multicultural education was seen as a *process* which was appropriate to all school policies and procedures and classroom programs and practices. The New South Wales policy recommended that schools incorporate multicultural perspectives to the curriculum. The process of bringing multicultural perspectives to the curriculum was defined as 'one of incorporating into these policies, practices, programs and experiences, *knowledge* and *attitudes* which reflect the multicultural nature of Australian society' (p. 3). Further, the policy stressed inter-cultural education which involved three interrelated concepts — inter-cultural interaction, communication, and understanding. Inter-cultural education was viewed as

> a process concerned with identifying the ethnic dimension to school life
> and developing skills and attitudes necessary to interact effectively in a
> multicultural society.

The importance of ethnicity was further emphasised in the policy objective of promoting ethnic studies. Rejecting static notions of ethnicity, the policy stressed that an Australian ethnic group was made up of individuals who shared a changing sub-national culture in their lives. While maintaining that ethnicity is an important factor in people's self-identification, the policy warned that 'people have many other overlapping identities such as those related to age, sex, occupation, social class, and place of residence'. The document did not however make it clear how these social categories might relate to each other.

The New South Wales Policy also saw the Teaching of English as a Second Language (TESL) as an important component of multicultural education. It justified TESL on the grounds that it enabled students to build on their 'linguistic and cultural identities' in order 'to foster the development of their self-esteem'. It also advocated the teaching of community languages as 'appropriate means of integrating the experiences of students and the wider community with those of the school'. The teaching of community languages also offered schools the opportunity 'to reflect and respond to the linguistic diversity of the community'.

The New South Wales Multicultural Education Policy statement clearly represented a major advance on the policies and programs which followed Galbally. It rejected simplistic ideas about the role of ethnicity in Australian society and its emphasis on a whole-school approach was clearly appropriate. However, the policy and its accompanying documents remained relatively silent on the issue of how schools might promote equality of outcomes. Its analysis of the links between ethnicity and economic inequalities remained inadequate. Nor did it make the role of ethnicity in Australian political life sufficiently clear. And whatever links it saw between inter-cultural education, ethnic studies, multicultural perspectives, TESL, the teaching of community languages and the principle of equality of opportunity, these remained obscure in the policy documents released.

New Initiatives

Since 1983, the five years of the Hawke Labor Government have seen a number of major developments in the area of multicultural education which, taken together, seem to indicate a policy shift, though the extent to which they have resulted in real changes in school practices remains unclear. First, the federal government's Participation and Equity Program (PEP) encouraged school and state education authorities to explore new directions in multiculturalism in which equity considerations were more directly confronted (see Rizvi and Kemmis, 1987). Second, the 1986 review of Multicultural and Migrant Program and Services (The Jupp Report) returned policy debate in multiculturalism to the concerns of the socially disadvantaged and discriminated against. Third, the establishment of the National Advisory and Consultative Committee on Multicultural Education (NACCME) led to the publication of a series of Research and Discussion Papers which attempted to move multicultural education away from liberal pluralist concerns towards the social-democratic objectives of social justice for disadvantaged ethnic groups. And fourth, the national policy on languages, released in 1987, no longer viewed the teaching of community languages largely as a way of ensuring the maintenance of diverse cultural traditions, but as a way of reconciling a range of demographic, economic and political interests. In the national policy on languages the issues of access to mainstream institutions played an overriding role. The language policy was developed in response to issues of pedagogy and questions of which educational practice was most effective in polyethnic and culturally diverse school populations where inequalities seemed to persist.

When launched in late 1983, the Hawke Government described PEP as the centre-piece of its youth policy. The program had two goals: increasing levels of participation in the post-compulsory years of secondary education; and, ensuring greater equity of outcome. The program stressed the need to link new PEP initiatives with existing programs of reform, including multicultural education. PEP was a school-based program and it enabled many schools throughout Australia to examine their practices and curriculum to see how they related to the principle of equality of outcome. In the process, many schools were able to shift the focuses of their multicultural education activities towards concerns of equity. And in a way, PEP's comprehensive approach to educational reform also provided schools with the opportunity to investigate, with fresh vigour, the possibilities of the whole-school approach to multicultural education. PEP, like other initiatives of the Hawke Labor Government, emphasised the idea of mainstreaming, that is, the view that educational programs should not be implemented through marginal programs, but through all aspects of the school's life: its discourse, practices and organisational forms.

PEP's emphasis on equity parallels the philosophical orientation of the Jupp Report (1986). Its title, *Don't Settle For Less*, is indicative of its emphasis on the equal provision of services to all minority groups. The Jupp Report emphasises political activism with its guiding principle, equitable participation, far removed from the pluralist and cultural maintenance concerns of liberal multiculturalism.

The same political principle has been evident in the numerous discussion and research papers written for NACCME. NACCME was set up by the Hawke Labor Government in 1984 under the chairmanship of Laksiri Jayasuriya. Its brief was to coordinate, monitor and review multicultural education programs and to sponsor information exchange on new developments in this area. NACCME saw these functions in terms of setting a new agenda for multicultural education. Most of the papers it sponsored were written by theorists who had already been identified as critics of the liberal theory of multicultural education. Central to their position was the view that multiculturalism, if it is to be a reforming policy, must incorporate concerns about equity. The revised policy must have a specifically political dimension; it must address issues of the nature and extent of disadvantage in Australian society.

The first NACCME Research Paper written by Jakubowicz (1986) set the tone for the papers that followed. The Jakubowicz paper located ethnicity within the dynamic political and economic context of Australian society, and suggested a view of multicultural education that involves students examining the form and causes of disadvantage in Australian society from a socio-political perspective. Another NACCME paper written by Kalantzis and Cope (1986) contrasted the liberal pluralist view of multiculturalism with what they called 'equitable multiculturalism'. Rejecting the pluralist view, Kalantzis and Cope explored the curriculum implications of equitable multiculturalism. They argued that

cultural variety in Australia needs to be understood both in the context of elements common to us all as humans and the structure and core culture of western industrialism in contemporary Australia.

If multicultural education is about understanding the complexities of Australian society in an effort to make it more socially just, then, they contended that students need to acquire skills of 'social literacy' in order to examine the nature of culture and cultural variety in its political and economic context and actively participate in reconstructing social relations along more equitable lines.

The idea of 'equitable multiculturalism' also appeared as a central theme in Jayasuriya's final NACCME report. The report, *Education in and for a Multicultural Society: Issues and Policies for Policy Making* (1987), argued for a redefinition of the field around four guiding principles — 'equity', 'understanding', 'identity' and 'unity'. These principles were integrated in proposing a comprehensive and coherent educational policy which acknowledged that the simplistic notion of ethnicity as an autonomous category, with which to describe social experience, must be rejected. The report maintained that an assessment of the complex interrelationships between factors such as class, gender, age, ethnicity and race is needed in order to arrive at a more satisfactory account of the reproduction of inequalities. It thus located multicultural education within the broader framework of the contemporary debate over the issue of social justice and the current economic crisis facing Australia.

New Agendas

In such a political climate, disadvantaged minority groups are most at risk. The policy agenda of the NACCME report is based on the premise that in the current restructuring of Australia's economic system ways must be found to protect the needs of the disadvantaged. It thus presented its proposals for multicultural education against a sense of economic realism as well as a commitment to emancipatory values. These proposals included a call for constructing links among emerging curriculum areas, a 'common curriculum' for students, more vigorous efforts to combat racism, teaching the skills that enables students to critically examine the nature and causes of social disadvantage and the cultural practices that help reproduce patterns of inequality, and the targeting of resources to attempt to achieve greater equality of outcome.

In a paper that discussed multiculturalism's emerging agenda, Castles (1987) endorsed many of the themes and proposals contained in the NACCME Report, *Education in and for a Multicultural Society*, which he described as an important contribution to the renovation of multicultural education in Australia. He also argued that, in 1987, multicultural education confronted a new set of problems and challenges to which it must respond. He identified these challenges as:

the changes in the economic situation;
the changes in migration processes and policies;
the realisation of the inappropriateness of the first-generation strategies;
the reappearance of racism in the public domain;
recent academic research showing that the idea of ethnic disadvantage needs to be disaggregated;
the federal Labor government's preparedness to effect substantial cuts to programs and services for ethnic minorities; and
the government's policy of mainstreaming, which implies that new initiatives have to target and receive support from the existing institutions.

Castles argued that the new agenda for multiculturalism should be based around a social-justice approach to the problems facing ethnic minorities. He endorsed the view of Jayasuriya who called for a

> new model of multiculturalism; a minority groups rights model attuned to the needs of the emerging future — to the needs of the second and third generation ethnic minorities, the non-Caucasian groups, the increasingly articulate and militant women, and the ethnic aged. Multiculturalism must be seen as a vehicle of change powered by the ideals of social justice.

Now, while this new agenda seems to point in the right direction, how might schools work towards a view of multicultural education 'powered by the ideals of social justice'? What might be the appropriate strategies? What kind of leadership might we require in order to move schools towards the social transformation that the principle of social justice implies?

In what follows, it will be argued that in order to examine these questions we need to look seriously at the structural features of Australian society and consider the issue of the relationship between schools and society — that is, we need to understand the social role of schooling in Australia. The chances of success of multiculturalism's new agenda are linked significantly, though not entirely, to the extent to which it is possible to effect real changes to the way schools are presently structured and the manner in which we currently conceive the social role of schools.

The Promise of Multiculturalism and the Structure of Schooling

In 1971, Smolicz wrote an influential article called 'Is the Australian School an Assimilative Agency?' The same question could be asked today with every likelihood that the answer would not be any different, even though more than a decade has passed since programs in multicultural education were first introduced to Australian schools. Despite the introduction of many discrete activities in multicultural education, by and large, the structure of Australian schools remains dominated by assumptions that serve the dominant Anglo-Australian group better than minority ethnic groups. So, as the Cahill Report (1984) demonstrated, while a great deal of energy has been expended, the changes have been relatively minor.

Of course, part of the explanation for this lies, as we have already seen, with the problems associated with the liberal formulation of multicultural education. And part of the difficulty lies in the fact that it takes a long time for programs like multicultural education to show results: structural and attitudinal reforms are inevitably slow. It would also be true to claim that despite the rhetoric of whole-school change, activities in multicultural education have been marginal to the mainstream activities of schools. Invariably, these have involved a few dedicated teachers, a few students, a few subject areas and only some school activities, and have not penetrated and affected the structure of schooling. However, the problem of reform in this area has also been due to the fact that insufficient attention has been paid by those proposing various views of multiculturalism to the issue of how, and indeed whether, it might be possible to achieve social change through education.

Schools in Society

The view that schools can in fact have an important role in transforming society has been questioned by a whole range of sociologists and historians of education. Bowles and Gintis (1976), for example, have argued that there is a *correspondence* between the requirements of the capitalist state and the structure and functions of schooling in Western countries. This and other *reproduction* theories of schooling link the form and substance of schooling to the capitalist mode of production. Giroux (1983:263) summarised a reproductive theory as involving the contention that:

> the underlying experience and relations of schooling are animated by the power of the capital to provide different skills, attitudes, and values to students of different classes, races, and genders. In effect, schools mirror not only the social division of labour but also the wider society's class structure.

What is being suggested by reproduction theorists is that schools structure the experiences of teachers and students in such a way as to reflect and recreate the patterns of relationships present in society: its economic structure, its social institutions and its ideological framework. Moreover, schools legitimate the dominant social ideology by fostering among individuals a form of compliant thinking which prevents the formation of critical understandings of social structure among groups of people so that they might mobilise themselves to change existing social conditions. Education systems, in other words, function as an ideological apparatus of the state, serving to maintain the pattern of inequalities existent in capitalist societies. Indeed, given this analysis, multicultural education appears as yet another ideology.

While the reproduction theory of Bowles and Gintis can be criticised for being excessively deterministic — for they seem to deny the very possibility of social change — the insights they provide about the structure of contemporary schools are, nevertheless, useful. They point to the assumptions which underlie the organisation of schools. Research in this area has revealed insights which are most useful in analysing developments in multicultural education. A most penetrating observation resulting from this research has exposed the contradictory nature of schooling's promise and reality. While, on the one hand, schools in Australia have stressed the values of individualism, democracy, creativity and cooperation, a scrutiny of their practices reveals structures that embody contrary values — obedience, bureaucracy, routine and conformity (D'Urso, 1979).

Practices

D'Urso (1974) has illuminated the social role schools plays through covert, and not so covert, messages of the curriculum. It has shown schools to be hierarchical, bureaucratic institutions organised around values that are contrary to the democratic ideals they often profess. More recent work on the curriculum's social role has shown that some of the experiences schools offer students are linked directly to the requirements of capitalist relations. As Giroux (1985) has pointed out, schools foster an ideology which is essential for defusing and obscuring the pattern of structural inequalities. Students are led to compete for limited rewards in a skewed competition that has the appearance of being based on terms that offer each student an equal chance of social rewards, but in reality school creates winners and losers. It seems that despite much talk about equality of opportunity, schools are in fact organised to reinforce political, cultural, social and economic inequalities. Students who cannot respond to a curriculum which teaches middle-class, white, Anglo-Australian and male values are disadvantaged.

While schools emphasise the goal of equality of educational opportunity, many of their practices remain competitive: designed to 'sift and sort'. Although many state departments of education have, in recent years, been experimenting with curriculum diversification, the competitive academic curriculum continues to dominate the experiences of most students. And while such a curriculum may cater adequately for the educational needs of a small minority of students, for most others, schools continue to provide an education which is inappropriate for their needs and interests. For a large number of students, the experience of failure seems inevitable, built into the very structure of schools. For these students schooling represents a system which demands routine, docility and obedience to an externally and hierarchically determined set of rules. Despite major efforts in this area, most schools provide little opportunity for students to have a real say in the educational decision-making that affects them.

It is not only through its curriculum that schooling works to perpetuate inequalities. Bates (1983) has demonstrated how the dominant traditions of theory and practice in educational administration also serve to justify patterns of control in schools and school systems that both mirror and reinforce patterns of inequality in the wider society. He has argued that the selection, organisation and evaluation of much of the knowledge presented in schools results from the demands of bureaucratic convenience, rather than some other rational criteria. Moreover, the bureaucratic structure of schools reflects features of social life in which inequalities play a crucial part. Thus, schools seem to imitate the patterns of dominance and subordination and the displacement of cultural concerns resulting in a tendency to favour the technical. Bureaucratic rationality (see Rizvi, 1986b), a mode of thinking and a way of approaching problems, structures much of the discourse of schools, where communication between teachers, students and parents is often unidirectional and acausal. An administration informed by bureaucratic rationality separates the technical issues of management from issues of culture and values. Such a system of administration lacks the capacity for developing forms of collective action and communal discourse. In it, differences, whether they be cultural or political, are not easily accommodated, except in certain symbolic ways.

These considerations may go some way towards explaining why multicultural education, and indeed many other programs of educational reform, has been unable to make the impact on schools anticipated by its designers. For purposes of convenient management, schools demand uniformity in curriculum and administration, and yet multicultural education emphasises the negotiation of cultural differences. Multicultural education stresses equality of educational opportunity, and yet, as has been shown, school systems are based on the notion of competition in such a way as to institutionalise failure on the part of a large majority of students, especially those who do not belong to the dominant culture. Multicultural education aims at the eradication of all forms of prejudice, and yet a great deal of what is presented as social knowledge in schools rests on a uniform set of assumptions. As Bourdieu and Passeron (1977) have maintained, cultural discrimination takes place in schools because the dominant culture is treated as *the* legitimate culture and all children are treated as if they had equal access to it. Despite its rhetoric about children from different backgrounds who bring different experiences, attitudes and values, contemporary schooling is structured around a set of uniform values. The conclusion which seems to follow from this analysis is that the structure of contemporary schooling conflicts with the key goals of multiculturalism.

Implications

It has been argued that there are a number of fundamental problems with the liberal theory of multiculturalism, and that even if multicultural education is reconstructed along the lines suggested by NACCME and other recent theorists, it is unlikely to lead to the kind of social change they propose. This is because the current structure of our schools does not easily permit social and educational reforms. The bureaucratic rationality that informs the strategies which most schools adopt for the administration of reform programs conflicts with the requirements of change. Where does this leave us?

Clearly, if our preceding arguments are valid, we would need to work on two (not unrelated) fronts. First, we would need revisions to the liberal theory of multiculturalism, which, as a number of authors have pointed out, is predicated upon assumptions about the nature of Australian society and does not question and, thus, legitimates the existing political and economic structure. And it is because of this that, while its rhetoric suggests that it is a reformist policy, multiculturalism has turned out to be an instrument of social control. It has served to defuse and obscure issues of structural inequalities in Australia, arguably the most fundamental problem facing many ethnic and other minority groups. And second, we would need to re-examine the nature of schooling and its social role. Equipped with this understanding we would then be in a better position to say what could be done in schools.

It has to be admitted that schools alone cannot transform the nature of society. However, if we reject the pronouncements of such neo-Marxist writers as Althusser and Bowles and Gintis that schooling inevitably serves the requirements of state capitalism, then it is possible to conceive of an important role for schools in, first, resisting the state's attempts at reproducing the existing social political order and, second, devising a new social role for schools that is more consistent with the ideals of democracy and equality: a role that is specifically educative and related to cultural rather than managerial concerns. Given the fact that in Western democracy schooling faces competing requirements, in order to obtain legitimacy and stability of the current socio-political order and also to afford citizens the right to change the existing social order, it is always possible for schools to exploit this contradiction. They can teach students the critical skills with which to analyse current patterns of social inequalities and develop a moral sense of living in a democratic multicultural society in which the community should be responsive to the needs of all, and not just a privileged few. Schools also need to model democracy: indeed, if the society's reproductive circuit, that functions to perpetuate inequalities, is to be broken the then democratisation of schools would appear to be an urgent task. For it is only by cutting loose from bureaucratic thinking and practices that schools can hope to initiate reforms of lasting significance — be they in the area of multiculturalism or any other.

Democratising Education

Any radical program in multicultural education must include efforts to democratise school practices, for unless schools actually practise democracy, no amount of teaching about ethnic cultures and cultural tolerance can lead students to develop a so-called 'multicultural attitude'. Students will simply 'see through' the contradictions between democratic ideals and undemocratic practices. Equality of opportunity cannot be achieved through schools whose practices remain dominated by the values of conformity and competition on the tacit terms of a set of centrally mandated goals. What then might be involved in democratising schools? Democratisation of schools means, above all, the democratisation of communication and social relations. Decisions about problems and how to solve them must be made on the basis of collective inputs. Decision-making about such matters as knowledge, pedagogy and evaluation must be devolved to the local school level: people should be given an opportunity to 'own' what goes on in schools.

Equality and democracy should be the central moral principles which guide educational action. By equality is not meant equality in the limited sense of equal opportunity through which equal access to goods is offered, but because some arrive at school without the prior training or culture upon which school life is based they have little prospect of successfully utilising these goods. If equality is to have any genuine meaning, social support systems enabling individuals to utilise social goods must exist. And the systems themselves must admit some degree of modification so that ever greater numbers can gain benefits from the goods they have on offer. If social systems are to change, then their possible futures need to be negotiated through democratic action.

However, the view of democracy advocated here is not akin to that involved in the policy of devolution being attempted in some states of Australia. In Victoria, for example, the Ministerial Papers (1984) have legitimated the idea of local decision-making through the work of school councils. The problem with the Victorian experiment is that, not only have the powers given to the school councils been restricted by numerous sets of central guidelines, but also the participation on the so-called 'representative' school councils has been confined to a few, who happen to be mostly male and Anglo. Many NESB parents, often because of language difficulties, have been shown, by a number of studies (e.g. Chapman, 1986) to shy away from such representative politics.

Participation

The view of democracy argued for in this chapter seeks to overcome many of the problems of limited forms of representative democracy identified by a number of social theorists including Pateman (1970), Barber (1984) and Williams (1984). This view, often referred to as 'participatory democracy', involves seeing patterns of relationships in any organisation, including schools, as continuous, reciprocal and involving all participants, not simply the elected elite. This view stresses *educative* aspects of the decision-making processes and involves conceiving of democracy as a total way of life, not simply activities which aim at producing a concrete decision. In this sense, democratisation refers to moving social and organisational life away from that pattern of relationships which involves uni-directional, closed and neutral communication to a way of seeing the human beings with whom we work and live in an open, committed and caring way (for a discussion of the distinction being suggested here, see Noddings, 1985). At a practical level, this view of democracy implies the expansion of public parti-cipation into broader arenas of social decision-making. Intricate forms of decision-making are not needed. Rather, the notion is to engage the community in direct participation whenever and wherever possible. It is to gradually extend the democratic forms we already have. There is no such thing as a 'perfect' democracy; practices and organisations are only more or less democratic. The extent to which practices are democratically organised is always a matter of judgment.

If this view of democracy is accepted, then the issues of the form of schooling that meets the needs of English and non-English-speaking Australian students equally must be brought, as far as practicable, to the local level: not in terms of a policy, externally devised and implemented but as a principle ex-plored, negotiated and tested for meaning and significance in the concrete circumstances in which people find themselves.

This conclusion suggests that we revise radically some of the practices that have developed around the notion of multicultural education. Multicultural education would no longer be a policy to be implemented, but a set of prac-tices that define certain forms of relationships within the school community.

Multiculturalism must be seen as being concerned with the entire range of practices that involve intercultural communication and understanding in people's lives, not simply an emphasis on ethnic histories, customs, religion, music and languages, as it seems to have become in many schools. Arguably, the current programs in multicultural education have led to a celebration of differences. The assumption has been that if people of different cultures know about each others' backgrounds then intercultural harmony will follow. It has been shown earlier how this assumption is mistaken. The common experiences and similarities across cultures are more profound than differences. And in a school committed to democracy, it is these similarities which ought to be the basis for further communication and dialogue. The experience of migration itself, of the way Australian institutions do and do not accommodate minorities and the way power operates in this country, could provide immediate starting points for ongoing dialogue. Cultures should not be seen as static, but as dynamic, constantly changing in response to the input of new ideas, the revision of old beliefs, the construction of new theories and the alteration of old practices. The emphasis should be on cultures being formed and reformed through what Walker (1987) has referred to as 'inter-cultural articulation'.

Given this emphasis on the need to begin with common concrete experiences to facilitate intercultural understanding, schools do not need definitive, centrally approved definitions of such terms as 'justice' or 'equality of educational opportunity' before they can apply these ideas to understand the nature of disadvantage in particular contexts. Many students belong to minority groups and their teachers already know a great deal about how material injustices and inequalities actually manifest themselves and what implications they have for educational opportunities. People who live them already know a great deal about poverty, long-term unemployment, indignity and the other manifestations of social injustice. This knowledge should be utilised more fully than it has been in schools, which often pretend that these problems do not exist. If multiculturalism is to mean anything then these experiences should be the focus of educational attention, and not reified cultural artifacts.

So instead of looking for abstract definitions, the focus of our attention should be on actual instances of injustices and on issues of how to oppose their reproduction through schooling rather than on some general definition of social justice for disadvantaged students. For one thing, such a definition may not be available. And, indeed, as the philosopher MacIntyre (1981:235) shows in his book, *After Virtue*, our society cannot hope to achieve moral consensus and that there are 'rival conceptions of justice formed by and informing the life of rival groups'. And for another, the discussion of terms such as 'equality', at this level, does not necessarily provide imperatives for action beyond such generalities as become encapsulated in such catch-cries as equal opportunities, outcomes and so on. We would be better employed to think about how it might be possible for schools to create conditions in which communities could negotiate what, for them, constitutes an injustice in their actual concrete circumstances.

In educational contexts, we could begin by investigating the actual circumstances in which students live and then proceed to examine how schools might have failed to take account of the facts of student lives and how they might implicitly contribute to the reproduction of social, political and economic injustices. It is only as a result of this kind of detailed collaborative research that we can find out how some groups of students do not get equal access to quality education and how, and possibly why, outcomes of schooling are unequally distributed.

Educative Leadership and Democratic Schools

What role might educative leadership have in a democratic school in which responsibility for initiating reforms would rest on its entire educational community? The democratisation thesis presented in this chapter would seem to suggest that a certain tension exists between the ideas of leadership and democracy. For after all, the traditional notions of leadership embody values of hierarchical authority and centralised power, while the concept of democracy highlights collaborative, caring and reciprocal relationships.

The way out of this dilemma is to deny the applicability, and desirability, of the traditional notions of administrative leadership in educational contexts. Watkins (1986) and Foster (1986) have demonstrated how much of the recent writings on educational leadership have been dominated by literature borrowed from management theory. They argue that leadership in education should be based on specifically educational criteria, rather than forms of technical/ managerialism that seem to have dominated thinking about educational adminis- tration. In schools committed to democracy, educative leadership should be seen as located neither in individuals nor in institutional positions, but in particular acts which serve to bring people together and make the possibility of inter- cultural understanding greater. Thus viewed, leadership may originate with any person within a community, and not just those who have been officially desig- nated as 'leaders'.

In our present context, however, principals would appear to be in the best position to offer educative leadership. Not only have they been mandated by the state for this responsibility, but also they are in an ideal position to overview the entire range of schools' activities and from that strategic vantage point can explore the possibilities for educative democratic action. This is consistent with the idea of collective leadership and individuals exercising initiatives that meet with group approval. Educative leadership may involve a whole host of initiat- ives or it may simply be one single act. The point here is that, apart from references to specific contexts, it may not be possible to determine what counts as a leadership act.

No set of traits or qualities can be prejudged as constituting educative leadership. The judgments we make about what is and is not 'educative leader- ship' are something that are subject to negotiation. This applies to all value judgments. The form of leadership required in particular circumstances, and fulfilment of particular goals, is always a matter of historical contingency. Thus, the most desirable form of educative leadership in our multicultural society is linked to a particular understanding of the cultural, political and economic developments currently taking place in Australia. Also, these suggestions are made against a set of theories about processes of social life generally, and social experiences in Australian schools in particular. In short, the view of educative leadership in a multicultural society presented here is historically specific.

In a democratic multicultural school, educative leadership should, above all, attempt to create conditions that enable school communities to collabor- atively understand, and hopefully oppose, the construction and maintenance of inequalities evident in their rituals, myths, traditions and practices. Ways must be found of challenging and, in time, replacing the bureaucratic and meritocratic ideology which has saturated the logic of schooling and school system, for if the argument in this chapter is valid, then it is this assimilatory logic that makes any radical program of educational reform extremely difficult to implement.

Clearly, for teachers, most of the action has to be at the local school and community level where students and teachers encounter injustices most directly. And it is here that a program of reform has most relevance and the greatest chance of success. The point, and the remarks about the need for greater participatory democracy in schools, should not, however, be seen as advocating some form of 'romantic localism'. We have to explore both the internal and external conditions that need to be created to enable the democratisation of schools, and thus facilitate the implementation of a more radical policy of multiculturalism than has henceforth been possible.

There is clearly an important role for governments and other decision-making agencies at a variety of other levels in our political system. However, the role of these bodies in redressing injustice is not at all easy to define. Certainly, political decisions that might result in a more equitable redistribution of general educational resources and provision of special funds for local initiatives would enhance the possibilities of reform. But equally, tightly monitored educational and political expectations of schools could also limit their capacity to initiate reforms which respond to locally articulated needs.

There also remains considerable tension between what is centrally pre-scribed and what actually happens as a result of local interpretations of policy guidelines. In Australian education, many centrally guided programs, like PEP, have had to be implemented to mesh in with local priorities, but the relationship between local and central priorities is never easy to define. To begin to under-stand these issues, we need to analyse the kind of pressures teachers work under and the kind of skills teachers need to 'run with the centrally prescribed pro-grams'. The social-psychology of the implementation process needs to be understood. But beyond this, the central administration still has the conceptual problem of when to intervene and how much latitude to afford to schools to learn from their errors.

To overcome the deficiencies of the centre-periphery model of educational reform, a more widespread initiative is required than those that have been tried in Australia since the first Karmel Report in 1973. Yet, it is improbable that in the present economic climate the funds needed for comprehensive programs of reform are likely to be made available. However, with only limited funds available the best option may be for teachers to reconsider their goals, pedago-gies and the structure of their schools, thus raising the parents' awareness of the present situation and giving students greater reflective and critical skills so that local initiatives can begin to address many of the more deeply rooted problems that children from minority groups face in schools. A policy most likely to meet the needs of NESB students that might also have some chance of success should perhaps best have its focus *in* schools and the lives of those who inhabit them and *on* things that teachers and administrators *do* and *think*. To a great extent PEP was moving in this direction, and the momentum it created needs to be harnessed.

Towards a Critical Interculturalism

The central task should be to reorientate *process* and *practice* so that notions of fairness, justice and equity become more important elements in our discourse about education and serve as criteria against which the success of schooling is judged. It is clear that the technical-managerial language in which much of education is discussed eschews issues of morality such as those involved in the policy of multiculturalism. We need to make moral discourse in schools respectable again. Only when this is done can we begin to make the more radical goals of multiculturalism a matter of important concern for all those who work in schools. As Hugh Stretton (1987:214) has recently pointed out, we should

> try, against fearful odds to reform the moral education, the technical training, the methodological self-knowledge and the hiring bias of our economists.

The same applies to teachers. They too need to become more proficient in discussions of social values and how they relate to education. It is only when they are able to identify instances of moral problems that teachers and other members of school communities can be expected to see how particular social arrangements embody serious inequalities that serve some of their students better than others, and how injustices may be built into the very logic of schooling. Of course, such 'self-knowledge' does not ensure greater equality or justice in society but it does go some way towards regenerating those traditions in which issues of morality, and more enlightened patterns of social life in and outside schools, are constantly and actively negotiated.

The issue of the education of teachers should be more seriously looked at. We need to ensure that not only are teachers being given skills of critical social and moral thinking but that they are also being adequately prepared to work in culturally diverse classrooms. As has already been shown, it requires particular moral sensitivities as well as a theoretical knowledge of how social institutions work to detect instances of racism that may be a source of many of the problems NESB children have. Many teachers in Australia, it seems, find any discussion of racism irrelevant and uncomfortable. For them and others in schools, there should be regular in-service courses whose purpose it is to examine the nature of institutional racism — that is to say, the form of discrimination established in the very assumptions upon which schools are organised.

Teaching remains a predominantly middle-class Anglo-Australian profession. Government departments of education could make greater efforts to attract bilingual and bicultural teachers who have had direct experiences of migration and intercultural communication. Many traditional schools are characterised by unidirectional discourse, where teachers are expected to 'impart' knowledge and culture to students. In democratic schools, educative leadership should involve the creation of structures that facilitate forms of multi-directional communication that are open and caring, enabling students, teachers and parents to share and test their cultural experiences against each other in an effort to actively construct new, more equal and fair cultural arrangements. Traditionally, teachers have viewed their role as being to educate students only. Perhaps, they should view it in broader terms to include the education of communities, to prepare parents and students so that all members of a community can take an active part in the life of a democratic school.

To facilitate intercultural understanding, educative leadership in a multicultural society must involve the establishment of closer links between the school and the community, between the teachers, pupils, non-teaching staff and the community outside, the parents, voluntary groups and official organisations. There must be a practical willingness to work with those who have criticisms of the system of schooling. Parents must not only be invited but also challenged to observe and critically debate the cultural processes operating in schools with teachers and students and each other. Parents should not only know about the content of the curriculum but should also contribute to it. Schools should use the knowledge and expertise of the community to the full.

Home-school communication is essential if we are to avoid the mistake of assuming stereotyped knowledge about the cultures and expectations of people from non-English-speaking backgrounds. School experience is so often based on assumptions which are seldom explored. Working with a particular model of a disadvantaged school in schools with a large proportion of NESB children, for example, some teachers may view their work more in a social-pastoral context rather than a skill- and knowledge-orientated one. They might believe that schools for the 'disadvantaged' are not places where high academic achievement can be expected. But here teachers' views may actually conflict with the expectations of parents for a vocationally useful academic knowledge. These problems can be a source of considerable anxiety, and the mismatch between school and home expectations can often result in a process of 'blaming each other'. Parents may wish for a traditional academic curriculum as a way of taking advantage of an education system which appears to offer social and economic rewards, while teachers may believe that such rewards are highly unlikely for any more than a small proportion of the students. Teachers may prefer to offer students a more 'relevant' curriculum, often dashing the aspirations of some parents. Conflicts such as this can be avoided if there is a greater input from the parents into curriculum decision-making, and a greater effort from the teachers to explain why they believe a competitive academic curriculum is not in the interests of all students.

There are no easy solutions to the problems and tensions that often exist between homes and schools in a multicultural society. The only practical option that is also fair to all parties would appear to be greater communication. And yet many of our schools presently lack structures that could be used to explain to parents why in the present economic and political context, promises of 'equal opportunity for all' are not possible in practice, and to discuss with them why the traditional academic curriculum may not be appropriate for all children in the technological society of the future. There is far too little exchange of ideas and educational debate in our school communities. Such debate would appear to be important in all schools, but especially in those ethnically diverse schools where chances of confusion about cultural expectations would seem to be very great.

The role of educative leadership in encouraging greater communication between cultures and between home and school is profound. Schools are sites where Australian culture is being constantly negotiated. They should also be places where traditions are critically examined and where all forms of discrimination, long entrenched cultural practices, no matter what their origin, are opposed in an effort to develop a more just society. In a democratic school, educative leadership should anticipate opportunities that may be utilised for teachers, parents and students to learn about different beliefs, values and traditions. Educative leadership should also involve the teaching of skills of analysis and criticism, as well as democratic practice, not only to the students but to the community generally. Schools alone cannot transform Australian society, but in order to develop an equitable multicultural society they can begin to educate citizens who are capable of clarifying misconceptions, challenging entrenched views and constantly seeking new solutions to the problems of creating a more socially just society.

Lead Author's Postscript, 1990

The preceding chapter was written in May 1987. Much has happened in the intervening period. My own thinking on the political and educational issues explored above has also developed. However, while I would now write the chapter in a very different way, I continue to subscribe to the main threads of the argument presented.

I remain convinced that the 'liberal' theory of multiculturalism is fundamentally flawed, and that a new approach is needed to address the issues of cultural diversity in schools and society. I still maintain that a policy of multiculturalism that takes the principle of social justice seriously must place democratisation of institutions at the centre of its concerns. A radical view of educative leadership in a multicultural society must, therefore, involve the creation of opportunities through which to facilitate 'inter-cultural articulation'. Ethnicity must be seen as a dynamic force, which is constantly changing in the emerging socio-political contexts, and which works in contingent ways with a variety of other social structures. I see schools as sites of both production and reproduction of culture, where educative leadership must ideally involve an understanding of the processes of change through which genuine equality between groups can be achieved.

Perhaps the most significant and relevant event that has occurred in Australia since 1987 has been Bicentenary celebrations in 1988. The Bicentenary brought the issues explored in this essay into a sharper focus. It provided an opportunity for the nation to explore the various contradictions that beset the policy of multiculturalism. In such an exploration, it became increasingly evident that the 'liberal' view of multiculturalism remained trapped within the contradictions of its two main thrusts: its sponsorship of ethnic politics and change, on the one hand; and ethnic pluralism and maintenance of the status quo, on the other. The tensions between its principles of maintenance of cultural identity, equality of opportunity and social cohesion also remained unresolved. Nor could the issue of the place of the specific and prior claims to Aboriginal land rights be accommodated with the framework of a policy that stressed equality of opportunity for all groups. As Castles *et al.* (1988:148) have pointed out, for Aboriginal people:

the Bicentenary became a lost cause. It changed from something with potential meaning to a public relations exercise.

The culture that the Bicentenary celebrated belonged to the white Anglo middle-class men, operating with a concept of the nation that was both ideological and exclusionary.

The cynicism thus generated resulted most evidently in the way many Australians withdrew their commitment from the policy of multiculturalism. Fitzgerald (1988:30) reported that few Australians understood what multiculturalism meant, and many who did, saw it as a social policy that promoted:

> community division and racial tension at the expense of our cultural heritage and national security.

Partly in response to these emerging sentiments, the Office of Multicultural Affairs released, in 1989, the *National Agenda for a Multicultural Australia*. This publication attempted to provide a more accurate definition of multiculturalism. But this definition did little to resolve the contradictions of multiculturalism identified above. It stressed the principles of cultural identity, social justice and economic efficiency, but exactly how these were to relate to each other was an issue that was left unexplored. The focus on economic efficiency, moreover, implied an instrumentalist politics which is fundamentally at odds with the view of educative leadership presented above.

References

AUSTRALIAN ETHNIC AFFAIRS COUNCIL (1977) *Australia as a Multicultural Society*, Canberra: Australian Government Publishing Service.

BARBER, B. (1984) *Strong Democracy*, Berkeley, CA: University of California Press.

BARTH, F. (Ed.) (1969) *Ethnic Groups and Boundaries: The Social Organization of Cultural Difference*, London: Allen and Unwin.

BATES, R.J. (1984) *Educational Administration and the Management of Knowledge*, Geelong: Deakin University.

BOSTOCK, W. (1981) *Alternatives of Ethnicity*, Melbourne: Corvus.

BOURDIEU, P. and PASSERON, J.C. (1977) *Reproduction in Education and Culture*, Sage: London.

BOWLES, S. and GINTIS, H. (1976) *Schooling in Capitalist America*, New York: Basic Books.

BULLIVANT, B. (1981) *The Pluralist Dilemma in Education: Six Case Studies*, Sydney: Allen and Unwin.

CAHILL REPORT (1984) *Review of the Multicultural Education Program*, Canberra: Commonwealth Schools Commission.

CASTLES, S. (1987) 'A New Agenda for Multiculturalism', paper presented at the conference, *Whither Multiculturalism?* La Trobe University, April.

CASTLES, S., KALANTZIS, M., COPE, B. and MORRISSEY, M. (1988) *Mistaken Identity*, Sydney: Pluto Press.

CASTLES, S. and KOSACK, G. (1973) *Immigrant Workers and Class Structure in Western Europe*, London: Oxford University Press.

CHAPMAN, I. (1986) 'The menace of multiculturalism', *Quadrant*, **24**, 10, 3–6.

CONNELL, R.W. (1977) *Ruling Class, Ruling Culture*, Cambridge: Cambridge University Press.

DE LEPERVANCHE, M. (1980) 'From race to ethnicity', *The Australian and New Zealand Journal of Sociology*, **16**, 1, 24–37.

DE LEPERVANCHE, M. (1984) 'Migrants and ethnic groups', in ENCEL, S. and BRYSON, L. (Eds) *Australian Society*, fourth edition, Melbourne: Longman-Cheshire.

D'URSO, S. (1974) 'Hidden realities within schooling', *Australian Journal of Social Issues*, **9**, 2, 108–17.

EDUCATION DEPARTMENT OF VICTORIA (1983) *Ministerial Papers Nos. 1–4*, Melbourne: Education Department.

FITZGERALD REPORT (1988) *Immigration: A Commitment to Australia*, Canberra: AGPS.

FOSTER, L.E. (1981) *Australian Education: A Sociological Perspective*, Sydney: Prentice-Hall.

FOSTER, L.E. and STOCKLEY, D. (1984) *Multiculturalism: The Changing Australian Paradigm*, Melbourne: Multilingual Matters.

FOSTER, W. (1986) *The Reconstruction of Leadership*, Geelong: Deakin University.

GALBALLY REPORT (1978) *Report of the Review of Post-Arrival Program and Services for Migrants, Migrant Services and Programs, Vol. 1*, Canberra: The Australian Government Publishing Service.

GIROUX, H. (1983) *Theory and Resistance in Education: A Pedagogy for the Opposition*, South Hadley, MA: Bergin and Garvey.

GLAZER, N. and MOYNIHAN (1970) *Beyond the Melting Pot*, Cambridge, MA: MIT Press.

GRASSBY, A.J. (1973) *A Multicultural Society for the Future*, Canberra: Australian Government Publishing Service.

HALL, S. (1980) 'Teaching race', *Multiracial Education*, **9**, 1.

HANNAN, L. (1983) 'Problems and issues for teachers making decisions on curriculum', in FALK, B. and HARRIS, J. (Eds) *Unity and Diversity: Multicultural Education in Australia*, Melbourne: The Australian College of Education.

ISAACS, E. (1976) *Greek Children in Sydney*, Canberra: ANU Press.

JAKUBOWICZ, A. (1981) 'State and ethnicity: Multiculturalism as ideology', *The Australian and New Zealand Journal of Sociology*, **17**, 3, 4–13.

JAKUBOWICZ, A. (1981) 'Multiculturalism and education', *NACCME Research Paper No. 1*.

JAYASURIYA, L. (1983) 'The facts, policies and rhetoric of multiculturalism', *Australian Society*, **2**, 6, 23–7.

JAYASURIYA, L. (1987) *Education in and for a Multicultural Society: Issues and Policies for Policy Making, NACCME Final Report*.

JUPP, J. (1966) *Arrivals and Departures*, Melbourne: Cheshire-Lansdowne.

JUPP REPORT (1986) *Don't Settle for Less*, Canberra: Australian Government Publishing Service.

KALANTZIS, M. and COPE, B. (1984) 'Multiculturalism and educational policy', in BOTTOMLEY, G. and DE LEPERVANCHE, M. (Eds) *Ethnicity and Gender in Australia*, Sydney: George Allen and Unwin.

KALANTZIS, M. and COPE, B. (1986) 'Pluralism and equitability: Multicultural curriculum strategies for schools', *NACCME Research Paper No. 3*.

KALDOR REPORT (1981) *Australian Ethnic Affairs Council Committee on Multicultural Education, Perspectives on Multicultural Education*, Canberra: Australian Government Publishing Service.

KEDDIE, N. (1973) *Tinker, Tailor . . . The Myth of Cultural Deprivation*, Penguin: London.

KNOPFELMACHER, F. (1982) 'The case against multiculturalism', in MANNE, R. (Ed.) *The New Conservatism in Australia*, Melbourne: Oxford University Press.

LIPPMAN, L. (1977) *The Aim is Understanding: Educational Techniques for a Multicultural Society*, Sydney: ANZ Book Co.

LIPPMAN, L. (1981) 'Multicultural society and its implication for education', in SHERWOOD, J. (Ed.) *Multicultural Education: Issues and Innovations*, Perth: Creative Press.

MACINTYRE, A. (1981) *After Virtue: A Study in Moral Theory*, London: Duckworth.

MARTIN, J. (1972) *Community and Identity: Refugee Groups in Adelaide*, Canberra: ANU Press.

MARTIN, J. (1978) *The Migrant Presence*, Sydney: George Allen and Unwin.

MILES, R. (1982) *Racism and Migrant Labour,* London: Routledge and Kegan Paul.

MILL, J.S. (1859) *On Liberty,* 1972 edition, London: J.M. Dent.

MULLARD, C. (1982) 'Approaches to multicultural education', in TIERNEY, J. (Ed.) *Race, Migration and Schooling,* London: Holt, Rinehart and Winston.

NEW SOUTH WALES DEPARTMENT OF EDUCATION (1983) *Multicultural Education Policy Statement*, Sydney: New South Wales Department of Education.

NODDINGS, N. (1985) *Caring*, Berkeley, CA: University of California Press.

OFFICE OF MULTICULTURAL AFFAIRS (1989) *National Agenda for a Multicultural Australia*, Canberra: AGPS.

PATEMAN, C. (1970) *Participation and Democratic Theory*, Cambridge: Cambridge University Press.

RIZVI, F.A. (1985) *Multiculturalism as an Educational Policy*, Geelong: Deakin University.

RIZVI, F.A. (1986a) *Ethnicity, Class and Multicultural Education*, Geelong: Deakin University.

RIZVI, F.A. (1986b) *Administrative Leadership and the Democratic Community as a Social Ideal*, Geelong: Deakin University.

RIZVI, F.A. and KEMMIS, S. (1988) *Dilemmas of Reform: Participation and Equity Program in Victorian Schools*, Geelong: Deakin Institute for Studies in Education.

SPEARS, A.K. (1978) 'Institutionalized racism and the education of blacks', *Anthropology and Education Quarterly,* **9**, 2, 219–39.

SMOLICZ, J.J. (1977) *Culture and Education in a Plural Society,* Canberra: Curriculum Development Centre.

SMOLICZ, J.J. (1984) 'Ethnic identity in Australia: Cohesive or divisive', in PHILLIPS, D.J. and HOUSTON, J. (Eds) *Australian Multicultural Society: Identity, Communication and Decision-Making,* Melbourne: Drummond.

STEINBERG, S. (1981) *The Ethnic Myth*, New York: Atheneum.

STRETTON, H. (1987) *Political Essays,* Melbourne: Drummond.

SYER, M. (1982) 'Racism, ways of thinking and school', in TIERNEY, J. (Ed.) *Race, Migration and Schooling,* London: Holt, Rinehart and Winston.

TIERNEY, J. (1982) 'Race, colonialism and migration', in TIERNEY, J. (Ed.) *Race, Migration and Schooling,* London: Holt, Rinehart and Winston.

VAN DEN BERGHE, P. (1981) *The Ethnic Phenomenon*, New York: Elsevier.

WALKER, J. (1987) *Educative Leadership and Curriculum Development*, Canberra: ACT Schools Authority.

WATKINS, P. (1986) *A Critical Review of Leadership Concepts and Research*, Geelong: Deakin University.

WILLIAMS, R. (1984) *Towards 2000*, London: Chatto and Windus.

WOOD, G.H. (1984) 'Schooling in a democracy: Transformation or reproduction?', *Educational Theory,* **34**, 3.

ZUBRZYCKI REPORT (1982) *Australian Council of Population and Ethnic Affairs, Multiculturalism for all Australians*, Canberra: Australian Government Publishing Service.

Chapter 7

A Practical Theory of Educative Leadership

P.A. Duignan and R.J.S. Macpherson

Introduction

This chapter develops a practical theory of educative leadership by conducting an ideas audit of the preceding chapters. It relies on a theme search to determine the structure of an appropriate argument. It also uses the emergent concepts and themes to test and develop the web of belief that the writers set out in Chapter 1. This process of theory construction was informed by the responses of over one thousand educational practitioners in various international workshops and conferences, and by the work of other theorists, especially the philosophical research program of Christopher Hodgkinson (1978; 1981; 1983; 1986).

New data and guidance on educative leadership are provided in Chapters 2 to 6. In Chapter 2, for example, it is argued that consequentialism which gives priority to the rights of clients should be the moral touchstone of any practical theory. A process and criteria for the creation and testing of trustworthy knowledge about educative leadership is developed in Chapter 3. Similarly, in Chapter 4, it is suggested that an effective theory should feature holistic constructivism and encompass all components of the administrative process, while in Chapters 5 and 6 it is demonstrated that the theory should interpret activity equally well at societal, systemic, institutional and team leadership levels.

Consistent with the design principles of the ELP, we grounded the analysis in the 'real world' of practice. We therefore begin by describing the metaphysics explicit in the arguments of Chapters 1–6, that is, the fundamental structure of thinking about the realities of educative leadership.

Realities

The exemplary practitioners and theorists involved in the ELP appear to integrate three major ways of seeing educative leadership; as an activity conducted in a material world, as cultural agency in a social world, and as reflective practice in an abstract realm of ideas, much as proposed by Hodgkinson (1979; 1981).

To be more specific, the first reality is the practical reality of physical behaviours and outcomes; reality as things. Seeing this world accurately usually means drawing on the traditions of the 'hard sciences' to invoke the knowledge system of empiricism. When Pettit *et al.* above discuss the econo-political context of rationalisation, for example, they demonstrate that education is partly but undeniably located in the realm of facts and material resources.

There are many reminders that educative leaders serve in a mechanistic and deterministic world of cause and effect. When Walker *et al.* discuss value orientations in curricula, they remind us that

> there is a real world out there which is ... the objective origin of the
> problems which our theories, methodologies and values are addressing.

They also argue that the appropriate level for effective action and decision making in curriculum matters is an empirical question which can be answered only by a careful analysis of the specific situation i.e. a situational analysis. Rizvi *et al.* remind us that disadvantage, racism and unequal powers are empirical realities in society and in education. The value of traditional scientific inquiry and explanation in this rational and material realm is therefore unquestioned. The better the explanations in this realm, the better it is for all in education in consequential and materialistic senses.

The second reality identified is the more arbitrary, estimated and probable social world that is appropriately and typically investigated by the qualitative methodologies of the social sciences. As the constructivist approach to improving the quality of teaching developed by Northfield *et al.* shows, the realities that count here are socially constructed, renegotiated and changed.

A major feature of thinking in this manner about reality is that there are degrees of freedom and partial definitions in use, despite the apparent rationality evident in the language used during interaction. Meanings generated to provide touchstone, as Walker *et al.* show, are shared and temporary social artefacts, not the facts of empiricism; however real they appear at the time or whatever their tangible impact.

The third way of understanding reality is to see it as a feature of personal experience (Greenfield, 1975; 1988). This was particularly evident when practitioners were writing and discussing case study materials. No less significant to them than the material and social realms they worked in, all involved in the ELP attested to the richness of their own phenomenological world; they spoke about imagining, valuing, speculating about and reflecting on educative leadership.

It was consistently reported by them, and evident in the chapters above, that this internal realm has distinct features. It is the mode of individual knowing that is potentially creative, free and voluntary. In Chapter 1 it is recommended as a way of seeing alternative realities of educative leadership; to inject excitement into routines, to create openness for negative feedback, and to question the continued appropriateness of organisational norms. Its value is demonstrated in Rizvi *et al.*'s argument about educative leaders helping a school's community to become aware of and to challenge anti-educative norms in society.

The differences between these three ways of thinking is a matter of some interest. In general terms, it is clear that the conceptual building blocks in the first material realm are 'things.' And while the key concepts in the second social world are cultural artefacts, the third personal and abstract world is built with ideas.

Each of these interconnected knowledge systems serve educative leaders in very important ways. Evers *et al.* and Pettit *et al.* argue that the 'facts of the matter,' as far as they can be determined, especially about consequences, are needed to provide external coherence to a policy proposal. Walker *et al.* show that multiple vertical and horizontal negotiating structures can strengthen the internal coherence and comprehensiveness of a curriculum policy proposal. Northfield *et al.* demonstrate that reflection on practice is an essential condition of professional development, while Rizvi *et al.* and Evers *et al.* also show that a philosophical attitude is a precursor to an educative praxis; the Aristotelian condition where practice and critical reflection are integrated.

> *Given the equally vital role played by each of these ways of thinking about the reality of educative leadership, we searched the arguments in earlier chapters for evidence of generative conditions.*
> *The findings were unequivocal:*
>> *the realm of ideas is evoked by reflection when people become concerned about what is right and what is significant for clients in education;*
>> *the social world of cultural elaboration is created by interaction when people become concerned about the alignment between new policy and the current meanings given to social reality, and about the legitimacy of their practices; and*
>> *the material world of things is generated by the reification of experience and its reduction to facts and figures, usually so that determined action can occur and be evaluated.*

These realisations about ways of thinking about educative leadership, their generative conditions and their unique forms of contribution have become major components of our web of belief. Each of these three components is now developed in detail.

The Realm of Ideas

In Chapter 1 it was argued that the two most difficult questions outstanding in educational administration are:

> *How will leaders in education know they are morally right when they act?*
> *How should they decide what is important?*

These questions concerning *values* and *significance* can now be attended to.

Values

The commonalities between the chapters above vastly outweigh the differences on the matter of an appropriate moral code for educative leaders. Evers *et al.*

provide the criteria by which educative leaders should be judged. It is important to note, we believe, that they identify neither principles nor consensus but consequentialism as the most educative approach to making judgments.

The specific criteria for consequentialism are identified in Chapter 2 and can be summarised here as questions; are the following ingredients — research, problem-solving, diversity, participation, criticism and reflection on practice — valued in the growth of knowledge, and, do the judgments made by leaders also contribute to long-term learning by clients, teachers and leaders?

In Chapter 3, Walker *et al.* apply this educative morality to curriculum development. Having spelled out the many values' orientations in curriculum, they then offer educative leaders a means of meeting Evers' moral criteria for responsible leadership in a plural context; the process of finding touchstone. In this regard, Rizvi *et al.* give high priority to the democratisation of communications and processes through which diverse learning communities negotiate organisational cultures and policies. Similarly, in Chapter 4, Northfield *et al.* recognise the plural expectations on teachers and recommend a constructivist approach to policy making in supportive social groups. These approaches are ways of finding touchstone.

However, to ensure there is external coherence to policy, double loop learning is also essential. Both the appropriateness of negotiated norms and the processes of touchstone in use must be regularly questioned to ensure that the prior rights of clients are respected. Walker *et al.* provide for this questioning by advocating multiple vertical and horizontal negotiating structures. Pettit *et al.* emphasise the importance of multiple links between planning and participatory processes to articulate priorities during rationalisation, but also to ensure that emerging agreements cohere with systemic and societal perspectives. An educative leader must accept responsibility for nurturing and protecting double loop learning.

> *To summarise the component of our web of belief concerned with appropriate values for educative leaders, we recommend:*
> > *consequentialism, specified as a concern for both the outcomes of learning and for responsiveness to clients' interests; and*
> > *that this concern be operationalised by the use of particular pragmatic processes and be evident as outcomes — touchstone and double loop learning.*

Significance

Taken as a whole, the evidence of the chapters above is that educative leaders should give balanced attention to a range of concerns across the three realms of ideas, culture and things. Walker *et al.* relate theories of knowledge to learning theories, and, via the social processes of touchstone, attend to the pragmatics of managing the trials of practical action. Pettit *et al.* use competing theories from political science to develop a practical strategy for managing rationalisation that integrates systematic planning with participation by stakeholders. They call for a responsible involvement by educative leaders in the politics of education; the articulation of interests and the process of distributing scarce societal resources in education.

The point here is that educative leaders appear to be successful in the abstractions of philosophy, adept in strategic appraisal and long-term planning, comfortable with political processes, able to inspire commitment to core values, and yet provide supportive and effective management techniques so that agreed aims are realised. This finding highlights the importance of strategic appraisal, that is, linking core values to what is achievable in a context of material and social contingencies. The crucial role of research, trustworthy information, and the rational analysis of options and likely consequences, is, therefore, apparent.

The importance of educative leaders facilitating the strategic evaluation of team, institutional and systemic development is also evident. The educative ideal is to have balanced attention given to the imperatives of each realm so that as many organisational members as possible fully participate in, and therefore understand, all components of policy making and implementation. This ideal appears achievable. Northfield *et al.* show how professionals can acquire a knowledge of and help improve teaching and learning through participation in team leadership in a supportive social group. Rizvi *et al.* argue for even wider empowerment through public participation in the broader questions and arenas of social decision making.

However, rather than partition knowledge about how groups, institutions and systems operate and evolve in social contexts, the scope and themes of the chapters above point to the need for a shared and more holistic perspective on change. We therefore argue that educative leaders should help balance the significance attributed to the realm of ideas (axiological and strategic appraisal), the realm of culture (social meanings and legitimacy), and the realm of things (management and the technologies of supporting and evaluating professional practice).

To summarise, strategic educative leadership provides crucial linkages between the production and value-based selection of significant ideas, and the cultural processes whereby they are transformed into taken-for-granted knowledge about structures and proper practices.

Simultaneously, strategic educative leadership generates double loop learning about both the significance of ideas in terms of consequences, and the appropriateness of the leadership services that the team, institution or system is experiencing.

The Realm of Culture

In all of the chapters above we note that there comes a phase in policy development and implementation when valued and significant but abstract concepts leave the realm of ideas and become cultural artefacts. We also note two general forms of activity concerned with the cultural elaboration of a policy; the realignment of meanings given to social reality, and the legitimation of changed professional practices. They can now be detailed.

The Realignment of Social Reality

There are many examples in the chapters above where the arts of diplomacy, explanation and articulation challenge taken-for-granted collective wisdom and language about what is significant and right in education. In our view, the challenge for educative leaders during this phase is to help achieve a new consensus about professional and collective identity, practices and consequences for clients. The standard phases can be described.

For a period, the meanings attributed to organisation and to professional self are destabilised. The ideals, beliefs, shared meanings and expectations, and their embodiment in symbolic devices, such as myths, rituals, ceremonies, stories, legends, jargon, customs, habits and traditions, lose coherence. As Pettit *et al.* point out, it can be a traumatic time for individuals. The standard patterns of relationships and practices and the symbolism of valued self and service fall apart. As social meanings become confused and ambiguous, it is common for people to defend the status quo and to threaten withdrawal.

Next, the intersubjective realities of the group, the institution and the system, are reconstructed to be aligned with the values of the new policy. Old assumptions, belief systems and structures are subjected to critical appraisal and then either set aside, subsumed or reinterpreted by the new policy. This reconstruction process is a search among plural perspectives for meanings that match the new policy. As Walker *et al.* point out, it is a phase where theories of social reality are in competition. They also note the crucial role played by situational analysis and touchstone during reconstruction; they are ways of articulating points of agreement and disagreement on matters of substance and method in order to develop shared meanings. Hence, a new cultural reality is elaborated to explain both personal and organisational aspects of communication, co-operation and progress.

It is also clear that cultural realignment is an intrinsically political process (Boyd, 1983). An early effect is the disturbance of power bases, coalitions and the perceptions of interests, as Pettit *et al.* demonstrate. The questioning, the renegotiation and the eventual redistribution of status, power and resources become real possibilities, as suggested by Rizvi *et al.* and Walker *et al.*

> *To summarise, cultural realignment has three major components:*
> *cultural destablisation, when the shared meanings of social reality, and their reproduction and legitimation, lose coherence;*
> *realignment, when intersubjective reality is realigned with the core values of the new policy; and*
> *renorming; when new norms emerge through political processes that reorder interests, their expression and the distribution of organisational resources.*

The Legitimation of Changed Practices

The weight of evidence in the chapters above suggests that the development of commitment to core values in a group, institution or system is a gradual cultural process, not an event (Fullan, 1983; 1985). People take time to negotiate and locate a new and valued self in an emergent culture. As the collective meanings of significance and rightness emerge, our view is that educative leaders should help ensure that the new consensus about valued professionalism and effective organisation coheres with the core values of the new policy.

Northfield *et al.* for example, show how the key meanings attributed to organisation and to a professional self, that are associated with quality teaching, can be coordinated and stabilised through personal sense making in a supportive social group. The process is clear; the imperatives of a new policy are made sense of in terms of personal and group experience, conceptualised by reflection on practice, transformed into trials, and when consequences for clients have been critically reviewed, gradually evidenced in changed practices, beliefs and attitudes.

Individuals' values change. Evers *et al.* show how the reformulation and elaboration of a personal web of belief, and the section of that web concerned with one's professional commitments, is driven by multiple inputs, particularly by feedback about consequences for clients. Although the components of a belief system concerned with professional self, and with being appropriately organised, might enjoy internal coherence and a high degree of comprehensiveness, it is the feedback from clients that provides for external coherence between the intentions and the outcomes of service.

Groups' values change. Through interaction, as Pettit *et al.* and Walker *et al.* demonstrate, teams, institutions and systems renegotiate ideals, beliefs, meanings and expectations. The changes become evident in the personal devices used to symbolise and celebrate commitment; titles, responsibilities, timetables, certificates, award ceremonies, parties, publicity and special assignments. They become evident in organisational metaphors used to explain valued practices, in particular the metaphors about professionalism, evaluation, and collaborative or corporate planning.

Institutions and systems change. As Rizvi *et al.* suggest, the nature and distribution of status, power and resources settle into new patterns that reflect the values embedded in priorities and rites, especially the rites of reproduction and legitimation. New perceptions of interests alter power bases and coalitions, as Pettit *et al.* demonstrate.

Typical indicators of change include fresh definitions of the situation, new understandings about personal service, and reformed expectations about the performance of institutions and systems. In cultural terms, there is, by now, one dominant theory of social reality, widely shared views on substantive and procedural matters, and, in particular, clarity over the criteria and processes of legitimation.

> *To summarise, the legitimation of changed practices follows, and partially locks in with degrees of consensus, the new operational norms of teams, institutions and systems. In philosophical terms, it appears that personal and shared webs of belief adjust to achieve external coherence. It is also a norming process that develops and extends commitment to agreed values into organisational structure.*
>
> *The cultural process establishes one dominant theory of social reality that coordinates views on substantive and process matters. We take the view that an educative leader should help create and sustain a hegemony of legitimation;*

> a knowledge system about forms of personal service and structures that
> maintains, reproduces and justifies changed professional practices and
> organisation.

The Realm of Things

It will be recalled that the key concerns of educative leadership in the realm of
ideas are rightness and significance. The section above identified consensus over
social meanings and legitimation as the primary focus of educative leadership in
the cultural realm.

The theme searches through the chapters above identified the importance of
attention also being given to the material and consequential realities of managerial and evaluative service. The basic focuses of managerial and evaluative
activity are the tangible consequences for long-term learning and for clients, and
how they cohere with conceptions of rightness and significance, and with the
nature of organisational culture.

Managerial Activity

In the chapters above, there is an explicit recognition of the crucial role played
by managerial support for professional activity. These conclusions were validated in discussions during the five ELP workshops, many seminars and conferences, and by reflection on our own experiences as educational administrators.
It is considered to be an activity which seeks to coordinate action and the use of
resources to educative ends.

Management is effective when it sustains a knowledge system that repro-
duces and justifies valued forms of professional practice and structures; structures defined as patterns of assumptions and relationships (Giddens, 1982). The
techniques involved have been well developed in the major texts in the field of
educational administration (e.g. Hoy and Miskel, 1987; Owens, 1987).

We agree with Northfield et al. Evers et al. and Walker et al. that the
touchstone of educative managerial service, such as the creation and maintenance of structure, is the extent to which it supports the development of learning
and teaching.

The knowledge system required to support appropriate management
technologies must, therefore, link professional practices (functions served) to
structures, but draw on alternatives to the traditional concepts of structural-
functionatism (Burrell and Morgan, 1979:25–28). Our preference is for educative techniques that are consistent with responsive and reflective bureaucracy
(Schon, 1983; Sergiovanni, 1987). These terms need to be explained.

Traditionally, in large complex institutions and systems, a functionalist form
of managerial service has tended to objectify and reduce structures to become
no more than lines of authority and has attempted to regulate professional
service by partitioning it into tasks and roles. A simplistic managerial technicism
often alienates educators (Beare, 1986). At its most extreme, as Rizvi et al.
point out, a bureaucratic rationality can systematically preclude alternative

explanations of the status quo, social order, consensus, integration, and solidarity, essentially by its primary focus on the effective regulation and control of social reality and ideas.

Despite the endurance and utility of this ideal type of organisation, as Evers *et al.* and Rizvi *et al.* show, there are fundamental flaws to bureaucracy. First is its dangerous inability to respond to feedback on rightness and significance, and second, is the extraordinary extent to which it objectifies social reality and fixates legitimation in lines of authority. We therefore argue that educative leaders should offer managerial services consistent with a responsive and reflective bureaucratic mindset. This means reconstructing Weber's (1947) ideal characteristics of bureaucratic organisation.

A responsive and reflective bureaucracy would justify and regularly review divisions of professional responsibilities into specialist services in terms of long-term educational consequences. As Walker *et al.* contend, any traditional hierarchy of authority needs to be developed into multiple vertical and horizontal patterns of double loop learning and accountability. Rigid systems of rules covering the rights and duties of employees would be replaced by negotiable performance contracts and other positive incentive regimes within 'good employer' guidelines. Standard procedures for dealing with work contingencies should be displaced by zones of professional discretion; zones that we hold should be governed by policy that has external coherence. Deliberately impersonal relationships should be reconstructed to feature open, respectful, responsive, responsible and democratic communications, as argued by Rizvi *et al.* The selection and promotion of professionals would move from being based on seniority and technical competence to advancement related to educative performance and outcomes.

Such an approach means making a selective use of managerial techniques. Planning, as a line function, can become a contested and expert support service linked to collaborative decision making occurring at team, institution and system locations, as demonstrated by Pettit *et al.* Coordination can cease being a line technique concerned with controlling the service of subordinates, and become the marshalling of commitment and resources to achieve valued ends so that those involved learn about self-coordination. The key point here is that educative leaders should use managerial techniques in ways that create and sustain a reflective culture in which structures and practices remain contestable and responsive.

> *To summarise, we argue that the touchstone of educative managerial activity is the extent to which it supports the development of learning and teaching. Professional practices must be linked to structures in ways that admit reflective and responsive thinking about being organised; to avoid reducing structures to lines of authority and arbitrarily partitioning service into tasks and roles in a hierarchy.*
>
> *Bureaucratic rationality inhibits feedback on rightness and significance, it objectifies social reality, and it fixates legitimation in lines of authority. Our view is that educative leaders should offer managerial services consistent with a responsive and reflective bureaucratic mindset. They should use managerial techniques to ensure that structures and practices remain contestable and responsive.*

Evaluative Activity

The need for evaluative activity by educative leaders is explicit in references to feedback, reflection on practices, responsiveness and double loop learning. It is equally clear that the two key core values of accountability are effectiveness and efficiency. Concerns for effectiveness focus on fidelity of outcomes in relation to goals (such as equity and excellence), whereas concerns for efficiency target the cost-benefits of means.

The arguments in the chapters above imply that an educative approach to evaluation begins at the point where teachers teach and learners learn. It relates intentions, cost-benefits of means, and outcomes concerning:

the quality of the relationship between the learner and the teacher;
the quality of the support services the relationship receives; and
the dedication of parents, community participants and administrators.

The most immediate organisational units that nurture the key teaching-learning relationship are supportive groups and institutions. The teacher-learner relationship is part of an institution-wide social system that reinforces assumptions about how teachers should teach and how learners learn. Improving the educative nature of relationships therefore means developing evaluative structures so that teachers accelerate their learning about teaching.

The ideal conditions for fostering improvement in institutions include leaders understanding and facilitating the process of change, and opportunities to reflect on accurate appraisals of their leadership. Evaluative structures, therefore, require a moral culture that defines rightness and significance. Evers *et al.* noted that educative leaders can and should be subjected to moral appraisal. They call on educative leaders to achieve at least two conditions to enhance learning;

first, develop clarity over responsibilities and expected performances so that evidence of success and failure can be applied, and
second, create procedures that provide opportunities for criticism in both theory and practice and a means of learning from such criticism.

We note that this also allows educative leaders to monitor the continuing appropriateness of the assumptions in structures and practices, and to review the philosophical questions of rightness and significance in policies.

These are important agendas given the recurrent attention drawn above to responsiveness, reflection on practice, and double loop learning. The next sections discuss these issues and link them to a means of relating educative performance to resources. To enhance responsiveness at all locations, we develop Walker *et al.*'s concept of multiple vertical and horizontal negotiating structures for accountability and feedback purposes. Vertical devices are needed to generate internal coherence between goals and outcomes across groups, institutions and systems. To do this, educative leaders in all units need to be held accountable for the extent to which they provide the conditions for learning about teaching and learning. Vertical communications are required to build a systemic mindset on appropriate forms of educative leadership and double loop learning.

Similarly, the trustees of education, such as school councillors, institutional governors and politicians, should be held accountable by their constituencies for the policy context that defines the appropriateness of leadership services. They also require effective vertical communications between local and central governance bodies to contest any provider capture of policy advice, to legitimate the organisational mindset, and to help account for, and advocate the use of, scarce public resources in education.

Horizontal feedback and accountability devices are needed to generate external policy coherence between each organisational unit, its community, and influences in the wider context, such as technological advances. As noted above, professionals have to be responsive to clients for the performance of learners, since life chances are directly affected by the performance of teachers and learners. An institution has to be responsive to its community's collective interests and for the wise use of resources. An organised system of institutions has to be responsive to ministers and governments since they hold a mandate to govern all social services.

Reflection on practice is also a crucial aspect of evaluative activity. Northfield *et al.* for example, contend that educative leaders should use a learning process that highlights the capacity and willingness of both individuals and groups to reflect on practice, to critically analyse it, and to experiment with new ways of thinking and acting. It can be concluded that evaluative reflection on professional performance is integral to teachers and leaders learning about change. Pettit *et al.* add that for personal growth to occur, double loop learning is essential, including an honest appraisal of one's personal skills, strengths and style of leadership.

It is our view that all members of an organisation should share the organisational memory of valued culture, particularly one that emphasises double loop learning and responsiveness. We therefore hold that educative leaders should systematically share knowledge about the organisation's learning systems (Schon, 1983:242). The ideal, in this respect, is creating what Morgan (1988) refers to as a holographic organisation.

Many summative and formative techniques of evaluation are alluded to above. The prior question to us, however, was what is to be achieved by evaluation? Pettit *et al.* gave one set of answers; educative leaders should help practitioners clarify their commitments, evaluate needs in human, financial and material terms, set deadlines, negotiate compromises and brain-storm solutions to any impediments to becoming an effective institution.

There is also good reason for developing evaluative techniques that reveal the educative nexus between professional and leadership development and the wise use of public resources. The approach we recommend is termed Educative Performance Budgeting (EPB) to distinguish it from program budgeting which is regarded by many as being a line management technique. EPB in education is the fact or act of budgeting for educative outcomes, and thereby, relating expenditure to valued performance in the areas of learning, teaching and leading. In principle, EPB should embody the spirit of zero-based budgeting by starting afresh each cycle; no distinction should be made between current and proposed initiatives requiring funding.

There are many reasons for introducing EPB into systems of education. One is that many administrators would come to appreciate the advantages of responsible freedom that comes with budgetary discretion. A sense of professional and managerial responsibility deserves reinforcement. A second reason for introducing EPB is that clarifying how expenditures relate to performance in education could have positive and important by-products; it could help promote public confidence in systems of institutions, community confidence in each institution, and parent and guardian confidence in professionals. A third reason is that EPB would build on and provide a major annual process of institutional self-renewal. It would closely link leadership, and professional and learning activity to the use of scarce resources. It would, therefore, promote more efficient services. It would also provide an incentive for better professional and more site-specific planning decisions, thereby promoting more effective leadership services.

More generally, EPB would offer a productive means of balancing local and state interests while giving formal leaders real discretion to respond to contingencies. With coordinatory system roles and management information systems, EPB processes should help achieve reasonable levels of coordination and consistency across systems of institutions, while also enhancing each institution's renewal capacities with devolved powers and supportive processes. A final advantage of EPB is that such a process accommodates growing diversity in institutional development while providing data that are crucial to the educative leadership of a system of institutions. EPB would also provide real incentives for the effective formative evaluation of policies by the central executive. EPB would also help:

> integrate all parts of the educative leadership model developed above;
> formalise concerns for educative effectiveness and efficiency;
> test for effective vertical and horizontal coherence; and
> provide double loop learning about the management information systems.

EPB would, therefore, target improvement at the most basic structure in education — the relationship and assumptions that exist between the teacher and the learner, by relating educative performance to the wise use of precious resources.

> *To summarise this section on evaluative activity, we argue that educative leaders need to develop structures and practices that integrate feedback, reflection on practices, responsiveness, and double loop learning for three reasons:*
>> *to monitor the key core values of effectiveness and efficiency;*
>> *to review critically the moral culture that defines rightness and significance; and*
>> *to ensure that educative leaders are subjected to moral appraisal.*
> *Various means of evaluative activity are recommended. Multiple vertical and horizontal structures, a holographic organisational memory of learning systems, and educative performance budgeting are suggested, since in combination they relate expenditure to valued performance in the areas of learning, teaching and leading.*

Figure 7.1: *A practical theory of educative leadership*

Summary of the Model

We have developed a holistic model of educative leadership in three meta-physical realms;

> activity conducted in a material world,
> cultural agency in a social world, and
> reflective practice in an abstract realm of ideas.

We recommend that educative leaders give balanced and integrated attention to the imperatives of all three realms. While others might have specialist commitments in large complex organisations and systems, educative leaders must provide a holistic view as indicated by the area of intersecting arcs in Figure 7.1.

> *The realm of ideas demands attention to what is right and what is significant at team, institutional and system locations. This requires philosophical and strategic appraisal of abstract issues and problems, prior to the development of new policy, in a way that links consequences to material and political contingencies. The tools of philosophy and the policy sciences are highly relevant.*
>
> *Another realm, the realm of social reality, begins where significant but abstract concepts cease being simply ideas and become valued cultural arte-facts. The cultural elaboration of a policy is achieved through the realignment of meanings given to social reality, and the legitimation of changed profes-sional practices. The tools of political science and social-psychology become more relevant.*
>
> *The final realm demands attention to the practical realities of performance, resources, and consequences; reality as things. In this realm, educative lead-ers devote themselves to managerial and evaluative activities to relate expendi-ture to valued outcomes in the areas of learning, teaching and leading. The tools of management science become relevant but require substantial reinter-pretation.*

We conclude that the educative leader, to ensure holographic conditions, must help create, maintain and develop the links between the three realms. For example, attention to the core values of effectiveness and efficiency, will help create coherence between:

> the production and selection of valued and significant ideas;
> managerial and evaluative activity; and
> question the continuing appropriateness of the organisational culture.

Similarly, collaborative decision making will help create coherence between the making of policy, its cultural elaboration, and, therefore, its implementation. Other mechanisms that serve the same integrative purposes include multiple vertical and horizontal structures, a holographic organisational memory, and educative performance budgeting.

Educative leadership should be, we believe, holistic, pragmatic, values-driven and cultural activity intended to enhance performance in the areas of learning, teaching and leading.

References

ARGYRIS, C. (1977) 'Double loop learning in organisations', *Harvard Business Re-view*, **55**, 5, 115–125.

ARGYRIS, C. (1982) *Reasoning, Learning and Action: Individual and Organisational*, San Francisco: Jossey-Bass.

ARGYRIS, C. and SCHON, D.A. (1978) *Organisational Learning: A Theory of Action Perspective*, Reading, MA: Addison-Wesley.

BEARE, H. (1986) 'Shared Meanings about Education: The Economic Paradigm Considered', The 1986 Buntine Oration, Joint National Conference of the Australian College of Education and the Australian Council of Educational Administration, Adelaide, September.

BOYD, W.L. (1983) 'Rethinking educational policy and management: Political science and educational administration', *American Journal of Education,* **92**, 1, 1–29.

BURRELL, G. and MORGAN, G. (1979) *Sociological Paradigms and Organisational Analysis,* London: Heinemann.

FULLAN, M. (1982) *The Meaning of Educational Change,* New York: Teachers College Press.

FULLAN, M. (1985) 'Integrating theory and practice', in HOPKINS, D. and REID, K. (Eds) *Rethinking Teacher Education,* London: Croom Helm

GIDDENS, A. (1982) *Sociology: A Brief But Critical Introduction,* New York: Harcourt, Brace and Jovanovich.

GREENFIELD, T.B. (1975) 'Theory about organisations: A new perspective and its implications for schools', in HUGHES, M.G. (Ed.) *Administering Education,* London: Althone Press.

GREENFIELD, T.B. (1988) 'The decline and fall of science in educational administration', in GRIFFITHS, D.E. STOUT, R.T. and FORSYTH, P.B. (Eds) *Leaders for America's Schools: The Report and Papers of the National Commission on Excellence in Educational Administration,* Berkeley: McCutchan.

HODGKINSON, C. (1978) *Towards a Philosophy of Administration,* Oxford: Basil Blackwell.

HODGKINSON, C. (1981) 'New taxonomy of administrative process', *Journal of Educational Administration,* **19**, 141–152.

HODGKINSON, C. (1983) *The Philosophy of Leadership,* London: Basil Blackwell.

HODGKINSON, C. (1986) 'New directions for research and leadership: The triplex value bases of organization theory and administration', *Educational Administration and Foundations,* **1**, 1, 4–15.

HOY, W.K. and MISKEL, C.G. (1987) *Educational Administration: Theory, Research and Practice,* third edition, New York: Random.

MORGAN, G. (1988) *Images of Organisation,* Newbury Park: Sage.

OWENS, R.G. (1987) *Organizational Behaviour in Education,* third edition, Englewood Cliffs, NJ: Prentice-Hall.

SCHON, D.A. (1983) *The Reflective Practitioner: How Professionals Think in Action,* New York: Basic Books.

SERGIOVANNI, T.J. (1987) *The Principalship: A Reflective Practice Perspective,* Boston: Allyn and Bacon.

Index